Raymond Pettibon
No Title (Long live crime...)
1982
Pen and ink on paper
11 x 8 1/2 inches
27.9 x 21.6 cm
Courtesy David Zwirner, New York

DISCO'S OUT...MURDER'S IN!

the true story of frank the shank and
L.A.'s deadliest punk rock gang

BY HEATH MATTIOLI AND DAVID SPACONE

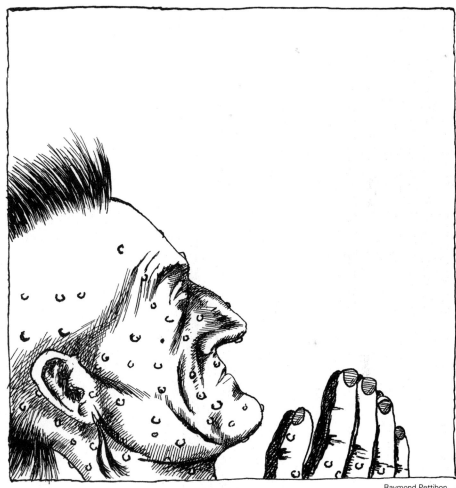

Raymond Pettibon
No Title
1982
Pen and ink on paper
11 x 8 1/2 inches
27.9 x 21.6 cm
Courtesy David Zwirner, New York

FERAL
HOUSE

Disco's Out ... Murder's In!
The true story of Frank the Shank
and L.A.'s deadliest punk rock gang
by Heath Mattioli & David Spacone
Disco's Out ... Murder's In!
© 2015 by Heath Mattioli & David Spacone, Feral House
All rights reserved
A Feral House book
ISBN 978-1627310185

Feral House
1240 W. Sims Way Suite 124
Port Townsend WA 98368
www.FeralHouse.com
design by D. Collins
illustration by Raymond Pettibon

10 9 8 7 6 5 4 3 2

CONTENTS

PROLOGUE

Make no mistake about it,
the faster you live ... the quicker you die.

980s LOS ANGELES was the epicenter of hardcore punk rock, arguably the most violent youth movement in American history. Most know about the music's impact, but virtually nothing is known about L.A.'s homicidal punk rock gangs, and the bodies they left in their wake.

Forest Lawn Long Beach was packed with beloved family and friends from all over Los Angeles. The deceased was a dear friend and just one of those guys. Sadly, his passing came too soon, like all those who burn too bright for others, but in the end have nothing left for themselves. After the sermon, after the memories, a number of us met back at a family member's house for a traditional wake, but this gathering was a bit different. Untraditional would describe it perfectly. Not since the 1980s had we seen this many infamous hoodlums of punk rock rallied together in one place. Most were dead, locked up, or had assimilated into normal society and disappeared long ago. After spending some time looking at sun-bleached photo albums and listening to good-humored stories, an old acquaintance named Frank made his presence known by striking up a conversation, asking if we wanted to catch a smoke out front. Both of us had known Frank from afar, and had heard more than a few accounts of his street legend. Clearly feeling nostalgic, and maybe a bit vulnerable due to the circumstance, Frank told us a hair-raising story of a homicidal night in Hollywood during the 1980s involving the deceased. Stories like this used to haunt us kids who lived on the sidelines. The whispers at shows and rumors throughout the city were true. If you were anywhere near L.A.'s hardcore punk rock scene back in the day, you knew you had to watch your back.

That late afternoon, we gave Frank a ride home and he opened up even more. Frank's stories were electrifying and shockingly explicit. He spoke of bloody murder in cold, detailed accounts. Looking into his eyes, hearing his voice, you knew he lived every moment and hadn't gone back to that place in a long time. Right then, we knew this needed to be put to paper. This was the meat missing from all the published stories about punk in Southern California—the awful history that made hardcore in Los Angeles without a doubt hardcore.

Entrusting us with the task of turning his vignettes into a publishable narrative was going to be a challenge. Frank worked the graveyard shift, so most of our interviews had to be done by phone, in the middle of the night or at dawn, making his admissions feel that much more chilling. Sometimes we would meet for breakfast, always at a different restaurant, somewhere off the 10 freeway near his work. These places he chose were usually uninhabited and depressing. Our original plan, before we got in-depth with Frank, was to do a nonfiction work about all the punk rock gangs of the time, but the more we pressed, the more substantial his story became. Frank's journey through punk rock was as magical as much as it was a nightmare, not to mention the authenticity of an old Hollywood landscape that has long since disappeared.

As Frank explained, of course there was blood and lots of it, but also much, much more. We felt that telling the story from Frank's perspective, as a kid, in the moment, was the only way to write this book—force readers to tie off and stick it in. Anything else would cheat the experience. During the lengthy five-year process, Frank was forced to take an honest look within and relive his horrific history—a history of abuse, a life of regret.

Writing this book was a chance to deliver an uncensored account of the L.A. punk scene from the trenches, from one of its infamous monsters ... Frank the Shank. Maybe this book can serve as a warning, a cautionary tale for future generations. Don't waste your youth.

N.B. Some names have been changed to protect the guilty and the thoughts and opinions expressed in this book are not necessarily those of the authors.

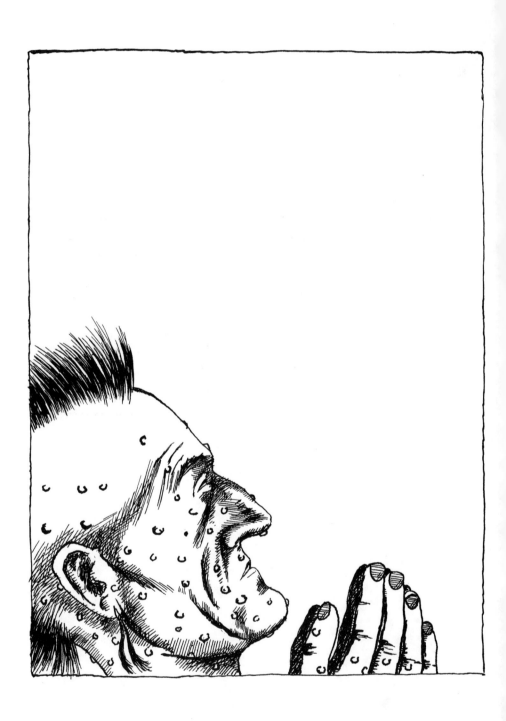

DISCO'S OUT...MURDER'S IN!

the true story of frank the shank and
L.A.'s deadliest punk rock gang

BY HEATH MATTIOLI AND DAVID SPACONE

CHAPTER 1
"THE SONS OF SID VICIOUS"

A SECTION OF THE SLAM PIT abruptly came to a halt and fanned out. Three from the Pig Children gang started to advance, and then another four moved on us. Each one was a true Philistine: sizable, smelly, disgusting. Santino pulled his box cutter out and started slicing and dicing at anything that moved. The Governor and I were pushing and kicking for more space. Every inch mattered. A few guys ran off bleeding. One Pig Child got hold of Santino, they struggled briefly, but the inevitable always happened ... blood poured.

I counted six slashes to the chest.

The guy's face turned white, reality set in, and down he went.

"LMP! Want some, get some!" threatened Santino.

Everybody backed the fuck up—the great equalizer once again proved its point. Shock seeped in as they surrounded their fallen.

Panic in Pig Park.

Santino, The Governor, and I stood tall—heads cocked back, eyes of evil. The Pig Children took an even harder look and realized there were only three of us, with no backup, and started to rally numbers. Next thing we knew, a good 30 or 40 guys were coming at us from every direction yelling, "Get 'em!"

We went at it.

I dropped one and then two, steady as ever. The Governor was trading bombs and holding his own. Santino nailed a few with his fists then sliced another. Funny thing was, the Pig Children were hitting their own people as much as us. That's what happens when you rage fight.

The Pig people kept coming and coming—it was time to retreat. We couldn't win and we knew it. Where the fuck were Sailor and Mongo when you needed them?

I pulled my butterfly, hoping to scare off the rest, but they didn't buy it. Out of the corner of my eye, a shiny metal object caught the moonlight, and disappeared into Santino's back. His face showed recognition of pain, but he somehow managed to fight off another ... and another.

I saw deep red.

Santino fell to one knee and then dropped out of sight.

Our blood in their water—Fuck that! Another minute and we were going to be in an all-out feeding frenzy.

I got a bead on the instigator calling for more guys to join the storm.

He was my Pig.

I rapidly advanced within striking distance. He saw my knife, but it was too late … closing time.

I shanked that dirty motherfucker, I stuck him deep, right in his sternum. My knife went right through. He let out a bloodcurdling scream at the top of his Pig lungs, then hit the ground convulsing—must have struck something vital, maybe his liver. His theatrics brought the party to a standstill. The Governor and I grabbed Santino and moved out. They were smart not to follow.

1978 is finally over. I'm Little League hero of my city but big deal. Our dollar plummets to an all-time low. Things I treasured as a boy mean zilch. The people Take Back the Night. My time in elementary school is almost up and I'm looking at life through an unfamiliar set of eyes. Test-tube babies. Dodgers lose the World Series to the Yankees again, so fucking what? I'm already used to that. John Wayne Gacy's a killer clown. Saving for a new BMX didn't matter as much as it did last month. A whopping 909 followers commit suicide for Jim Jones. Chalk it up to puberty or whatever, but this young man is on the hunt for something new. Don't drink the Kool-Aid. Toga! Toga! Toga!

I started spending afternoons hanging around a fringe record store in La Mirada called the Magic Mushroom, wandering the aisles, checking out hot chicks on album covers … satin pants and high heels. Strange experimental music played as a balding clerk sat on a stool watching foreign splatter films. Every now and then, he would jump from his seat, yelling "Stab her already!"

My world got flipped on its axis the day my neighbor Marla walked into the record shop. She was several years older than me and I never thought much about her until that afternoon. Marla was all sleazed up in torn fishnets, patent leather, bleached hair, and extra slutty makeup—way ahead of her time. There were two older teenage guys with her, sporting Indian-style Mohawks over a foot high, held up by Krazy Glue or maybe varnish. One wore a plaid kilt over his torn-up Levis, and both had on motorcycle boots with chains connected to their belts. I did my best to get as close as possible without pissing them off. I had never seen anything that cool or original before. Hypnotized … it stuck in my head.

Within a week, I saw Marla again at the record store. She was alone this time. I gathered up the courage and said something.

"How's it goin' Marla, you still allowed in school?"

She looked me up and down with an air of distrust.

"I know you ... maybe?"

"Yeah, I live around the block from you, I'm Frank." She was unimpressed.

"That's cool ... I guess."

"What records are you listening to?" I asked.

"The only records," Marla growled, "Sex Pistols, Black Flag, the Germs!"

I got confused. "What's that?"

She started to walk away, but something compelled her to educate me.

"Punk music, it's all that matters—throw everything else away."

"Whoa, that sounds cool man. But I'm broke."

Marla scrutinized me a second time.

"I could let you borrow some ... Just don't you fucking dare scratch them!"

She lent me a Black Flag record called *Nervous Breakdown*, along with Sex Pistols' *Never Mind the Bollocks*, and the Germs' *GI*. I never liked rock 'n' roll, so after hearing this stuff, I found exactly what I needed—music that spoke to me in loud, fast, and aggressive ways; guys who cursed and screamed about not taking any shit, that politics were a sham, that it was time to toss the whole world in the trash. This attitude felt dangerous. I loved it.

I started buying a few of my own records with saved-up lunch money, and got completely addicted to the sound and message. Unfortunately, very few punk bands had albums or even singles available. Record companies weren't willing to take a chance on this niche genre. Kids in Los Angeles who wanted to embrace the movement had one saving grace: Rodney Bingen-heimer. On Sunday nights between 8 p.m. and 10 p.m., he hosted a radio show that played punk rock music emerging from the scene. Cutting-edge bands that no one else had access to; local demos, cheap four-track record-ings, interviews, imports—a virtual goldmine for all of us looking for that sound. I taped his radio show religiously, and then traded the cassettes back and forth with a couple of 'posers' at school.

Almost everyone, including myself, was a poser when we first got into punk rock. You secretly listened to the music without committing to the look. Parents, teachers, and most importantly, your peers didn't accept the radical change in appearance. Haircuts above the ears were for momma's boys and dorks. Secondhand-store clothes, homemade T-shirts, and big black boots were a recipe for weirdo. Time away from school was spent hanging out at Skate City Skatepark on Telegraph Boulevard in Whittier. I never really had enough money to skate there full-time; mostly hung out with my wannabe punk friends, lying to each other about a scene we knew nothing of.

During the summer of 1979, I saw something on television that shoved me into taking the next step. A Chicago radio station held an event at a baseball game in Comiskey Park called "Disco Demolition Night." They put together a giant pile of disco records in the middle of the outfield and blew it up before the game. Veritable mayhem ensued when the bomb went off. It looked like fun to me. People rushed the field, tore things down, and lit fires. Everyone was fed up with disco and wanted it destroyed. Outside of the shiny bimbos, I hated everything about disco. That John Travolta pimp bravado was flat-out lame. "Disco Demolition Night's" spectacle fueled my desire to blow up the status quo governing my own life.

After summer school let out next day, I took a look in the mirror, grabbed my crappy skateboard, and headed over to my buddy Gary's house in La Habra. There was me, Gary, a kid named Chuck and another one called Mikey sitting around his room, ready to take the big plunge. Gary broke out the clippers and hit the switch. This was it.

"Who's goin' first? I'm givin' the haircuts, so I go last."

Chuck sucked in a big gulp of oxygen. "My dad's gonna kill me."

"Whose isn't?" I reminded him.

Mikey put it simple, "Everyone is gonna hate us. We're dead meat!"

Some nervous laughter erupted.

"Fuck it, I'll go," Chuck postured.

Gary slipped on the quarter-inch attachment and went to work. The anxiety on Chuck's face said it all. I knew there was no coming back.

Having your head shaved was really asking for it. This was not an easy time for social acceptance. The whole human race still wore its hair long in 1979. Whether you were a rocker, biker, hippie, burnout, surfer, skateboarder, lowrider, disco beaner, fob, or even a standard black guy into kung fu, you were not happy having a few freaks around you with shaved heads. All gave punk rockers some kind of shit. We were outcasts from that moment on. The four of us quietly sat for a moment, staring at each other with our quarter-inch hair standing on end, taking in all the possible consequences. Mikey looked over to Gary and passively asked, "Are we really punkers now?"

After cutting my hair that day I returned home and stared in the mirror. For the first time I actually saw someone I liked.

The toughest lesson I learned as a punk rocker would be the most common in my crowd for years to come. My drunken father took one look at me, his eyes on fire, and hurled a freshly cracked beer right at my skull. I lost my balance trying to protect my face as the beer hit me square in the shoulder.

"No drugs in this house, you fuckin' loser!"

As I picked myself up from the floor, Dad walked right up and started kicking me in the side.

"Washout! Shitheel! Bum!"

Punks began making headlines, and the media found a new boogeyman, pegging punk rockers as antisocial psychopaths on dope:

Kids Riot at Punk Rock Concert, Sex Pistols Stormed in New Battle of the Alamo, Enemies of the World, Drugs Kill Punk Star Sid Vicious.

My father, like everyone over 30, had the opinion that all punks were losers and dope addicts. He figured he could beat some sense into me.

"Grow your hair back or join the fuckin' Marines. No son of mine is gonna look like this!"

His blows hurt a little less than usual. I expected it. But one beating sent me to the hospital with a bruised rib and a few stitches, marking my first step into manhood. None of the doctors even asked me how it happened. I desperately wanted to crucify my father, but instead wimped out and told them I crashed my bike. I was never able to look my father square in the eyes ever again. He hated me. I hated him more.

I never let my hair grow out. Just kept clipping it down as more beatings happened, from almost everyone. A simple thing like walking down the street resulted in a pounding. Carloads of much older and bigger hippies trolled my neighborhood looking for trouble, or money to get loaded. They frequently pulled over and jumped me for no reason other than my short hair. If you were punk rock, everyone with long hair was after you. Our local hippies called themselves the RCP Gang, which stood for Rock Creek Park. They named it in double honor of rock 'n' roll and Creek Park, a local park a few blocks from my house in La Mirada that they had claimed as their turf in the early '70s. Difficulty with them began when I was eight years old. These long-haired, low-life burnouts, ages 17 to 21, made a living picking on little kids. Kids on my block were always on the lookout for RCP. They took our allowance or our bikes and sold them cheap for booze, weed, or downers. Now RCP started zeroing in on punk rock kids. If you were punk, they called you faggot, made you beg, and still punched your face in. They felt like tough guys doing this. It made no difference to them how old we were.

One year, maybe two, and I would be strong enough to give them a go for the money they stole from us. If I was going to keep my head shaved, I had to bide my time.

Thanksgiving 1979. Another boring day with the family and their friends; at least that's what I thought sitting at the kids' table, surrounded by spastic children. Can't believe these kids are my same age. What a bunch of retards. Right before the turkey dinner was served, my half cousins, Janet and Fay, walked in the house. The only seats left were in the kids' section. Disappointed eyes and concerned looks from the adults followed them all the way to our table. They sat right across from me.

I hadn't seen them in two years and had no idea they were so with it. Janet wore a fitted black motorcycle jacket, tight jeans, pointed boots, and straight jet-black hair with chopped China bangs. Fay dyed her cropped hair platinum blonde and had on an Exene Cervenka-style dress with tube sox and biker boots. Janet was 24, slim, and petite. Fay was almost 18, kinda tall, and amply stacked. Both were a maniac's wet dream. Right away they noticed my shaved head.

"Nice hair, bet mom and dad are thrilled," Janet commented.

I put on the act.

"I just had to do it, you know?"

"That's sooo intense, Frankie," Fay cracked.

"Do you go to punk rock concerts?" I quizzed.

"They're called gigs, and yes we do."

I lost it.

"Take me—you gotta take me! I'm sick of being a poser! That's all I listen to. The Germs, Black Flag, Rodney on the ROQ—come on!"

Amused with my rampant enthusiasm, Janet and Fay could no longer contain their laughter and started throwing olives at me.

I pestered Janet and Fay for over six months with phone calls, pleading to let me tag along to a gig. Finally they agreed to take me, under one condition: it could positively never come back to haunt them. If our family ever found out, they could get into big trouble, ostracized even. Snitching was not in my blood, my father made sure of that.

X was playing at the Whisky a Go-Go on one Friday night; the sisters gave in and decided to take me and my pal Gary. Janet and Fay said it would be "cute" to have a couple of little shaved-head kids with them. Gary got permission to stay at my house, where it was easy to sneak out after bedtime. Janet and Fay planned it all out. They'd pick us up one block away at the liquor store, stock up on booze and cigarettes, and "ease on down the road."

This was my first trip to Hollywood. I had no idea what was in store. A million ideas ran through my head from all the movies and stories of La-La Land. Without saying a word, Fay handed Gary and me each a Lowenbrau as the Germs blared from the car speakers. Halfway through our second beer, we were halfway to Hollywood. Janet pulled a joint from her leather and sparked it up, took a couple tokes, then passed it to me.

"Tell me you've been stoned before."

"Sure I've seen weed before," was my "I'm with it" response.

"Not seen it! Smoked it?" Fay taunted.

Disregarding grownup advice, I said yes and took a hit. Smoke filled my lungs. I tried to hold it in like I saw the stoners at the park do, but to no avail.

Gary snatched the joint from my hand, bragging, "I smoked my brother's weed, he's a hippie."

I coughed out smoke from my virgin lungs as Fay busted up.

"It's madness, reefer madness.... "

A big swig of beer soothed my parched throat while the new sensation took over.

From Hollywood Boulevard to Sunset Boulevard was a three-ring circus of hookers, freaks, and neon slime. Old classic history dismantled, overrun with smut. The days change at night. Change in an instant. Parking the car momentarily halted the lurid kaleidoscope in my brain. I walked up to the Whisky, high as a kite, anticipation killing me. Punks were everywhere, smoking cigarettes and cloves, looking cooler than anything on the planet. All of them seemed to get a real goof on a pair of shaved-headed kids strolling up with hot older chicks. The girls had some pull at the door and we walked in for free, totally buzzed, feeling famous. X was setting up, the headliner everyone came to see.

Janet and Fay knew a lot of people inside and always made sure to introduce me as their "cousin Frankie." The place smelled all kinds of weird. I tried to count the number of punks inside—must have been nearly three hundred. The number of Blacks, Asians, Mexicans, and Whites appeared to be almost equal. This mix of races was not what I expected. The only time I saw races share common ground in L.A. was at Dodgers, Lakers, or Rams games. Here, I found a movement based on togetherness; we were all in the same tribe. Color, race, and religion meant nil; this representation filled me with pride.

When X hit their first note, the whole place became a wild frenzy. I knew about "the pogo" and "the worm" but witnessing these punk dances up close overwhelmed me. I wanted to join, except the mix of beer and grass was a curveball. My brains said go while my body told me to stay put or puke. Punks were jumping straight up in the air, making jerky spasmodic moves to the noise. Some were at the edges, rolling and convulsing on the floor like they were being electrocuted. The rest of the crowd bumped and bounced against them, creating an explosion of individual expression—a true modern art painting come to life.

Awestruck, I turned to Gary and said, "The scene is really growing, huh?" Like I knew.

Gary slobbered out, "I'm fucking wasted ... X rules. Exene is the finest chick in the world!"

I fought to contain myself. I was losing it inside.

"This is where we belong Gary, we're real punks now!"

Gary's face went deathly white as he proceeded to vomit all over the floor.

Janet and Fay loved taking me to gigs. I was the kid brother they never had. Every few weeks I snuck out, got picked up at the liquor store, and was off to another night of privileged exhilaration at a punk show. My mom and dad had no clue. This continued well into 1980 as the two girls brought me to all the hot spots of the day: Hollywood Palladium, Florentine Gardens, Starwood, and the Vex. I even went on road trips to San Francisco's Mabuhay Gardens.

Meanwhile, beatings at home continued. My drunken father would drag me into the backyard and challenge me to a fight, the same way his old man did to him. He made me fight. Many times. He was never happy. Dad only smiled when telling that same old story of leaving Detroit in 1960 at the age of 28. His accent always came back strong while talking about his old days.

"I'm at my routine cocktail lounge on my lucky stool when the bartender started up with 'Hey Jack, how 'bout tellin' that one again about the spook and the chink double dutchin' at the pearly gates?' I was well into my second malt celebrating my second divorce. 'You're the bartender, you guys are supposed to tell the jokes.' A few 'work' associates had stopped by for our mandatory happy hour. Blackie Lapicola was my best pal and saw to it I got good 'n loaded considering my circumstances. He always knew how to cheer me up. Closin' time came and I stumbled outside onto a crowded sidewalk. Some guy bumped into me, putting his hands all over me. Detroit protocol: you bump, I swing. I threw a monster hook and caught the pickpocket square in the jaw. Out cold. Blackie and the guys took one look at him and hurried me away. Now, I'm even more irate that my pals didn't let me take his money for tryin' to thieve me. Blackie set me straight: 'That was no pickpocket, Jack, that was a Detroit cop, in full uniform no less!' Next day, I'm nursin' my hangover, when I get information that I'm no longer welcome in Detroit."

His only option was to start anew on the West Coast, or suffer endless harassment from Detroit police ... or worse. Back then he was actually a well-liked guy who hung around a number of mob men from Detroit's south side, occasionally driving for them. Some people would call that "connected." Being 100% Italian, my dad fit right in. When it came time to relocate to California, they hooked him up with their people in the L.A. family, who offered him work at one of their businesses: Lads Trucking Co.

I got stubborn. The more Dad beat me, the more dedicated to my music and scene I became. No longer safe in the streets or my own home, my life at this point was an exercise in bloodshed. Punk's raw power and attitude, along with lyrics that stood for something, gave me purpose. Dad's poundings couldn't wear me down any more. The chip on my shoulder decided to develop a personality. I made friends, similar to myself, whose folks also tried to punish the punk out of them. Since there were only a small number of punks around at the time, we all stuck together. Kids like us became even more dedicated to the cause in order to put up with the constant abuse.

Fay began dating an older punk named Eddie, who partied at the original punk clubs before my time: the Masque, the Fleetwood, and Club 88. Eddie was around during the infancy of punk rock and schooled me in the history of the music. He told me how the rock bands of the '70s influenced punk's first defining band, the Sex Pistols, and how they loved the New York Dolls, Iggy and the Stooges, and most importantly, the Ramones.

Eddie bragged of early punk's energy overwhelming people. He even witnessed hippies cut off all their hair at gigs before entering. Eddie had a shifty appearance: narrow shoulders, long limbs, misguided eyes, hair dyed jet-black and slicked to his neck. He was the only punk I ever knew who made it to the last Sex Pistols show in San Francisco. Eddie showed me around Hollywood without the girls, sometimes making me drive when he got too drunk. It made no difference to him I was only 13 and he was 25. Fay told me he was dishonorably discharged from the Army after spitting in his staff sergeant's face for waking him up too early. She warned me to never bring it up.

We went to other famous clubs together: Madame Wong's, the Hideaway, the Cuckoo's Nest, and the Anti-Club. The guy had been around so long he knew everyone from managers to bouncers to bands. Now they were letting me on the stage during gigs and backstage afterwards to drink more beer with bands like Circle Jerks, Dead Kennedys, and L.A.'s Wasted Youth.

Eddie and the girls did narcotics whenever they could get their hands on them. This required frequent trips to the "Confederate House" off Euclid Street in Fullerton near Janet's. Every punk within a 30-mile radius went there to score. The place functioned as a full-service flophouse and self-medication emporium. If you were punk rock, the welcome mat was always out to come inside, get what you need, party if you want, crash if you have to. First-generation punks ran the joint, paying rent by selling any obtainable drugs: Whites, Reds, Black Beauties, Cross Tops, weed, LSD, even mushrooms. There were never available seats on the two couches, eternally filled with unemployed, ambitionless, slutty outcasts in crazy makeup. Random sex noise could be heard at any given moment from one of the three occupied bedrooms.

From the street, Confederate House blended well with the neighborhood. Its stucco, paint, and yard were reasonably maintained so no one hassled the tinfoil-covered windows. Girls who stayed there got a real kick out of aggressively flirting with me, much to the chagrin of Janet and Fay. Even though they shared drugs with me, dirty girls were against their rules. Lucky for me, whenever the two left the living room, corrupting claws came out. One of the girls with vampire makeup slipped her tongue in my ear and sucked on my earlobe. Another girl, who always wore bondage clothes, lifted her plaid skirt and flashed the goods.

"Beautiful, isn't it? One day I'll let you play with it."

Outside of a dirty magazine, that was the first time I saw IT ... leaving me speechless. To this day, I've never had the chance to say thank you.

Eddie also took me to an abandoned hotel, behind the landmark Grauman's Chinese Theatre on Hollywood Boulevard, to party or flop after shows. All kinds of punks would stop by to get sanctuary from the street and share their stories. The spot was a barren shithole littered with dead cockroaches; you know you're in a nasty place when even the bugs choose to die. Abject graffiti added to the motif. "Disco's out Murder's in!" was the one that stuck with me. The hangout always smelled of rot and housed a number of runaways who told tales of bodies being dumped. Those who squatted there more permanently dubbed it "Motel Hell."

MOM AND DAD, THE LOVING DAYS.

My folks were going through a divorce due to my dad's drinking and abuse. He was now out of the picture. Mom started working 12-hour shifts to make ends meet, allowing me to be away from home at will. Parental supervision and control were at a minimum—fuck, yeah! Eddie and I scored "pick-me-ups" at Motel Hell and partied there from Friday until Sunday. The squats always had some kind of hustle going. Even in Hollywood, punk rockers were still not a common sight. Tourists paid a dollar to take a "picture with a punker" outside the Chinese Theatre. We were honest-to-goodness freaks from outer space, providing big laughs for their hick friends back home. At the end of a day's work on the Walk of Fame, you had enough money for food, beer, drugs, and cover charge for that night's show.

partied with Eddie sometimes at a club called Seven Seas, owned by powerful Palestinian drug kingpin Eddie Nash, who also owned the Starwood. Mr. Nash took pleasure in catering to the young nightlife of Hollywood. He was always behind the bar at his clubs, watching everything, making sure no one got out of line. Eddie drank so much at Mr. Nash's clubs that they were on a first-name basis. He even introduced me to him. By this time Eddie Nash was already famous for the Wonderland murders. Amateur coke dealers from Wonderland Avenue pulled off a strong-arm robbery at his home. He returned the favor by having a crew of thugs bludgeon them to death with lead pipes … allegedly. Porn legend and coke freak John Holmes was placed at the scene of both crimes, but never found guilty of any wrongdoing. To this day it is still considered the bloodiest crime scene in L.A. history. A lot of drugs in the punk scene came from Wonderland Avenue because of its close proximity to the Sunset Boulevard clubs the Whisky, the Roxy, and Gazzarri's. My pal Eddie took the news hard, having to now find a new connection.

Violence was sporadic in the punk scene at this time, yet frequent enough to warrant a need for numbers, strength, and protection. Select punks were lashing out, developing mutual contempt for one another. Naturally a handful of punk rock street gangs formed. One of the oldest and largest came from my home city. They were called LMP gang, which stood for La Mirada Punks. Their exploits became known in my area at the tail end of 1979 when the gang was constructed, which is a story in itself.

City of La Mirada is in Los Angeles County, bordered by Whittier, Santa Fe Springs, Norwalk, Cerritos, and Buena Park. Some of these cities, like most suburbs of Los Angeles, had sketchy areas with cholo gangs who had shot, stabbed, and beaten the shit out of each other for generations. La Mirada was no different. Even though most of the city was middle- to upper-middle-class, the east end was plain shitty. Most houses there were shabby or falling down, hemmed in by oil fields and wrecking yards.

LMP gang's founder and driving force was known as Santino, taking his name from *The Godfather* movie. At 15, he was already sizable, standing 5'10", weighing 175 pounds, and in better shape than most teens. Santino established himself as a legend at Skate City Skateboard Park, where I first saw him shredding in 1978. Not many kids got big air out of the pool like him. Unfortunately, he hit a growth spurt that forced him to quit skating. At 16, he was suddenly 6'0", weighing 200 pounds, with nothing to harness his aggression.

I watched Santino pass time at Skate City, patiently waiting for someone to slam down on the concrete. He swiftly walked up to the injured and offered his own special brand of help when their arm or leg looked busted.

"Are you okay man? I'm sure I could get that bone back in place for you" always sounded good to a fallen skater, relieved that a Good Samaritan was offering medical assistance.

Santino carefully placed his hands on the injured spot, secured his grip, then began to squeeze and twist until the pain caused awful screams. Kids watched in horror as Santino grinned at his prey, only letting go after he got a sadistic fix. I saw this happen numerous times, before kids wised up and refused his help. Every time some youngster ate it, they jumped to their feet, busted bone and all, before Santino could reach them. It kind of freaked me out, but also kind of made me laugh too. Kids un-casually spoke about how he loved punching people who wore eyeglasses, just to see the lenses bust out.

"Stay away" was the word.

When Santino's look and style changed that year, gossip spread among the youth about him putting together a punk rock gang.

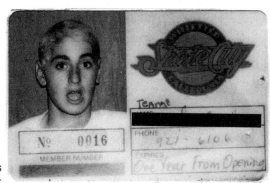

SANTINO'S
SKATE CITY ID CARD.

antino had olive skin and a Roman nose, giving him an almost Italian appearance. Shaving his head highlighted his strong, cold features and big ears, which he covered with a low bandana. This looked extra menacing with his punk uniform of army jacket, Levis, and combat boots. Life on his street was full of gangster drama. The neighborhood was part of CV3 gang, which stood for Compton Varrio Tres. Members from Compton had moved to East La Mirada and started a chapter there many years earlier. CV3 cholos gathered on Santino's lawn nightly, waiting for his father to get home from work. Those who came by his home for advice on personal matters and gang life

15.

knew Santino's dad as "The Godfather." He was a former vato from East L.A., which carried a lot of respect. Less than two blocks away was the rival gang VLM, which stood for Varrio La Mirada. The two gangs were constantly at war in the neighborhood, often right in front of the house. It wasn't hard to figure out where The Godfather's loyalty lay. When his local Neighborhood Watch recruited him to help fight crime in the area, The Godfather used the information to tip off CV3, so they could do their dirty work without getting caught.

CV3 actively tried recruiting Santino because of his special street-fighting capabilities, not to mention their relationship with his dad. Santino, however, had ideas of his own. Why be a soldier in someone else's gang when you can lead one that is like no other? The energy and violence of punk as it was portrayed in the news got him all worked up. Images of anarchy, lewd behavior, and scared authority, along with music that sent his blood pumping, were heart-stirring alternatives to the traditional cholo lifestyle.

Here was his chance to do something groundbreaking. Why be just another gangbanger in your neighborhood when you can run wild in the streets of Hollywood? The punk rock scene was ready-made, wide-open territory. Santino's local group of teen hoodlums was determined to establish the name LMP as an infamous violent force.

Over the next year, LMP claimed La Mirada Regional Park pool as turf. Our city emptied the pool due to drought conditions in 1979, leaving it abandoned to skate and graffiti. LMP tags, anarchy signs, backward swastikas, and other symbols of hate lined the pool, solely intended to freak people out. Santino allowed kids to skate the pool with no hassles if they were punk rockers. Gary and I skated there a few times without any problems. LMP kept a watchful eye, but never gave us the time of day.

Word floated around school, the skate park, and our local record store that year: "LMP is fighting back and fucking hippies up!" LMP became true folk heroes to us punk rock kids who were sick of taking hippie shit. I began asking Janet, Fay, and Eddie if they knew any LMPs. The sisters knew two: one called "Sailor" and another named "Joker." Both said they hated Sailor, who was ridiculously drunk and fighting all the time. Joker gave them the creeps, because he always leered at their tits.

Eddie partied with Sailor at gigs sometimes and was familiar with his story: "He gets so drunk, he just sails away...."

16.

Paul Krappman photo

$1,000 reward

A sight like this has become rare in La Mirada since the city started offering a $1000 reward to anyone providing information that leads to the arrest and conviction of anybody who destroys or defaces property by means of graffiti within the city limits. The city urges those with information to call the Sheriffs Dept. at (213) 863-8711.

LMP CLAIMING TERRITORY.

Sailor often pedaled around East La Mirada on a rusty beach cruiser looking for beer and trouble. At 6'4", 280 pounds, he was way too big for that bike. His light brown hair was spiked and clipped, which made him look like a surfer turned punk. Even though Eddie was from Orange County, he buddied up with Sailor and partied among other LMPs in order to stay out of their line of fire.

I was super intrigued by this punk rock gang thing and would hassle Eddie for details. He had befriended members of other gangs that had sprung up in the scene. One of the most recognized was the L.A. Death Squad. On the street they were simply called "The LADS." Strong allies from the get-go with LMP, they had members living in Hollywood and parts of the South Bay. Certain LADS wore skull-and-crossbones armbands and dressed in all black. LMP, along with LADS, started making waves in the city, at shows, and most punk hotspots. Eddie had grown up near Vicious Circle gang, a tough little force that held their own from the beach cities, but maintained their strong core in Long Beach. Their name originated from a band that once boasted Jack Grisham as lead singer. Jack later became the frontman and throttle of the mighty T.S.O.L. band. Eddie also spoke of another outfit that just formed called Circle One, similarly named after a band they followed. Their gang members were easily spotted in white long-sleeved button-ups with tails bearing an insignia on the arm. Violence and destruction at Circle One shows were often attributed to the gang's antics.

Hollywood's punk music scene kept moving forward, with local bands playing harder and faster than any other bands in the genre. Even bands in England weren't playing with such ferocity. In L.A., it became known as "Hardcore Punk" due to this new style. Things were changing; first-wave punk had ended, and 1980 was in full swing. A new generation of people and bands were venturing onto a scene driven by changing times. Reagan was on his way in, vowing to take down the evil commies and force the freeloaders off welfare. Our country was fed up with pussy-ass Jimmy Carter for botching the Iran hostage crisis and putting us in a recession. Americans welcomed Reagan's conservative message with open arms. Time for a crackdown on the riff-raff; if you weren't some kind of preppy, you were a target for the authorities.

Punk in L.A. answered the whole thing with Hardcore and a big Fuck You! An intense form of nihilism took hold of the scene. Everyone started dropping the Sid Vicious look, favoring a more confrontational military style, complete with buzz cuts and combat boots, similar to Shawn Kerri's skanking punk logo for the Circle Jerks. Orange County also produced a lot of bands during this time. Most of them sucked and OC became the inventors of what we called "Bubblegum Punk." Punks from OC like my pal Eddie were friends with the Hollywood crowd, but most of their bands weren't welcomed in Los Angeles. The bands almost always stayed on their side of So Cal, playing shows in Costa Mesa at a club called the Cuckoo's Nest. The same acts played there every week. T.S.O.L. and the Adolescents were really the only OC bands embraced in Hollywood.

ACTION AT THE CUCKOO'S NEST, PHOTO BY MONK ROCK.

ince venues in Hollywood were hard to come by, hardcore groups came from all over the Los Angeles area and played in cities like Long Beach, San Pedro, Compton, East L.A., Pasadena, Pomona, and the San Fernando Valley. Nine times out of ten, booking punk bands resulted in destruction of club property and injury to employees. There was simply no profit in it. Tiny clubs, overfilled with bodies crammed in front of the stage, pushing and shoving during the set as others still tried to pogo up and down. This combination of enthusiasm and expression in front of the stage gave birth to "Slam Dancing." Punks now assailed each other with elbows, kicks, forearm shivers, and flailing fists. No one was really trying to hurt each other, but rather pump each other up to see how much we could dish out and take in an area termed "The Slam Pit." Only punks understood.

uring the school week, my mother started keeping a more watchful eye on me, making it nearly impossible to slip out of the house. Once, Eddie planned a trip to the Whisky a Go Go on a Thursday. That night became legend throughout the punk community for years to come … and I missed it. The Whisky was a notorious breeding ground for discord. There was always a ton of punks and street freaks hanging out in front, still amped up from the show. Five gung-ho Marines showed up after the gig, starting fights with everyone outside. Sailor was leaving the Whisky when one of the jarheads decided to taunt him. He lost his temper on the dot and challenged all five to fight. In front of the entire punk rock world, Sailor went to work. The Marines were well-trained, landing quality blows, but their attack had the reverse effect of feeding his fury. He distributed a combination of ferocious head butts and accurate power shots, destroying them in a matter of minutes. Once they were out cold on their backs, Sailor gave merciless boot kicks to each so hard that the crowd heard ribs cracking and limbs breaking. Eddie said members from the LADS and Circle One gangs just stood there, mouths agape, in awe of his brutal street-fighting skills. Sailor's reputation proliferated from Hollywood out to the Valley, and all the way to the beach cities, letting everyone know LMPs were bad news.

During this time, the LMP gang was getting known as heavy-duty players in the violence game. Word spread around that they were responsible for killing somebody on Sunset Boulevard. The story went that somebody mouthed off too much and ended up stabbed to death. I heard many versions, but they all ended in murder. It happened opening night of the movie *Friday the 13th*. Nobody actually came out and took credit for the homicide, though LMP were the only crew seen in the area.

LMPs could be found stirring up trouble all over Hollywood, loitering in the parking lot across the street from the Whisky a Go-Go, or partying at legendary actor/sleazeball Errol Flynn's dilapidated estate. Errol Flynn's was an infamous gathering site for all sorts of derelicts and reckless youth, located in the hills north of Franklin Avenue, where Fuller Street ends. On the front gate, spray-painted in large letters, were the words "La Mirada Punks." No one ever messed with it. LMP held down this notable danger zone for some time.

You could also find the gang hanging out, scaring customers away at the well-known punk spot Oki-Dog hot dog stand on Santa Monica Boulevard. Behind Oki-Dog, down off the alley, was another original hangout known as "Punk Park." One of Hollywood's first actual punk rock gang fights took place there between LMP and Circle One. Disciples from both gangs clashed at a gig in Hollywood, putting two from Circle One in the hospital. A few weeks later both crews ran into each other at full strength. Circle One chose not to tangle and disappeared. Later that night, with most of their numbers intact, they regrouped at Punk Park. Circle One gang were still fuming over their two casualties. A smaller group of LMPs showed up, thinking Circle One had split. Circle One saw their chance for revenge and attacked hard with fists, bottles, and whatever they could get their hands on. The LMPs were momentarily caught off guard, but some of their best fighters were there to even the odds. After a knock-your-teeth-out and drag-you-down-the-gutter skirmish, Circle One fled the scene.

Next weekend, LMP came to Hollywood nearly 30 strong, wanting Circle One blood. LMP considered them pussies for attacking when they were outnumbered, so now it was all-out war. Both clans were attending a show at full strength when LMP located the leader of Circle One. Numerous LMP members began staring him down, specifically making cold gestures of slitting their throats and blowing their brains out. The leader, who was no wimp by any means, knew that LMP would surely kill him first, and wanted no part of this. Circle One sent over a neutral friend of both gangs to confirm they wanted no problems with LMP ever again. Santino sent word back that their leader and anyone with him would die a painful death if they stuck around Hollywood. Circle One took the threat seriously, disappearing from the gig that night and, as a matter of record, gone from the entire city.

LMPs were so riled up and high on thoughts of violence, they ended up stabbing two beach city punks who unfortunately wanted beef after the show. One victim ran off after being knifed in the lower chest cavity, collapsing a couple of blocks away. He died in the street alone. No one found out what happened to the other guy, who ran off into the night dripping blood, making animal sounds, never to be seen again. Very few punks from the beach ever considered the fact that some gangs played for keeps. For days after, the scene buzzed about the stabbings. Everyone was talking about the La Mirada Punks and their murderous ways. You can bet Circle One heard about all of it, knowing they had escaped death by the skin of their teeth. For a number of years they kept the peace, and their distance from LMP.

Weeks later, I was hanging out with Eddie, Janet, and Fay at Oki-Dog. Amidst the constant crowd of losers and boulevard trash were a few recognizable LMPs, including Sailor. A group of OC punks that Eddie and the girls knew were prancing around, doing their best to draw attention to themselves. One in particular went on and on yammering louder than anyone else about who was who and what was what in the punk scene. We recognized him to be Tony Cadena, lead singer of the Adolescents. In the middle of his theatrics, he spoke some bullshit about LMP. Bad idea. Janet and Fay despised violence and both started throwing food at each other to distract from the situation. Punk rock's most feared street fighter, Sailor, walked right over to tiny Tony, picked him up by the neck one-handed, and stuffed him into a trash can. He put the lid on top and sat down on it, all 6'4", 280 pounds of him. Tony screamed and beat against the lid while Sailor simply sat there drinking beer out of a paper bag. His friends made no attempt to rescue him or plead his case. After an hour, Tony began whimpering and crying out loud like a baby. It was hilarious; everyone around started cracking up and pointing at the garbage can ... nobody cared how good his bad was. The four of us made a move to split. As we left I looked back and noticed Sailor sadistically tapping on the lid. Wish I had that guy on my side.

Sunday, December 7, 1980—a date which will live in infamy. Darby Crash, singer of the Germs, is found dead of a heroin overdose, just like Sid Vicious. The news got overshadowed by the fatal shooting of John Lennon, leader of the hippie crusade. Now both leaders of our movement were gone. Darby and Sid made a heavy impact on our scene with their outrageous behavior, style, and fuck-everyone attitude. All punks wanted to dress and act like those two ultimate antiheroes who scared mainstream society. Darby's death hit home with everyone who participated in the L.A. punk scene. He had a special connection with all of us who watched him perform. I was fortunate enough to have met him. The night before he died, Sailor bullied Darby outside Oki-Dog, pushing him around to the point of tears. Later on that same evening, a loaded Darby pleaded with Joker of LMP to sell him a gun. Darby Crash often romanticized about dying young; most of us thought of it as dramatics. We never figured out what exactly the gun was for—protection from Sailor or a means to commit suicide? These deaths left a legitimate void in my life at the end of 1980, though little did I know the adventure had just begun. No one could deny the Sex Pistols belonged to the first generation, but we were all sons of Sid Vicious.

CHAPTER 2
"YOUTH GONE MAD"

ARCH 1981, PRESIDENT REAGAN GOT SHOT. Ha ha ha! The papers said triggerman John Hinckley Jr. was trying to impress Jodie Foster, à la Travis Bickle, by offing the president. He had watched *Taxi Driver* 15 times in a row just before his big moment. How appropriate, Ronald Reagan's would-be assassin was a punk rocker.

School sucks as usual and I'm a marked man. Teachers, principals, teenage narcs, everyone was just waiting for me to step out of line so they can put me in cuffs, or worse. Every day I did barely enough to get by and keep 'em all off my back. That weekend Gary and I decided to go to the swap meet and see if we could pick up some metal studs for our jackets. Time to step up our look. La Mirada swap meet, like all swap meets, was a great place for low-rents to get separated from their cash. Aisles of crap you eventually regretted buying. Our swap meet's special sideshow attraction featured the "Cambodian Swamp Rat" booth. Like some shitty carnival, you paid one dollar to step inside and view a preserved dead rat four feet in length. A long line of sucker children and slow parents waited patiently for a sick thrill. We were too hip for that scam. The booth with studs and spikes was all that mattered. We knew we could get them from Bobbo, a soldier-of-fortune hippie who sold knives, custom leather goods, and military patches.

Approaching his section, we noticed something had changed. Sailor was now splitting the booth and had set up a makeshift barber chair with a sign reading "Punk Rock Haircuts 10 Bucks." The both of them were already drunk by 11 a.m. and feeling good. Gary and I were looking over the merchandise when Sailor began giving us the hard sell.

"You need Sailor's signature Mohawk to go with those studs. You can't buy Bobbo the hippie's stuff and not get a haircut!"

Bobbo smirked, going along with Sailor's bully tactics while I picked through the goods.

Sailor homed in on Gary.

"Don't you want a Mohawk to scare everybody with?"

Gary hesitated, looking for a way out. "I only got eight bucks."

Sailor eyeballed me.

"Bet your buddy here will loan you a couple bucks, he looks totally stand-up to me."

I turned to Gary to see if he was serious as Sailor persisted.

"Come on, cough up some bucks, afraid he's gonna be more punk than you?"

I countered, "I won't have enough money for studs."

"So? Bobbo's not going anywhere. Look at him...."

What could I do? My customized jacket could wait a week. Watching Gary get a Mohawk was going to be one for the books.

Sailor took our money, sat Gary in the chair, and told him, "Just hold up for a minute, let a crowd gather around, they really get a kick out of this shit."

Bobbo put in his two cents.

"We would have twice the crowd if we were over by that fucking Cambodian rat booth, someone needs to shut that sideshow down. It's a Vietnam flashback waiting to happen ... it's irresponsible!"

After about ten minutes and two more beers a small crowd gathered around. Sailor addressed his audience, "This kid here is no pussy like most of you—he's got balls!"

People began pointing and clamoring as Sailor took his time giving the perfect Mohawk. When he finished I jealously spoke up.

"All the chicks at the Palladium tonight are gonna think you're from England."

Sailor lifted his brow, "Palladium? Who has the wheels? I'm in!"

That's all it took. I was now officially hanging out with Sailor, brawling legend of LMP.

We had to pick Sailor up that night in deep, deep LMP/CV3 territory. Sailor said drive directly to his house, pull in the driveway, and stay in the car since his street was hot. After Gary idled his truck for several minutes, Sailor walked outside and hopped in the bed, holding a 12-pack, no questions asked. I jumped in back with him so he didn't have to ride alone. Plus it was a chance to see first-hand what the legend was all about.

Suburban homes along the I-5 freeway transitioned to the manufacturing district, then the housing projects, in one energizing blur until we hit the 101. It was a real rush soaring up the freeway drinking beers with Sailor. All of a sudden, Sailor says to me, "Watch this," and climbed out of the truck bed. Motoring at freeway speed he stood on the edge of the back bumper, holding the tailgate with one hand, guzzling beer with the other. Sailor surfed the bumper for a good ten minutes, scaring other drivers to death. I couldn't believe my eyes; a stuntman at least would've used a harness. Gary was sweating bullets behind the wheel. Sailor gripped the tailgate like an enemy's throat, as he savored his last few drops of beer. In a tantrum, he hurled his can fanatically at the other cars trying to swerve away from us, climbed back in the truck, then sat down next to me and opened another beer.

"That was pretty stupid, huh?"

At 13 years of age, I was in no position to agree or disagree with him. I knew then, Sailor the brawling legend was crazy, too.

Once we arrived at the Palladium parking lot, I noticed Gary was still on edge.

"Hey, I want to show you something, come take a look at this." Gary pointed to the tailgate, gave it a tap with his fist, and BANG it crashed open.

"It's fucking busted, there's no way that should have stayed shut."

Sailor hardly reacted. "Come on, let's go beat some ass."

SAILOR, THE
BRAWLING LEGEND.

I nside the Palladium, the slam pit was expanding and churning at fever pitch. I watched everyone push, shove, hit, and kick anyone within range. I'd been in more than a few regular-size pits, and one crazy one at Hong Kong Café where somebody threw a bar stool in the middle ... but this was the Hollywood Palladium. More punks equal more punishment. I wound up in the pit stomping, bashing, and thrashing when this big fat guy openly blindsided me to the floor.

Sailor picked me up in step with the body storm and told me to "Get some payback!"

Shit, how did I get put in this position? I couldn't cheese in front of the legend. What he forgot to tell me was the fatso was his buddy from LMP's Norwalk Dukes chapter. I started slamming again and noticed the fat guy breathing heavy, chugging a beer at the side of the pit. My eyes locked in on him. He put the can to his mouth and I charged. I caught fatso off guard. Slugged him square in the stomach. Out of shape and drunk he nearly hit the floor. Next thing I knew, he was catching up to me in the pit threatening to kill me. He slickly kicked some kid's feet out from under him, thinking it was me. It caused a small uproar and some punk chick got in his face. The timely diversion was over before it got started, but it allowed me to avoid that cheapshot artist for the rest of the show. Sailor laughed his ass off about it all the way home.

"You two looked like a punk rock Laurel and Hardy. You're lucky you gave that dude the slip; if he had grabbed a hold of you, he would have shown no mercy, believe that."

"Screw that tub-o-lard, he hit me from behind!"

"That tub-o-lard is my pal from our Norwalk chapter and he's stone cold as they come."

He handed me his half-empty beer and slapped me on the back.

"You did good. I'll give you a Mohawk for half price."

L ate that night, awake in bed, I watched a B-movie on TV called *The Car*. A sinister chopped '71 Lincoln with no driver was terrorizing a small desert town, randomly running over innocent people. The raven-black car was possessed by Satan and totally unstoppable. Stephen King's *Christine* felt like a cheap knockoff; the plot was similar but nowhere near as scary. Images of people being brutally killed tweaked my sleep till morning. That evil car stuck with me in the weirdest way.

Next day, half asleep, I rode my skateboard through the streets of East Whittier. The whole time, it felt like somebody was watching me. I couldn't shake the paranoia. I started to cut down a side street, hopped off a curb, and munched it. Hard. I picked up my broken skateboard, stunned by what I saw … did I just crack my crown? Was this the result of a concussion? Felt like I was in a daze, because right behind me sat "The Car" itself, menacing blacked-out glass and all. Panic.

I started to book it when the window came down and a girl's voice called out, "Hey, get in. We'll give you a ride."

I paused. They looked like punk rockers. Pretty sure I saw them around La Mirada before, but never in that fucking scary Lincoln. The guy waved me over and opened the door. Convinced they were local punks, I got inside, no reservations.

Leather seats, dingle balls, power windows, "The Car" was fully custom. Wow, one night I'm watching the movie, next day I'm in the back seat of the most evil wheels ever … driven by punks! The driver told me her name was Sickness; the passenger's name was Vitamin Ena and they were in a punk rock band called Youth Gone Mad. Sickness was a tall, slim, white girl with hard features, but pretty. She looked hardcore in her Levis, boots, and purposely smeared eye makeup. Vitamin Ena was a European mutt, way over six feet tall, bony, hunched over, and creepy ugly—like Ramones ugly. Looking at him, you would say he was born to be punk rock. He dressed like Sid Vicious—black leather and band buttons all over his jacket, with a skeleton key padlock around his neck. Both were already out of high school. On the way home they invited me to their band practice and made plans to pick me up later that evening. When we pulled up to my house, I asked Sickness, "Where did you get this badass car?"

She replied matter-of-factly, "I fucked some Hollywood producer for it."

As "The Car" pulled away I noticed the license plate read "MR 666" and the license plate frame said "Lucifer's Limousine."

MOVIE STILL
FROM *THE CAR*, 1977.

fter I shoveled down a quick dinner, my new pals were at the house to pick me up. I climbed into the back seat and sat down next to a short, dark-haired beauty, pale as a corpse, with the foulest mouth I've ever heard. The girl spewed cusswords a mile a minute, then turned to me, without missing a beat: "They call me Donna the Dead."

Donna claimed to be "honorary" president of Youth Gone Mad's fan club and she was determined to make it bigger than the Misfits Fiend Club. I already knew of Donna; her reputation preceded her as a solid street fighter who could beat guys up. She was an LMP member like the rest of Youth Gone Mad. Donna's fighting skills, paired with a nasty temper, made her the most unpredictable of all the girls in LMP. Other punk rock gangs had girls who hung out, but weren't actual members. LMP had female members like lowrider gangs. Donna the Dead was 17 and 100% aggro. Barely five feet tall, we called her "Itsy-bitsy" behind her back. No one had the stones to say it to her face.

On the way to Vitamin Ena's garage, she whispered in my ear, "You sure are a cute little punk rocker." It was love at first sight for the two of us. From then on Donna the Dead and I were inseparable. We even looked related, so we always told people we were siblings. She lived near my junior high, making it easy to cut class and spend the entire day at her house having fun. We drank, got high, cooked some food, and then sat on her couch watching her dad's X-rated movies. She loved the acting—and hated the sex.

eading into the summer of 1981, early evenings were spent in La Habra Heights watching Youth Gone Mad practice while we got fucked up on drugs and alcohol. When the band got bored, it was off to Hollywoodland loaded. Every time we left the neighborhood, people stared out their windows, fearful of "The Car" and its satanic presence. Sickness wasn't any kind of devil worshiper, but she enjoyed giving people the idea she was. Wherever she parked the vehicle, it ended up covered in Christian pamphlets with warnings to repent. Giving people the creeps never got old.

Hollywood became our playground. It was easy to get away with ridiculous behavior due to a lack of cops patrolling the city. LAPD seemed okay with the insanity so long as it stayed there, without spilling into suburban areas of affluence. Tourists generally kept away, especially at night; Tinseltown was too seedy and dangerous. We wandered through the freak show from club to club, maybe catching a gig, or up to Errol Flynn's with more booze and drugs, then back down to Oki-Dog to eat and hang out. Oki-Dog was located on the main drag, where all the gay bars were. A dollar bought you a bag of huge, long, heavy French fries—not for eating but for throwing. Our night usually ended driving down Santa Monica Boulevard, chucking ketchup-drenched fries at the homosexuals who walked the street cruising for sex. Pelting them all summer long was an LMP tradition.

One afternoon, a punk rocker I recognized from around La Mirada showed up at the liquor store where I played arcade games. He offered to smoke me out with homegrown pot he ripped off from his brother. After getting stoned, the two of us realized we lived only four blocks away from each other. He told me he was from LMP and his name was Youngblood. The kid was narrow, with arms too skinny for his body, which complemented his droopy eyes. We were the same age, about the same height, and both wore a traditional look of cuffed Levis, engineer boots, and plain white T-shirts. Youngblood drove around in a red four-door '68 Oldsmobile with a British Union Jack flag painted on the roof. His car was punk rock trash that stood out a mile away. Inside, the seats were missing, replaced with five folding beach chairs that slid all over when you turned corners. It was a hectic deathtrap, making every trip an act of courage. Even more ridiculous, Youngblood was two years too young to get a legal driver's license.

Youngblood and I started spending a lot of time together at his house, where the parents had no control over what went on. At the time, I had never seen anything like it. His 19-year-old brother was an original LMP named Boxer. He made a living working construction and weird odd jobs. According to Youngblood, Boxer loved throwing blows but was never satisfied with just winning. He critiqued his every performance like a pro. Boxer even had the intimidating face of an Irish mug. His bedroom was an LMP clubhouse where all the originals congregated. A colossal, floor-to-ceiling British flag was painted on one wall. LMP was written neighborhood-style down the side, with every member listed below. In one corner stood a giant pot plant. In the other corner, a mini-refrigerator with a beer keg inside, and a tap at the top ready to serve.

After Boxer left for work in the morning, Youngblood and I broke into his room and stole weed harvested from his plant. We each filled up a plastic gallon milk container full of beer, then the day was ours to party at Donna the Dead's or the Youth Gone Mad garage. Late afternoon it was back to Youngblood's. Boxer returned home from work about that time, always with a few different LMP members. All of us kicked our feet up together and watched a newly premiered TV channel called MTV. They showed nothing but music videos from crummy '70s corporate rock bands all of us hated. Music television was downright bizarre … but we were addicted. The channel bombarded you with wild visual styles and hot chicks with stupid hair. Sensory overload.

Youngblood and Boxer were always stealing from each other: weed, beer, pills, food, girls, and most of all, gasoline. Many times I sat quietly while Youngblood took a shower and watched Boxer slip outside with a hose and siphon the gas out of his brother's Oldsmobile. Twenty minutes later it was Boxer's turn to shower. Then, Youngblood would sneak outside and siphon Boxer's car, never realizing he was only stealing back his own gasoline. This went on every day for years. Out of pure selfish enjoyment, I never said anything to either of them.

Youngblood and I ran together all summer long. Money came first. Then fun. We walked Hollywood Boulevard to Sunset, scouting and scheming. Night after night, we were hobnobbing with the depraved. Hollywood was dangerous and people looking for danger were around every corner. One evening, some old character followed us down the "Walk of Fame," out of place and stiff. Every now and then he ducked down or hid in the corners. Once eye contact was made, the deviant came up to us, mumbling.

"They won't let me in all the cool places. I want some and I got the money for it."

No need to confer with Youngblood; we were connected, fast minds on the same page.

"What you looking for?"

The sick pervert got enthusiastic. "I want something naughty. Really naughty."

Youngblood spoke up, "We can take care of you, no problem. What do you want? Girl or boy?"

"I want a homeless girl to punch me in the face."

I stepped in to close the deal.

"We can set that up, just give us something so she knows you're for real."

He produced a ten-dollar bill from a Velcro wallet.

Youngblood shook his head.

"It'll take more than that to get her interested."

He anxiously handed over another ten bucks, no questions asked.

"Okay, wait right over there, we'll be back in ten minutes. For the right amount of money this girl will bust you up good."

He waited there, fixing his hair and clothes, readying himself for a hot date. Youngblood and I vanished as soon as we turned the corner. We could have found a runaway skank to do it cheap, but why bother? Easy money. That kind of amusement happened all the time.

Another broke night doing the Grauman's Chinese bit, Eddie, Youngblood, and I posed for snapshots with all sorts of out-of-towners. Tourists made me want to vomit. At least Eddie always offered up some insider gossip on punk and the streets in general. He laughed about fucking this rich punk slut, her father being the one and only actor who portrayed a bumbling foreign detective in the movies. His daughter was allegedly the girl L.A.'s Wasted Youth wrote a song about titled "Uni-High Beefrag."

"She's getting richer day by day
She really makes me sick
Uni-High Beefrag
She's getting money every day
She really makes me sick
Uni-High Beefrag
She's Uni-High's richest punk rocker
She's Uni-High's wealthiest slut
She is a stuck-up cunt
It's Clitoria!"

"Any punk can fuck her," Eddie said, "If she comes your way, make her pay you."

The warm night drifted. Dollars were starting to add up when a woman in a simple white cotton dress and sandals walked by. Her eyes were hidden behind dark sunglasses but I could tell she was looking right at me. Something made me talk.

"Hey, don't you want a picture with a real live punk rocker?"

She laughed. "No, not really … it doesn't impress me."

I thought for a quick comeback as I approached her.

"Don't you want to scare your friends back home?"

"Home is three blocks away," the woman playfully retorted as she lowered her glasses. I noticed she was definitely in her mid-20s and definitely amused.

"Don't you want to help me save up to go to college?"

She half laughed, "Doubt you'll make it through high school."

"I'm Frank, what's your name?"

She shook my hand just long enough to give me hope.

"Not this time, Frank, I'm not into boulevard come-ons...."

Her words put my hope on hold as she walked away.

"You catch that, Youngblood? That woman was all over me."

"Oh, I saw all right ... you ain't got a shot in hell; she was like twice your age."

"So what, I'm in love!"

Dark hair and light eyes always did something to me. As a young boy, my father brought me to his truck yard in the city of Vernon, where I got into all kinds of mischief while he went out on deliveries. I regularly snuck into the parts room and leafed through their Playboy magazine collection when they weren't looking. The pale-eyed brunettes were hypnotizing. One day I painstakingly cut out all their pictures and smuggled them home. Those naked girls ended up taped all over my bedroom walls that same night. My mother saw them and almost had a heart attack. She tore the naked ladies down and threw them in the garbage.

"You and Sam need to be better influences, he's at an impressionable age; he should learn to respect women."

My dad and his boss Sam Sciortino got a big kick out of it. Somehow the magazines at his work were still left in plain sight for me to swipe.

CHAPTER 3
"THE BOYS NEXT DOOR"

pparently, I was under the watchful eye of original LMP members the whole time Youngblood and I were hanging out. Youngblood religiously gave them updates of how I handled myself on the streets and in the scene. What I thought was another ordinary day, waiting for Boxer to leave so we could steal his beer, turned into much more.

Into the room walked a fistful of LMPs giving me the eye up and down. I searched Youngblood's face to see if he knew what was up. Four original LMPs stood over me: X-man, Santino, Boxer, and Joker. I quickly sized them all up. X-man was Costa Rican, way more a lover than a fighter. Revolving women were his preoccupation so I wasn't concerned. The other three were pure poison. I had heard the stories of Santino and even witnessed him bounce a big cinder block off someone's back when they were already down. Delivering sound, accurate punches was a point of pride with Boxer and I'm sure he pegged me for the missing beer and weed. Joker had a real face of death, which worried me.

Santino spoke up.

"You know the rules if you're gonna keep hanging out."

Boxer took off his flight jacket; Joker moved the chairs out of the way.

Youngblood chimed in, "Do it, Frank, this is your chance!"

Conflicting thoughts ran through my mind. This was it. LMP members were all I'd been hanging out with for quite some time. Getting jumped in was just a formality. The guys started to circle; I put 'em up and braced for the attack. Punches came in bunches. A dense cloud of knuckles and flesh tried to bury me. I countered best I could as the blows kept coming. A crate of records got in my way, tripping me and sending me to the floor. Boot kicks nailed me in the ribs, back, and stomach. Lying there, all I saw were the "Royal Colors" of the British flag painted on the wall before blacking out.

Channel 3's "I've Got a Gun" roaring from Boxer's speakers opened my eyes.

"City boy hit the downtown streets, be wise don't go it alone
Helping hand is at your fingertips, lock the door and pick up the phone
Dial 1 800 999 865 654 28, C.O.D. through the UPS
Smith and Wesson Magnum point 38

This punk's got an equalizer, all it takes a little loot
That's right it's your turn to hide, the shoe's on the other foot

I got a gun, looking out for number one
I got a gun man, manslaughter can be fun..."

Who knows how long I was out? Above me, my new gang pounded beers, cheered, and yelled. Still foggy, I lay there while the originals reminisced about other jump-ins and how they took it easy on me.

"Usually it's one minute minimum," Santino proclaimed, "but I didn't want to trash Boxer's room. This is my home away from home." I stayed comfortable on the carpet, contemplating my future as the cobwebs began to clear. In an instant all the hair-raising details of LMP nights in Hollywood came back to me. My personal journey into mayhem and murder was about to begin.

LMP gang already had multiple parts to it. One crew in my home city of La Mirada, one in Whittier, and one in Norwalk. All were causing chaos in the scene independently, but still functioned as one gang when need be. Each city was geographically hooked together. Each clique had 20–25 members per city. The numbers were about to grow to 40–50 in La Mirada and Whittier. A new chapter in the city of La Habra was getting underway with about 20 members. The Norwalk clique stayed small, tight-knit, and lethal. LMP also forged stronger ties with LADS. No single gang in the scene could stop us. Everybody had to shut up and take it. Thugsey of LMP used to say, "We will go down in history as the largest and deadliest punk rock gang or all of our enemies will join forces and destroy us."

gangs garnering local attention

La Habra Police Department collection of weapons confiscated from punkers includes many handmade weapons

Staff photo / Juaquine Matthews

WHATEVER LMP COULD GET THEIR HANDS ON. NOTICE "POSER BEATER" WRITTEN ON BAT (TOP OF PHOTO).

unk rock gang growth turned epidemic in La Mirada at a time when the sight of one punk in any city was uncommon. Only at a gig could you find more punk rock gang members. The place became a spawning ground for violent punks; too many sharks in the same tank. Youth unrest, close proximity to L.A.'s gang banging neighborhoods, and the punk movement proved to be a malignant cocktail. Nobody knew how badly this would escalate in the years to come. I don't know how one city ended up so unlucky.

My neighborhood in La Mirada was thick with LMP members. Santino lived on an infamous block we called "Easy Street." At the end were brothers Bumper and Barney. Two houses down lived The Captain. Across the road was Thugsey. Sailor stayed a block away and Magnum was two streets over. Popeye, brothers Shadow and Bubbles, Wank, Cooper, Larry, Dale, Pino, X-man, Willy, along with brothers Boxer and Youngblood, were also in the same section. At least 15 more resided in a one-mile radius. Not to mention plenty of female LMP members lived nearby—Crescent, Linda, Mel, Big Annie, Wanda, Scary Sherry, Donna the Dead, Sickness, Gilligan, Marie, and at least five or six more whose names I don't remember.

SANTINO,
EASY STREET.

LMP was like one big unhappy family. You never knew when a situation would turn into the disturbed and unimaginable. Behind Santino's street lived Willy, who came from punk's first wave, like Eddie. Willy, an LMP original, was phasing out. His dad got injured on the job and, being the good son, he took care of him. Willy never took off his filthy construction clothes and stopped going to gigs altogether. Everyone loved him anyway. He unexpectedly decided to host a pre-Youth Gone Mad show gathering. It was customary for someone to throw a party in the neighborhood before a gig. Right off the bat, I noticed Willy had tiptoed off to his bedroom with Sickness. Next thing I knew, he came running back—screaming like a banshee.

Santino wanted answers.

"What the fuck you yelling for? What happened?"

He answered by taking down his pants. Nobody wanted to look, but how could we resist? Willy pulled out his willy and carved on the top of it was a fresh bloody X.

"Look what she did to me!"

I spit out my beer laughing as the whole room erupted in unison. Santino demanded what we all wanted to know.

"How the fuck did that happen?"

Still in shock, Willy replied, "She used a razor blade on it."

Santino questioned him further.

"Why didn't you move or get out? You some kind of sick fag?"

"No ... I ... I ... I was too scared, her green pussy frightened me—I couldn't move, I was too freaked to move," is all he kept saying over and over.

After that it took a long time before any LMP considered getting Sickness into bed. I had to admit, dyeing her pubic hair fluorescent green was as punk as it got.

Sickness wasn't crazy, she just did crazy things. Sailor's neighbor, Responsibility, and most loyal sidekick Magnum, on the other hand, was state-certified 5150. The Norwalk State Metropolitan Mental Hospital wound up being his second home. We referred to that place as the "ding module." No one could count how many times he had been in there. Magnum was legal drinking age and an intimidating six-foot-tall punk. Everyone thought his mother was the meanest lady alive, identical to Sissy Spacek's mom in *Carrie*.

He loved telling people, "I'm really Johnny Rotten, singer of the Sex Pistols."

His favorite topic of conversation was jerking off. His favorite line with girls: "You know, my hand gives me more pleasure than your pussy ever could!"

Sitting in the back of a covered pickup, en route to Hollywood, Santino decided to provoke Magnum. Our favorite mental case happened to be sitting next an uninformed female LMP member.

"Gilligan here really wants you to jerk your meat for her."

Before she could dispute the request, his pants were down around his ankles and he was off to the races. Jerk-off Magnum stared right into Gilligan's pupils and robotically masturbated to her frozen face. We let him go for a minute, then decided to cover him up with an old furni pad. He didn't stop. Gilligan had no sense of humor and started kicking Magnum's jack-off tent, trying to make him quit. He merely grunted after every boot, until he reached the finish line.

Countless times during the night, Magnum would ride his bike to the mental hospital, located about a mile from our neighborhood. He ritually knocked on the door, and pleaded with the staff to commit him.

"Let me in, I want to be me again, I don't deserve to be out here!"

Hospital protocol forced them to turn him away, even though he clearly needed psychiatric attention. One night, after getting customarily turned away, he piloted his bicycle straight to Winchell's Donut House. There he spotted two local sheriffs inside eating doughnuts, drinking coffee. Magnum walked right up to the window and tapped on the glass with a pair of homemade nunchucks.

The police report stated:

Male suspect dressed in punker attire, wearing a "Fuck Iran" shirt, pro-
voked my partner Deputy Riggs and I. Suspect began taunting us with a dan-
gerous weapon known as nunchucks, as we filled out reports at a local coffee
shop. Following his threatening behavior, the two of us exited the premises
in an attempt to contact the male suspect. We asked him his name. He stated
"Ace." "Ace what is your last name?" I questioned. Male subject replied, "Ace
you out motherfuckers!" He then started twirling and spinning his weapon in
an aggressive manner as he moved toward us. During this threatening dem-
onstration we moved in to detain him. After a brief struggle in which Deputy
Riggs deployed his mace, we subdued and cuffed the male suspect.

Magnum got what he wanted—an E-ticket ride to the ding module. Unfortunately, a tough police trimming that included a separated shoulder came
along with it.

Nothing slowed him down. After his release, he believed he was a karate
expert. We saw him, for what must have been six straight hours, crossing a
busy street back and forth. Magnum kept pressing the walk button, making traffic stop, then showing off his focused karate kicks and chops in the middle of
the intersection. He even attempted to communicate with drivers in Japanese.
Santino, two Norwalk LMPs, and I came back later that day to check on him.

Our two comrades asked Santino, "Can he get arrested for this?"

Santino replied, "He's not hurting anyone and it's legal to cross the street
speaking Japanese, right?"

I didn't see a problem either; at least he wasn't jerking off at traffic. When
we arrived back in our neighborhood, Santino told our crew what Magnum was
up to. Boxer said he saw Magnum at the same intersection last week, only that
time he had a whistle in his mouth while directing traffic.

"I yelled at him, what the fuck are you doing? He yelled back at me, I'm
working for the police now! They're paying me to eat burgers, drink coffee, and
direct traffic!"

Everybody wished that we could get Magnum the help he needed. Especially Sailor. The ding module equaled a dead end.

When our crew ran out of liquor-buying options, we had a trump card
known as "The Captain," still in his teens but looked close to 30. Short, stocky,
with a five o'clock shadow that looked like it was growing right in front of you.
Even the backs of his fingers and thumbs were covered with hair. Santino's

dad said he was a dead ringer for a 1940s wrestling villain. Once he got tightened up, he morphed into "Captain Out of Hand," the woman-hating drunkard. When women rejected him, it sparked something heinous inside. He made them pay. Where these reactions came from is anybody's guess.

Captain was at a bar in the guts of Hollywood, well into a three-day bender. A girl who was way out of his league tried to walk by. What should've been a normal pass at a hot girl shifted sour in an instant.

Captain Out of Hand grabbed hold of her wrist.

"You goin' my way? Huh? Huh? Because I ain't asking you, I know you've tasted the dirty before!"

Mortified, she yanked loose and sidestepped past him. Captain Out of Hand retaliated with a solid punch to the back that sent her flying. Barney and I tackled him right out the door before the bouncers went George Foreman on us.

Getting back to the car we asked him, "What for?"

"'Cause she's scared to take her clothes off … they're all scared to take their clothes off!"

A couple weeks later, Captain's alter ego struck again. I was returning home with him from a show at Dancing Waters, San Pedro, sound asleep in the back of his car. A girl from our block sat in the passenger seat. Yelling suddenly opened my eyes.

"A deal's a deal! I give you a ride to the gig, you eat my cock, you wench!"

His hand was palming her head, pushing it down toward his crotch.

"Ewww, what are you doing! Let go of me, you crazy asshole!!"

As he turned the steering wheel, she squirmed loose.

"Stop this car … pull over … let me out now!!"

She cracked the door open, hoping he would stop.

It worked in reverse.

"You don't go down, then you go out!"

Captain Out of Hand gave her a big-time boot shove right out the door. She hit the pavement hard and tumbled down the street. I looked out the rear window in equal parts horror and amazement. Captain Out of Hand drove on, completely at ease with himself, like nothing ever happened.

Shadow and his brother Bubbles lived a short distance from The Captain. One Friday night, Captain showed up to their home while the brothers were out causing trouble. He walked right inside unannounced and made his way to the TV room. Their mother was enjoying chocolate ice cream, watching the Million

Dollar Movie while lounging in her bathrobe. During a commercial break she glanced away from the screen and saw The Captain standing in the room with an overeager look on his face. She hopped up from the couch.

"The boys are out. What are you doing here?"

He flatly replied, "I'm going to rape you, bitch."

Alarmed, she bolted directly to her bedroom and locked the door. Captain walked out of the house, straight to the liquor store for more beer, then to Santino's and met up with us. Santino asked him where he'd been all night.

Captain answered, "Out fucking this old bag for a couple hours."

We figured he was just telling more fish stories of pussy from his drunken imagination.

Shadow and Bubbles found out next morning that Captain got way out of hand with their mother. Bubbles procured a shotgun tout de suite to "shoot him on sight." Fellow LMP meant nothing. At that point Captain Out of Hand disappeared from our scene for a while.

Money was always an issue. None of us wanted a job, plus punk rockers scared customers away from businesses, making us virtually unemployable. Instead, we lived a pirate's life in Hollywood. No more scrounging from tourists in front of the Chinese Theatre; that was for sucker punks and homeless kids. Now I had a rep to protect and a crew to run with. The streets provided the rest. Gasoline was always free; we just siphoned it from some sap. Local news eventually did stories on gas-stealing prevention measures to utilize in Los Angeles. Wow, if they only knew what else we were up to.

Hollywood was chock-full of marks. One of our easiest spots became the alley behind Oki-Dog on Santa Monica Boulevard. Rock-paper-scissors determined who played the bait. Everyone hated playing bait. My first time doing it, "lucky me," I was the forbidden fruit. Go figure. Our game: stand on the boulevard and entice homosexuals into the alley. Seeing a teenage boy standing all alone, smiling, was too much temptation. They fell for it every time like clockwork. Queers made a beeline right to the alley where we waited in the shadows behind trash cans. Soon as they came close, our pack jumped out and gave the prey a swift ass-kicking. We took their money, drugs, even their leather jackets to sell. If they put up any kind of fight, the beating got serious.

LMP Barney didn't care about getting their money or valuables. He loved the sport. Barney was known for his "Gomer Pyle" flattop and the Louisville

Slugger he labeled his "Magic Stick." Barney's game: have Sickness or Young-blood drive close to the curb while he leaned out the window and nailed queers with his bat as they strutted the boulevard. He felt throwing French fries at them was a waste of money. It should be noted that intolerance ruled the '80s; homosexuality was still widely frowned upon. Nobody seemed to care that jocks, rednecks, and punks alike harassed them to no end. Protecting homosexuals was at the bottom of the police agenda. Besides, if they did, everyone would know LAPD played for the pink team.

unk rock was here to stay. More bands, more kids joined the ranks. Bands from the West Coast, East Coast, and the UK were bringing new intense sounds to the movement. Now there were many options, and hardcore was becoming diverse by the end of summer 1981. Among the luminaries we listened to and watched play were: The Adicts, the Adolescents, Agent Orange, Angry Samoans, Anti-Nowhere League, Anti-Pasti, Alice Bag Band, Bad Brains, Bad Religion, Black Flag, Channel 3, the Cheifs, China White, Circle Jerks, the Clash, Cockney Rejects, Christian Death, Crass, Dead Kennedys, the Descendents, Discharge, Dischords, D.O.A., the Exploited, Fear, 45 Grave, Generation X, the Germs, Ill Repute, Jodie Foster's Army, L.A.'s Wasted Youth, Manson Youth, MDC, Middle Class, Minor Threat, the Minutemen, the Misfits, Powerless Flowers, the Professionals, Public Image Ltd, Reagan Youth, Siouxsie & the Banshees, T.S.O.L., Twisted Roots, UK Subs, Vice Squad, and Vox Pop.

CIRCLE JERKS,
WHISKY A GO-GO,
WEST HOLLYWOOD,
CALIFORNIA, 1981 PHOTO
BY EDWARD COLVER.

HOLLYWOOD BOULEVARD LOOKING EAST, 1980.
PREMIERE OF *THE DECLINE OF WESTERN CIVILIZATION*. PHOTO BY EDWARD COLVER.

Penelope Spheeris' documentary *The Decline of Western Civilization* starring Black Flag, Fear, the Germs, and X among others, was popping up on public television and being passed around on videocassette, giving kids everywhere a taste of L.A. punk life. More youth wanted in. Hardcore punk was in full swing with more shows and bigger crowds all over Los Angeles. More youth, more trouble. If you were part of a crew, you had responsibilities. When you went to a gig you checked in with your gang; this was mandatory for all four city chapters of LMP. If Santino wasn't there, another vet commanded the soldiers. When an incident started brewing, or another gang was around, the war faces were on. You stayed with your crew the whole night, which meant forget about getting laid. Our veterans always had to know the numbers in case someone stepped stupid with us during a show. If the coast was clear, we were free to do our own thing. Veterans carried the heavy load to keep the situation in check while our young contingent enjoyed adolescence, knowing it would be us running the show one day.

In Movieland, our crew sat in cars or outside in parking lots partying, then habitually walked Sunset Boulevard and Hollywood Boulevard, drinking beer, smoking pot, and tripping on LSD. When we saw a punk who looked unfamiliar we invited him or her over, handed them a beer or a joint and hung out. This is the way the scene was originally meant to be—a movement of unity and individualism against authority, against the norm. You ran into these people again and they always returned the favor, offering us beer, drugs or a ride home. Some weren't even punks, just Hollywood types who hung out in the scene.

All this interaction provided us the opportunity to scam on girls from all over So Cal. Not only punk rock girls, but all sorts who wanted cheap thrills with something unsafe they were told to stay away from. We gave them exactly what they were looking for—a toilet fantasy fulfilled up at Errol Flynn's estate. Our kingdom provided a magnificent view of the city, a grimy empty swimming pool, broken-down tennis courts, and a junked white Fiat rumored to belong to Errol Flynn's son. Turned out, Errol never even owned the property, but rented the pool house in 1957 from a friend and started throwing wild orgy parties. After our own fumbled orgies there on top of dead grass and broken beer bottles, we dropped the girls off at their cars or back on the boulevard where we had found them.

Flipside Magazine covered all things punk rock since its origins in 1977. A photo of our gang slam dancing and going berserk at a warehouse show in Pomona appeared in a new issue with a blurb about our activity that night. LMP considered the recognition a formal validation from the self-appointed punk rock intelligentsia. Not like our crew needed it, but it certainly meant the whole state of hardcore knew who we were. Their idea of us in the magazine, however, was vague at best.

"This was LMP night! The friendly people from La Mirada were there, we missed the opening band but LMP said "THEY SUCKED!" Will we ever see LMP again? I hope so!"

Oh, just you wait, *Flipside* … Just you wait.

Hanging out with our main Hollywood allies was always an amusing display of similarities and differences (nothing like a little friendly competition amongst punk gangsters). There were five of us—Sailor, Joker, two from their crew, and me at some Hollywood dive. We knew the bartender, who also bounced punk gigs for extra bucks. Right when a little boredom set in, one of us lit a match.

"Let's go kick someone's ass!"

Then came, "Fuck that, let's go run someone over."

"I ain't fucking my car up, how 'bout we eat some LSD and mug some tourists?"

Right on schedule someone poured gas on the fire.

"That's kid shit … let's kill somebody tonight."

BAD RELIGION, THE HAT-
___ T.S.O.L.   VEX 4/30 by Al
___ushed in only to make a double
___ on the place - Vex alright, but why
all the black lights, and who is this band
playing heavy metal thru my ears????
Well it was Funeral, with so many great
bands to choose from in L.A., I can see
why not a whole lot of people showed
interest in this group. Day-glo painted
shirts, very guitar oriented sound and
way too long of a set - not my cup of
tea. Bad Religion were a surprise,
they must have been added at the last
minute - they do a fast punk set, the
singer is great, kinda sounds like John
(Genoside) Patterson, but the band is
much more into loud fast music. They
just started wailing into some great songs
when we were told the police had come
and told them to turn down - they did
try that for a song - then turned it up
to end the set. The Hated came on, they
're a good punk band with an added lead
guitar taht plays all kinds of familiar
leads - way too many songs so I got
bored until they played the single which
was great - great full sound. TSOL......
finally, their last 2 shows got cancelled, but this one went on. They had a
terrible sound - NO guitar, something
happened to the PA or something. Jack
was his usual weird looking self with
his usual white f__ paint, but he always
manages to m___self look different.
Anyways ___ ___ off the ep sounded
___ ___ the audience loved
___ drummer.

SUN RA   April 2   Myrons Ballroom
1 Day After April Fools   by Dave
Sun Ra's Astro Infinity Omniverse Ark-
estra wasn't as weird and noisy as I
hoped it would be. But he was plenty
far-out. First of all a guy comes out
and tells everyone to stand back from the
stage so Ra could do his thing. So everyone does this and at the same time evry-
one sits down on the floor. So the bands
making jazz-noise whatever with three
drum kits, trumpets, horns of all sorts,
whatever. Finally Sun Ra comes out
and says "Some call me Mister Re. You
can call me Mister Mystery." Also I'm
taping it see, and this guy comes up
to me and tells me to stop taping because it'll make Sun Ra nervous. So I
quit taping for a second, stuck it under-
neith a table in front of me and kept on
taping, see I like to respect people's
wishes but at the same time I like to do
what I goddamn well feel like. Anyway,
you are asking what the fuck does this
have to do with punk? How the fuck
should I know?!! So like Ra has all these
millions of costumes and at one point he
comes out with what looks like a pot-
holder with holes for the eyes over his
face. Anyway I've gone on too long - - -
"Space is the place"............

___Los Tazers
___   by Al
___w it's gonna be
___e gigs atArt's
___s way out in Pom-
ona, ___ ___ is worth it - where
else is there a club in a shopping mall?
Onwards - - - we missed Los Tazers,
but the friendly people from La Mirada told us they were just a cover band.
This was La Mirada punk (LMP) night,
and the next two band were from that
area. Raw Sewage are a three piece band

and are pretty raw and 'garage', the
singer was pretty good - but he had a
moustache which looked kinda weird,
I've gotta admit, I haven't seen that before (Darby never had one!). Born Against were the headliners, and were a
bit better. They weren't as raw all the
time and even did a few great covers
like 'Time Of T'___ h really
sounded good,
too. Now, will w__
I hope so!!!!

LMP NIGHT, *FLIPSIDE*.

All it ever took was one knucklehead to raise the stakes and just like that, some poor guy's life was on the line.

We spilled out of the joint and into the back alley off Vine Avenue. I started to take a piss next to Sailor when the distinct rat-a-tat of a Vespa scooter overpowered our urine hitting concrete. A Mod, dressed to the nines in penny loafers, parka, and porkpie hat came putting by on his two-tone bike with too many mirrors attached. Mods were nothing more than spineless kids whose parents wouldn't let them be punk. Our two allies took off after him, shouting their disgust.

"Pussy fucking loverboy!"

"All Mods die!"

"Slow down you sissy, we only wanna ride your scooter!"

Realizing madmen were after him, the guy throttled it for all he was worth. We zipped our trousers and joined the chase. The two, clad in signature black, were wearing out their boot soles with little chance of catching the scooter. By good luck though, Satan rewarded our hate for Mods with an obstacle that slowed the Vespa. Running at full force, one of our comrades pulled out a long knife and stuck the Mod deep in his ribcage. His wounded side stiffened up as he let out a grisly wail. The scooter wobbled nearly 50 feet before it collided with a wall, and ejected the victim hard to the pavement.

Our Hollywood allies took a moment to catch their breath and admire their work. As Sailor, Joker, and I reached closer, they informed us to clear out with a hand signal. From about ten feet away his condition looked grave. A pool of blood outlined his body. Our two associates picked up their new Vespa, kick-started it, and sped off. I looked at the Mod on the ground and watched his breathing become shallow. I couldn't articulate what I was feeling. Intimate stories of homicide from other LMPs had desensitized me. The veterans of my gang looked at death no differently than an ass beating, a simple act of murder. Strangely enough, it wasn't the blood that tickled me the most ... It was how ridiculous those hardcore punks looked riding double down the alley, as their tail light got smaller and smaller... and smaller and smaller.

CHAPTER 4
"UNFAIR WARNING"

og days of summer were no more. September landed and school was back in session. Graduating from junior high school turned out insignificant. No one from my family showed up and neither did I. Dad was a selfish rummy, Mom needed to pay the bills. The only significant change to my life occurred after what I saw in the alley. It came in the form of my first knife. Not too big, not too small, a folding switchblade with wood inlay. Cost me $7.99 and I never left home without it.

As a freshman in high school, your first year was supposed to be wrought with terror from upperclassmen, but not me. Jocks and hippies populated the campus, but LMP came with a threat-filled edge. People knew I ran with crazies. They knew I was in a gang. The veteran LMPs who had already passed through this institutional joke either dropped out or got kicked out. We established a reputation of resistance.

When Oingo Boingo played a lunchtime set in the quad, all active members from my gang walked on campus in a show of force, even though it was a New Wave dork band. Santino knew teens from L.A. to Orange County would show up, using the opportunity to let everyone know it was our punk rock gang turf. Every instructor, disciplinarian, coach, and teacher's pet had a look of distress. Kids stayed the fuck away. Security stood close but never made eye contact. No one dared to phone the police and acknowledge City of La Mirada had a problem on their hands. On local law enforcement radar, LMP was still a mere blip. We were doing all our deadly damage in the Hollywood scene. LAPD knew there was ghastly punk rock violence going on, but had no idea who was doing what to whom.

In La Mirada our activity was sporadic, not too sensational. Youngblood and I were getting busted around our neighborhood for little stuff—vandalism, truancy, and curfew. A bunch of posers from OC started a new gang bent on instant status. They called themselves DYG, which stood for Destructive Youth Gang. Members were 11th and 12th graders from surrounding cities behind the Orange Curtain. A proper punk rocker from one of their high schools informed us that only a year earlier, the guys were all punk-music-hating jocks and prep-

(LEFT) FRANK, FRESHMAN YEAR;
(RIGHT) LMP GRAFFITI, WHITTIER CHAPTER.

pies. They were now punk rock gangsters. DYG spray-painted their name everywhere we congregated, crossed out LMP, and proclaimed they would destroy La Mirada.

Groups of them started showing up at local hangouts when we were elsewhere. Santino spotted their so-called leader at Skate City, nonchalantly pulled a hatchet from his car, and chased the imposter down the street declaring war on DYG. We knew there were roughly 20 of them, so no need to involve the Whittier, Norwalk or La Habra chapters. Regardless, Whittier LMPs happened upon them first and threw that plan right out the window. DYG got all dolled up for a show and walked in like they owned the joint. Dressing punk rock for the night made a jock or preppy feel like the real deal... until they met the real deal. Then it was too late. On their way to establishing themselves at the edge of the pit, all were confronted by several Whittier LMPs. Frantic fists started flying. Noses got twisted, lips busted. Before you knew it, a couple of them were a bloody, laid-out mess. Others ran out of the venue and took off, leaving their wounded behind.

The following week I got tipped off DYG were hanging out in our city—unacceptable! Santino and I found two of them putting on the punk act in front of our local record store. Santino goaded them into fighting. We wasted them even-steven, delivering enough boot kicks to permanently diminish their brain cell count.

The store clerk came outside yelling "Don't kill them in front of my store; do it down the road at my competition's!"

Fighting side by side with the leader of LMP was something I knew I would hold close for years to come. I definitely used all the moves I had rehearsed alone in my bedroom. Needed to send my own message.

Give or take a few weeks, they regrouped and pumped themselves up to retaliate. Youngblood was making time with a girl at a party on the border of Orange County when some opportunists from that clique tried to jump him. DYG wanted to settle the score like cowards. They snuck up and started pushing Youngblood and his girl around. No class. He took a collection of solid shots to his head that put him on the verge of unconsciousness. Left with no choice, Youngblood stabbed his way out of the predicament. He pulled his knife and sunk it into one of them, twice. First sight of blood sent the rat pack fleeing in every direction. None of them had the stomach for it. Youngblood and his girl smoothly strolled to his car and drove off.

We were told DYG let their hair grow out and immediately switched back to their jock/preppy ways. Nevertheless, someone from the party recognized Youngblood and squealed to the authorities—just the name of the game. His self-defense case worked and they put Youngblood in juvenile hall for a year. Lucky for him the kid didn't die; it would've been a murder conviction with a direct trip to YA, then the state pen for his 18th birthday present.

Youngblood was always closer to Santino. Now, with him gone, I became the rising star. Santino took me under his wing and passed down the codes of gang life his father instilled in him. Hanging out all the time, I was constantly schooled on how to live life according to the politics of the neighborhood: learning how disputes were solved within a clique; whether to have a sit-down or fight it out; and knowing who is in charge, along with all the ins and outs of how each one of us fit in.

Next, I was introduced to the CV3 gang who LMP shared the neighborhood with. Our relationship was truly special and historically pioneer. Nowhere else did a punk rock gang and cholo gang share territory, becoming actual affiliates. CV3, together with LMP, were spray-painted everywhere. Varrio La Mirada/VLM was the only other gang in our city. CV3 were their sworn enemy, thus so were we.

The old neighborhood was split into two sections, the east side and the west side. A concrete river full of slimy algae ran through the middle. Both sections were controlled by CV3. Our crew usually hung out on the west side where Santino lived. Members of CV3 from that confined area were called "Dead Ends." All the blocks were dead-end streets, held down by a young crop of hoods like Youngblood and me.

The older veterans who lived on the east side were known as "The Tinys," all big scary guys that had been to prison. Sporting double-breasted jackets, three-piece suits, trench coats, Stacy Adams, and hats, they were the best-dressed gang I ever saw. Their side of the neighborhood was markedly more dangerous with its narrow streets. Once another gang entered, the only way out was to back up pronto, or drive through and suffer the consequences.

Another geographical advantage was the dairy overlooking the whole east side. Moisture from its nonstop cow manure created a dense fog from fall to spring. Grotesque stench, combined with a lack of visibility, brought a John Carpenter horror aesthetic to the entire place. Knowing that CV3's gun-toting gangsters surrounded you in the fog only added another layer of fright. Rival gangs like VLM, South Side Whittier, and Carmellas didn't take the risk and only attacked from the west.

Before long, CV3 became inquisitive about our punk rock lifestyle.

"We wanna see that crazy slam-shit, ese!"

LMP brought CV3 members along to many gigs, causing people in the scene to mouth off.

"LMP are a bunch of cholos into punk rock."

This was far from the truth. We were genuine punks from lowrider neighborhoods, mostly white, but with a range of ethnicities. Having a group of classically dressed Chicano gangsters alongside us at gigs must've been a unique sight, to say the least. Watching punks slam dance to mucho loco music, then engage in brutal free-for-all gang fights afterward, was pure entertainment to them.

My 14th birthday arrived Sunday, October 4, 1981—it's a teenage warning. Mom took off early to work and left me a grocery store cake with 14 candles haphazardly on top. Also, a card sat next to it with 20 bucks inside wishing me "Happy Birthday! You are a good son, Love Mom."

I casually messed around with a girl named Josette who felt like celebrating that afternoon. We decided to catch the movie *D.O.A.: A Rite of Passage*, a documentary that followed the Sex Pistols around on their only American tour.

The picture was a real dud except for the Sid and Nancy interview. Nancy kept blabbing nonsense while Sid tried to nod out on the bed like an honest dope fiend. No wonder he eventually stabbed her.

Bubblegum punk from Orange County was trying to blend into our L.A. scene and pass itself off as hardcore, much like DYG did with their bubblegum gang. On a night with nothing else to do in Hollywood, we ended up at the Whisky. Social Distortion was playing, OC's most impotent wannabe punk band of all time. Everyone involved in the L.A. scene knew they were Dubble Bubble personified. That night, frontman Mike Ness was getting showered in saliva. His face kept contorting in distress, nothing punk about his conduct at all. If you were a punk band playing at an L.A. venue, the crowd spat on you to show appreciation or hatred, it didn't matter. Barely halfway through his set, loogies began to take their toll. After pleading with the crowd to cut him some slack, the "boo"s grew deafening. More spit, coupled with trash, came flying at Mike. He momentarily sulked, then walked backstage. L.A. punks didn't tolerate any soft musicians. Whenever Fear played, it was a downpour of mucus. Lee Ving embraced it. Milky globs hung all over his face through the entire set, including the encore. Lee kept singing in a coated frenzy, earning our love and returning the favor with power.

One night when Fear was headlining the Whisky, our crew made plans to meet out front before the band came on. We were out loitering on the sidewalk, associating with hardcore's finest, when a flashy hot rod abruptly pulled up to the curb blasting idiot rock music. "Diamond" David Lee Roth of Van Halen got out of the passenger seat, dressed in striped spandex and mirrored shades, with his hair flowing everywhere. Behind the wheel, Eddie Van Halen waited for the valet.

Diamond Dave yelled out, arms wide open, "Look who's heeeere!" to the crowd.

His publicist obviously forgot to tell him who was playing that night. The grand entrance was greeted with dead quiet from a stunned throng of dedicated punks.

Out of the brief silence someone sounded off, "You fucked up!"

A surge of laughter erupted followed by an onslaught of beer and spittle taking to the air. Hands shoved David Lee Roth all around like a live pinball on the verge of tilt.

Quickly realizing he was in enemy territory, Roth jumped back in the car and yelled at Eddie, "Step on it for Chrissakes!"

Heavy metal had their turn. Now, it was ours.

A new gang from Venice Beach also wanted their turn. They claimed the name Suicidal after a band they dressed like called Suicidal Tendencies. We labeled them "Sueys," like an old-time pig farmer call: "Suey pig-pig-pig! Suey pig-pig-pig!" Hated from the moment they showed their faces, that nickname stuck for good. Original crews considered them a joke, even though some of their members were legitimately dicey. Suicidal had the nerve to let kids who weren't jumped-in gang members tag along, to fake big numbers, so long as they had the look. The actual gang was small. Kids brand-new to the world were enamored with the band's and gang's mix of punk and L.A. cholo style— bandana pulled low to hide the eyes, long white T's or button-downs, baggy creased Dickies instead of pegged, shorts past the knee with high tube sox, and a baseball cap flipped up with "Suicidal" written across it gang-style for every-one to see. The singer, Mike Muir, routinely rounded up maybe ten gang mem-bers along with 40–50 followers in requisite attire for any show they played.

Next, he would instruct them to run through the hallways yelling "Suicidal! Suicidal! Suicidal!" repeatedly, like a battle cry in a mock gesture of war.

After all that posturing, they found somewhere to sit down and do nothing.

If our crew couldn't or wouldn't pay for cover, the outside of any venue was as action-packed as the performance inside. On a night we were celebrating something I thought at the time to be monumental, me and about dozen LMPs were posted up across the street from Cathay de Grande, another one of our favorite Hollywood rattraps that provided live music. As I spied the city's con-crete happenings, I noticed five of our cronies from the LADS camped out on the curb, having a good ole time, too drunk to stand. Moments later, I spotted a group of Sueys and their obvious followers surrounding them with bad inten-tions. Trouble was brewing. Things were about to get ugly real fast.

Our pack made a clandestine move across the street to head off a sure attack. We materialized out of the streetlights from all sides before they knew their situation was deep shit. Sailor let loose a clubbing shot that folded their biggest guy. I came with a running haymaker that removed another Suey from his feet. Right when they thought they got the drop, they were getting dropped. Witnessing a few of their role models fall to the pavement sent Suicidal's fol-lowers retreating every which way. In spite of the dustup, our oblivious L.A. Death Squad buddies never budged from their drunken lounge act on the curb. Topping it all off, one of our guys appropriately hollered out "Suey pig-pig-pig!

Suey pig-pig-pig!" Chasing after them was useless, so all joined in on the hog call instead. People talked about it for weeks after, but it really wasn't much. I thought it was going to be my first real punk rock gang-fight ... but it was more like *West Side Story*.

Suicidal battled LADS over the next couple years, yet never had the nerve to declare war on us. LMP and LADS, however, fought side by side throughout the hard fast '80s. We considered them brothers in arms who, just like us, craved the action.

The Los Angeles punk rock push now had a significant number of organized gangs, though only a few were achieving notoriety for their exploits—LMP, LADS, Vicious Circle, Suicidal, and Circle One.

The singer of Circle One, John Macias, started a splinter crew called The Family, a group of veterans out in force who protected kids new to our movement from mounting violence. He now approached the punk scene as a faith-based Christian peacemaker. One night Suicidal had LMP seriously outnumbered, thinking they would get the big payback over the Cathay incident. John Macias took their leader aside and gave it to him point-blank.

"Look, you might have caught these La Mirada guys with less tonight and will probably win, but what about tomorrow, or next week? What then? They will come for blood. Just let it ride; walk away."

John spoke volumes. Suicidal did the wise thing and let it go. What a shame mental imbalance ultimately got the best of him. During a bipolar rampage some years later on Santa Monica Pier, Macias threw some man over the top railing into the ocean, then charged a line of police pistols and riot guns. He didn't stand a chance. Cold-blooded murder from an insensitive police squad never sat well with anybody who knew John or felt his influence.

In San Fernando Valley, a group of affluent jock kids turned punk, then tossed their hat in the ring and started up FFF—Fight for Freedom. Copying the Suey template, they adopted punk lowrider style, even wore flipped-up caps with FFF scrawled across the bill.

Common talk in the scene was, "FFF carries all kinds of guns at all times."

No one reputable ever witnessed them shoot anybody or saw a big cache of firearms. Their presence in Hollywood at that moment was rare. Most considered them rich kids who were trying to play the part of punk rock gangster.

A new crew called Mid City Punks began spray-painting their name up at some of the traditional locales and alleyways around Hollywood: Cathay de Grande, the

Whisky, the Roxy, and Errol Flynn's, among others. Membership was diffuse, ranging from Chatsworth to Culver City. It was a tough gang to identify, which could have been purposeful, since they dressed like run-of-the-mill traditional punks. You only knew who they were when they started trouble. Not one of them was friendly with us and that's how we liked it. LMP simply added 'em to the RIP list.

(LEFT) FRANK IN CUSTOM BLITZ JACKET. BACK OF THE ROXY, 1982;
(RIGHT) GODZILLA'S, SUN VALLEY, CALIFORNIA 1982–83. PHOTO BY EDWARD COLVER.

So much hate, so much fun. Our world was getting better and better. Godzilla's opened in Sun Valley as 1982 came to a close with the upstart efforts of L.A. punk band Youth Brigade. Godzilla's was now the biggest location to consistently throw shows thus far: pinball, snack bar, several side rooms, and very easy for us to sneak into—it was one big punk rock playground. Big-name bands played at an affordable cover charge, giving the rest of the kids a break. Godzilla's was for punks, run by punks, the answer to the greed creeping into the scene.

982 started with a dress code overhaul for LMP. The look of our whole gang changed to one with a style similar to skinheads of the "Oi!" movement. As soon as we obtained records from Cockney Rejects and 4-Skins, along with the compilation albums *Oi!* and *Strength Thru Oi!*—it was on. Our outward blueprint shifted when we saw pictures of these guys from across the pond, listened to their music, and heard a new message that complemented our own actions on the streets of L.A. These weren't racist skinheads, but rather working-class pro-Brit youth with a uniform look who disrupted soci-

ety through violence. "BIC" bald heads, DM boots, suspenders, white T's, Fred Perry, and Ben Sherman shirts or rolled-up long-sleeved button-downs—they scared the crap out of England and fought anybody who tried to shut 'em down or move 'em along. Bands called the Strike, Infa Riot, and Criminal Class with their songs "Gang Warfare," "We Outnumber You," and "Blood on the Streets" became the soundtrack of our lives. No one else in punk was telling you verbatim to resist society with violence. Dressing like these guys was only natural.

Showing off our new look at Little Tokyo's Atomic Café, we ran into original punk Don Bolles and asked him to join us for dinner. Since the downfall of the Germs, he was playing drums for 45 Grave and Vox Pop. Don was cool, but very eccentric, dressed in subtle drag and wearing makeup. Overanxious, I started talking at him right away about the Oi! movement.

"The scene really needed this shot in the arm! The music is so strong and powerful and full of meaning—anyone that's against us gets a beating!"

Sickness added, "It's true, a lot of the Oi bands are better than most punk bands."

Don played along, barely listening, "Yeah that's cool."

Sailor finished his double helping of fried rice and started to get restless.

"Hey Don, why don't you let me take a razor to your head? What you got going on don't make no sense."

Don took a sober look at all five of us in our standard skinhead attire and shiny heads. His face changed. Now he was paying attention.

"I'm cool for right now, thanks," then started eating his greasy noodles at an accelerated rate.

Sickness frowned.

Don stood up, still chewing his food. "Thanks for the grub, guys, I got to go ... see you around."

In hindsight I could see how the guy felt cornered, but Don obviously didn't get the memo ... punk rock was in our hands.

The Captain came out of hiding to see if he could somehow smooth things over. I was over at Santino's acquiring homemade brass knuckles when he showed up to throw himself at the mercy of the court.

"I blacked out that night, Santino, I went over my limit ... don't remember any of it."

Santino let him have it.

"You walked right in without saying a word and threatened to rape their mother. They want your ass, what do you expect? You're lucky they haven't camped out in front of your house."

Captain pleaded, "I'm sleeping at different people's houses, I'm hearing things, I'm afraid for my life."

Santino was somewhat stumped. Everyone loved The Captain and his alter ego Captain Out of Hand, but this was a personal issue, not an ordinary gang matter.

"I don't know man, you really fucked up; keep laying low until I figure this one out."

I proposed a possible solution.

"What about writing an apology to their parents letting them know how sorry he is? That he was under the influence—he was going through some stuff."

Santino pondered my suggestion.

"You know, Frank, that's a good idea. Their dad's an old-time high rider. That's showing respect, totally his generation, and Captain Out of Hand here really never even touched his wife."

Captain's eyes lit up. "I'll do it! I'll go get on it right now!"

Santino added, "Put in there you'll never go anywhere near their house again. Take your time with it. Make sure shit's spelled right. I'll get it to them as soon as you're done, you fucking moron."

No one really knew if it was going to work at all. Santino had little tolerance for dissension within our ranks. He made the issue a priority and gave it to Shadow and Bubbles' parents within the week. Turned out they had no reservations accepting the apology letter, contingent on that he never showed his face anywhere near their house again. The brothers still had a problem with the whole thing but our leader wanted it buried. Santino notified Captain Out of Hand that getting shot is no longer a concern. Now it would be okay to show his face around La Mirada again, as long as he kept a safe distance from Shadow and Bubbles.

As ringleader, Santino always had his work cut out for him. Some of his troops were too punk for their own good. Their interpretation of the movement was to annihilate everything. Bands were telling you to destroy society. LMPs took this message literally. It was a major part of what bonded us together. Popeye was a shining example of this mentality. Mid-20s, living at home, no job, and pissed off for being born with nerve damage in his face. One side of his mouth didn't work when he spoke, making it look as if he chewed on an invisible pipe like Popeye the Sailor Man. His repayment to the world was to set it on fire. Numerous times we stopped him from burning down some of our favorite establishments. Popeye had a serious axe to grind with Oki-Dog. He swore they ruined his shot with Belinda Carlisle, famous frontgirl of the Go-Go's.

Somehow Popeye wound up at one of those hip industry parties in the Hollywood hills shortly after dining at Oki-Dog. Supposedly, at the height of the party, he was making serious time with Belinda. She still had a real thing for punk rockers, being she came from the Masque days and all. Belinda was sharing her blow; all his best material was working, when without warning he had to use the restroom. What Popeye thought was going to be a momentary inconvenience turned into a nearly 20-minute Oki-Dog explosion. People pounded on the door as angry voices yelled "Hurry up!" while he desperately tried to muffle his flatulence by running the water and flushing the toilet repeatedly. When the ordeal was all over, airing it out was impossible. No windows, no ventilation, no matches—flat-out fucked. Hoping the coast was clear, Popeye opened the door to a smiling Belinda Carlisle. Offensive party-clearing smell flooded the entire hallway, cutting off all oxygen. Belinda's pleasant expression morphed to pained proctophobia—the fear of rectums—causing her to slam the door in his face, take off down the hallway, gagging and choking, trying not to puke.

Not too long after the incident, we were at Oki-Dog, as usual, when Sickness warningly gave me a sharp elbow and uttered in my ear, "I knew it, I knew it, what an asshole."

I turned to see Popeye gripping a pint of Bacardi 151 with a bandana sticking out, all set to light and toss his Molotov cocktail onto the roof of Oki-Dog. He was mumbling Belinda's name profusely, shaking his lighter, trying to get it to work. A couple of us hurried to take him down, but Sailor just snatched the bottle from his hand, pulled out the bandana, and started drinking up. The whole lot of us busted out laughing, making Popeye storm off, unwilling to let bygones be bygones.

Later that same week he openly threatened to burn an enemy's house to the ground. Next day, he followed through like a first-class arsonist, torching the place. Cops were on the case right away looking to haul him in for his pyromania. Popeye fled to a relative's in Texas, which proved to be another big mistake that further affirmed his guilt in the eyes of the authorities. Soon as he stepped off the plane they were waiting for him. He was found guilty of arson, narrowly escaping attempted murder since the house was empty. Judge sentenced him to a number of years in the state pen. Popeye's LMP career was over for the time being.

Joker also thought ultra-violence was the answer. It wasn't about collecting buttons and shit like that for him either. Not the biggest guy by any means, but he would argue that too. His mouth was to blame for many a confrontation. You know the type; except Joker possessed a killer's rationale, the kind that results from witnessing your grandmother bludgeon your dad to death with a household iron in grade school. According to the grapevine, she became hell-bent over his father gambling away the family home and decided to play executioner. Grandma got sent up for life. Joker definitely lost more than he won with his fists, but never with his knife.

I witnessed Joker's great equalizer out at the punk rock hotspot, the Music Box. Unfortunately, the fire marshal came and pulled the plug on the show after the first opening band. Everyone at the venue was booted without a refund, putting a pile of hate-filled punks outside with nothing to do but stew over it. Five bucks was a lot of money to have nabbed from you, considering punks were pretty much unemployable. No one got their fix, which made the waters around the venue treacherous. Talk was floating around that club ownership regularly called the fire department so they could stiff the bands and rip off those who had paid to get in. People were openly talking riot after the fire department left. Arguments started breaking out, guys were mad-dogging one another, girls started to get mouthy, bottles were being thrown at the club, showering glass on the crowd. Santino was in the midst of it, assembling our crew, when I spotted Joker getting heated with some big masher skinhead donning a stainless chain from nose to cheek to ear. Evidently, Joker pushed the wrong buttons. A grudgeful right fist from the skinhead let him know. The shot caught Joker square in the nose as a loud pop echoed throughout the crowd. He buckled to his knees nearly finished, blood sprayed all over his black studded jacket.

Time stood still precisely long enough for me to utter, "Uh-oh."

With animal quickness, Joker sprang to his feet and shanked this poor fool who thought it was going to be a fair fight. The skinhead's mouth gulped for air like a man drowning. I counted the knife go in his stomach six times. Each time with such barbarism, Joker's entire fist disappeared into the skinhead's guts. After the third penetration, his face had indicated he was approaching death, off on a trip to a faraway land. A piercing scream curved everyone's attention toward the action as the skinhead turned into lifeless putty. Once again, all of punk rock witnessed LMP kill like it was no big deal. Little did they know we were just getting warmed up.

CHAPTER 5
"YOUNG, LOUD, AND NAUGHTY"

KUNTFIGHT WERE MY FAVORITE PUNK BAND that never got their shot. Eddie introduced me to this band after a Circle Jerks show where they gave me a demo tape. Just two songs, both were less than a minute long. Get in, destroy, and get out. Kuntfight's singer Trina was the hottest punk rock girl with liberty spikes I ever saw. Their sound was faster and harder than anything I ever heard locally until that summer. I made it over to a few of their practices, all of which were shut down before they even got going. It only took ten minutes for the cops to show up and threaten to confiscate their instruments due to noise pollution. Trina's neighbor next door hated punk music and squealed any time they played. The tattler was some white-trash inventor named Larry, who was always out in his backyard drinking Miller High Life while tinkering with a homemade hot-air balloon contraption. We had no idea what it was, nor cared. The guy and his loudmouth girlfriend thought they were in charge of the entire neighborhood.

Shortly after another fink episode, I got a call from Kuntfight's singer Trina, telling me that her jerk-off punk-rock-hating rat neighbor was planning to fly his invention out of the backyard the next day. She wanted me and some LMPs to come over and shoot him out of the sky for his transgressions against her band. I let Trina know it would be an honor. Plus I wanted to screw her.

Next morning, me, Sailor, Sickness, Donna the Dead, along with this punk I met the night before who called himself Degenerate, piled in "The Car." We brought serious artillery for the job: two BB guns, one pellet rifle, and a .22 pistol, in case something more powerful was needed. At the Kuntfight house, a small gathering of punk rock refuse was enjoying the good life, drinking blue-label beer and barbecuing. A few of Trina's cohorts also brought air rifles to participate in the turkey shoot. Donna the Dead got extra drunk, being she was the only one without a gun. She broke her shooting hand the week before fighting two cholas for cutting in line at Pup 'n' Taco. She won.

Every ten minutes one of us peeked over the fence, up to the moment asshole Larry finished filling his weather balloons with helium, ready for takeoff. Just as planned, balloons ascended above the fence, lifting a backyard lawn chair with stool pigeon Larry strapped to it. All of us scrambled around to find a choice hiding spot to sharp-shoot from. He hovered at about 50 feet up; a rope anchored him to the ground. I had perfect cover from a bushy tree and dead aim at one of his balloons.

Larry pointed to someone in his yard and yelled, "Cut the rope! Cut the rope!"

The hot-air throne took off like a skyrocket rising hundreds of feet in seconds. Rapid shots broke out from every corner of the backyard. Air rifles had no chance in hell of hitting the balloons. Degenerate unloaded his .22 pistol yet nothing came close. With all the commotion, we couldn't get a clean shot. Now Larry was nearly out of sight. Baffled by how fast Larry disappeared, we resumed our beer drinking and put some fresh meat on the grill.

The guy completely vanished. That day "Lawnchair Larry" made national headlines, maneuvering his fantasy ship three miles high, drifting into federal airspace over Long Beach Airport's primary approach. The CB radio he brought along proved to be his true stroke of genius that prevented him from getting shot down by the military as a possible spy craft. Nearly an hour into the flight, Larry conjured up enough courage to start popping balloons, and lowered himself to safety where the cops were waiting with handcuffs. All the media attention stirred up by the event put the final nail in the coffin for Kuntfight. Curiosity-seekers, news crews, and beat cops crowded their neighborhood for months, making band rehearsal impossible. Someone was always around to shut them down. Kuntfight sold their instruments and said fuck it.

Youngblood was able to get released from juvie early by telling probation counselors whatever they wanted to hear. He regurgitated the issues of right, wrong, remorse, and regret until they were satisfied. My freshman year was over and I was thrilled to have an LMP my age to run with again in time for summer.

First night home, the two of us headed straight to Errol Flynn's in celebration of being back on the streets. We were set up for the night with some Mickey's Big Mouths and a little bit of hash I held onto for a special occasion. Sitting at the edge of the abandoned pool, high above Hollywood, I got the skinny on juvie. Youngblood's shaved skull kept the cholos, Crips, and Bloods, along with the white trash loadie kids, at bay. He just made mad faces all the time. Why mess with a youth who looks dangerous when there's much easier prey? He found the place severely boring, outside of the occasional flash-in-the-pan knuckle-up and the time some Piru Blood split open a counselor's nose with a Rubik's Cube.

Sitting at the pool and looking out over Fuller Street, we noticed a BMW and a Porsche pull up and park at the entrance. Five privileged types with feathered hair and Izod shirts exited their cars then hopped the gate. They made the walk up the shadowy trail that wound its way to the pool. Overgrown, dying trees lined the old road, giving rise to a "Sleepy Hollow" environment. This generally scared most people away, unless you found some kind of comfort in that evil. We did. Youngblood and I polished off our last beers as we kept tabs on the group coming toward us. When they arrived at the pool area, we noticed they were college boys, already loaded from a bottle of gin being passed around. Although the preppies pretended to ignore us, their eyes flashed trouble. Right off we heard some hateful whispering. Tension blanketed us. Clearly overmatched, Youngblood and I decided to relocate to another part of the estate. The college fellas blatantly followed as we quickened our pace. We saw our chance and slipped into the brush.

They ran by us, yelling out in the blackness, "Kill the punkers!"

"Yeah fucking punker fucks!"

"Kill! Kill! Kill!"

Youngblood and I stayed hidden until they finally gave up, thinking we got away. Our antagonists walked back past us bragging about how "lucky" we were.

From the cover of bushes, I stayed as still as possible and listened to how they were going to "make an example" out of us, that "Punkers are losers and deserve to be tortured!"

When the coast was clear, we retreated back down the road to our car, pulled out a bumper jack and bat from our trunk, then proceeded to "Trash! Trash! Trash!" their cars. With pure joy, we rearranged their preppy machines all to hell and spray-painted LMP on them for added insult. From the pool area above, they could perfectly see their vehicles under the streetlight, getting 100% vandalized. Powerless to stop us, they threw even bigger fits and charged down the hill. We popped every tire, making it impossible for them to chase us. Youngblood and I leaped into our Oldsmobile and tore ass out of there. My patio chair seat toppled over, dumping me to the floor as Youngblood fishtailed his way down Fuller. Just like expected, the gruesome twosome were back.

odney Bingenheimer put Youth Gone Mad's song "Oki Dogs" in his weekly rotation, creating a local hit. Youth Gone Mad practices were something you didn't want to miss anymore. Sessions at Vitamin Ena's house became tightly focused instead of some drunk-fest. From that point on, I made sure to arrive on time to hear the entire set.

At their first new and improved rehearsal, Sickness greeted me with "Hey Frank, say hello to yourself."

She pointed over to some dude leaning against the wall. Holy shit, she was dead on. It really tripped me out for a minute, like looking into a funhouse mirror. He looked just like me, same height, but thinner. After getting introduced, I realized it was a kid from my last Little League team that won the city championship. He always got on base. His name was Jim. Sickness picked him up off the street in "The Car," thinking it was me. Exactly like she did me. We hit it off, going right back to where we left off in Little League. Instead of baseball, it was punk rock and rottenness.

Jim was a perfect addition to Youngblood and me. He grasped our particularized punk rock ways very quickly, consistently showed up to mandatory gigs and parties, made sure to watch our backs, learned how to act around the vets, and understood who to watch out for. Jim resembled a chemotherapy patient, being he was so thin with a shaved head. His fair skin was the tipping point. We officially changed his name to Chemo. He hated it. Chemo loved to be underestimated and followed through on any dare with panache. He got off on calling your bluff.

A friend of mine worked at the Magic Mountain theme park ticket booth that summer. She invited Chemo, Youngblood, and me to check out "New Wave

Night" for free on a Saturday. All three of us thought it would be a great opportunity to scam on New Wave chicks and cause uproar ... free is free. There was also a concert in the amphitheater that evening. Upon entering the park, all the teens were buzzing about this band from the UK called Talk Talk. I snuck in a short bottle of hard booze that got us trashed as we made our way to the venue. Inside it was New Wave hell—fat girls in weird makeup, brooches pinned on sweaters, dorks with bi-level hair in multicolored fashion, sunglasses, romantic posing, and every look from MTV times ten. Soon as the band started, everyone broke out their best overly dramatic dances, stomps, spins, and swayed hyperactively to the beat. We ended up stuck in the middle without any idea what to do. Girls treated us like we had the plague. They only wanted their kind. Youngblood dared Chemo to sneak up on stage and sock the singer. The light bulb went on in Chemo's brain and a cat-that-ate-the-canary grin developed on his face. He disappeared into the black hole of New Wave fantasy, resurfacing a few minutes later on the side of the stage. In one quick move he climbed up and charged the singer as security tried to apprehend him. A behemoth-sized member of the event staff tackled Chemo right as he got his clutches on the singer. The momentum toppled all three to the ground. Talk Talk's frontman had no idea how close he came to getting laid out and brushed the whole thing off like it was some fanatic trying to hug him. He went right back to his set while security escorted our compadre out of the amphitheater. We followed Chemo to the guard shack where they made him sign a piece of paper declaring, "You will never come within 1,000 feet of the Magic Mountain theme park." Chemo smiled at the dumbass security staff and signed their no trespassing form with the name "Travis Bickle."

Three nights later, Chemo, Youngblood, and I went to Cathay de Grande for a Battalion of Saints gig. They played so fast I thought the band was going to burst into flames. Slam dancing was downright warfare. Hardcore had reached another plateau of sound and fury. Southern California bands were fully committed to taking punk to dangerous levels in order to match the Oi and thrash bands of the UK. Once again, L.A. drastically improved punk rock, and everyone who attended turned it into a pain game. Every other kid that night wore the face of a hardened inmate, like they had never been babies. None of them were faking it. I guess musicians never considered, nor really cared, about the effects their music was having on the youth who attended gigs and the possible aftermath—but *c'est la vie*.

We exited that show feeling bulletproof. Our trio ached for more action. We walked down a side street to our car. Both Youngblood and I looked at each other, knowing it was time. I slapped the cigarette out of Chemo's hand to get his attention.

"Decide right now if you are LMP or not. Make a decision."

Youngblood simply let him know, "This is the only way you can keep hanging out."

I made it clear: "The free ride is over."

Chemo visibly began to comprehend the moment, weighing the pros and cons of what was at stake, when Youngblood landed a quick pop to his mouth. He now grasped the situation completely and took a step back to get 'em up. My knee found his gut as he swung desperately to keep us away. Youngblood hit him with a flurry as I kicked Chemo's feet out from underneath. Both of us booted him with force repeatedly for a strong 30 seconds. Out of breath, we figured he had enough.

Chemo rose up like nothing happened and tried to high-five us proclaiming, "I'm LMP —yeeeeah! I'm LMP!"

We felt ridiculed by his lack of pain. I focused in on his jaw, hitting him with my best overhand right that erased his enthusiasm immediately. Youngblood was on the same wavelength and hooked his kidney hard, causing a nasty grunt. The two of us put on the finishing touches and made every hit count. We tackled him headfirst into a car, severely denting the door. Crumpled on the ground, he coughed in agony trying to grab his breath. Someone from a passing car yelled out, "Get up, you pussy!" and hurled a bottle that sailed overhead narrowly missing us. It took Chemo effort to get into our car, where we folded the lawn chairs, making room for him to recline. He lay there in a heap, finished for the night.

Heading toward the 101 freeway, Chemo cursed every time we hit a pothole. Youngblood went out of his way to drive over every crater in the road, putting a smile on my face. As we were about to merge onto the freeway, I noticed that same woman I met in front of the Chinese Theatre who refused to give me her name. She was driving a late-model Toyota sedan, singing to some tune on the radio, carefree, twirling her hair.

I shouted, "Stop the car. It's her! Turn around!"

Too late, Youngblood hit the on-ramp. I thought about that lady for days after meeting her, wondering if I would ever see her again. She was a woman, different than the usual girls I found myself with. All the way home I tuned out Chemo's moans and Youngblood's banter. How would I find her? Could she see past my punk rock ways?

CHEMO, ALWAYS IN
THE BACK SEAT, 1982.

oungblood and I decided to not bother running Chemo's membership up the ladder. It was our moment to make an executive decision. We put in our time and knew it was in the gang's best interest to start increasing ranks with an injection of youth. Chemo was out of the rotation a while. Standard jump-in recovery time was two to four weeks. He was out nearly four with a twisted knee, bruised ribs, plus a concussion. When Santino got informed, he reminded us that recruiting tough, moldable punks our age was always his plan.

As soon as Chemo recovered, he started throwing LMP parties on weekends when his mom left town, which was often. I never saw his dad around or even in family photos, only him and his mom posing with random relatives. If Dad were in the picture, he would've had a coronary the way our gang used to fuck that house up, leaving holes everywhere. One time, high on PCP, Youngblood put his head through the bathroom wall. Chemo's mom put up with our wild behavior like a saint. If we were too wasted to drive Youngblood's car home from wherever, she just picked us up, no questions asked. His mom was a well put-together woman who looked her best at all times. I came to find out she was quite lonely and frequently dated, looking to find that father figure for Chemo. His mother also traveled with her square dance troupe on a continual basis, providing Chemo with a life every kid dreamed of ... an empty home on weekends and no parental guidance.

My supervision wasn't a priority at Dad's work when I was a boy. His boss, Sam Sciortino, left me to amuse myself with his trusty German shepherd, also named Frank, while he tended to business and Dad went on deliveries for him. The two of us Franks had our run of the place, playing hide and seek, fetch, building cardboard forts, always on adventures like Tom Sawyer and Huck Finn. I started noticing peculiar things that went on at Lads Trucking.

One afternoon I watched men in suits take pictures of the truck yard from a neighboring rooftop.

Sam came out of his office, flipped 'em the bird and shouted, "Fucking feds!" then gave me a wink and went back to work.

I climbed up top of the highest truck I could get on, waited for those guys in suits to notice, then gave them the finger shouting, "Fucking feds!"

I constantly looked forward to going to the truck yard, watching Sam tell people how it was, durably convinced we were the good guys.

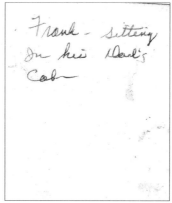

Frank - sitting in his Dad's cab

YOUNG FRANK,
ADVENTURES
AT UNCLE SAM
SCIORTINO'S,
LADS TRUCKING CO.

Youngblood, Chemo, and I took a sundown drive through the neighborhood to study all the cholos positioned on porches, readying themselves for the night. About four blocks away from my house and one over from Youngblood's, I noticed some punk rocker we never saw before, kicking a chain-link fence. We quietly stopped our car to watch this angry kid taunt, spit, and bark at a big Rottweiler that was even angrier. I wondered for a moment, if the dog were to get loose, who I would fight side by side with? Youngblood hit the horn and waved him over. As he cautiously walked to the car, a cloud of dirt and gnats walked with him. If Pigpen from "Peanuts" were punk rock, it would be this kid. He wore a disheveled version of the prototypical boots, jeans, and leather jacket, topped with short dingy hair pretending to be a flattop.

I spoke first, "Hey, are you new around here?"

"Noooo. I'm Norman," was the reply.

His face looked like he was searching for the answer to a deep question that nobody asked. We found out over time that this expression was permanent. The three of us inquisitively stared, waiting for him to say something. I quickly came to the conclusion this boy had no social skills whatsoever and the dog he was tormenting possessed a higher IQ than him. This kid was a perfect fit for us, even though he knew nothing about punk rock. I opened my door and told him to hop in. Norman became a semi-regular fixture with us from that day on. He stayed with his family in a pleasant two-story home in the Creek Park section of La Mirada. No one ever discovered how long Norman lived in our neighborhood or where he came from.

The new routine went something like this: Youngblood siphoned his gas back from his brother, picked me up, swung by Chemo's, and then over to Norman's, where things got a little tricky. You knocked on the door, sometimes nobody answered, even though the lights were on and cars were in the driveway. Other times, after knocking, a muffled voice spoke to you, sounding identical to the teacher from "Peanuts."

"Squawk, squawk, squawk," minutes passed, nobody opened the door, and you split.

Or, "squawk, squawk, squawk," a couple minutes later, out came Norman with the deadbolt locking behind him.

After hanging out with us for two months strong, he told us he wanted to be jumped into LMP. We took Norman's application to the higher-ups.

Boxer was firm, "You're kidding me, no fucking way, he's too stupid and he'll talk shit to the wrong people. Look at this guy...."

X-man said nothing, just shook disapproval at all of us, including Norman, who was right there in the room with that confused mouse-in-a-maze look on his face.

Youngblood and I answered back, "We'll take him to Santino, he's the boss."

"If he says he's in, then he's in, bottom line."

X-man elaborated, "He'll have to be in our crew, he lives in our part of the woods, giving us the right to veto Santino's decision. Unless our people from Norwalk or La Habra want him in their crew, which we all know they won't—this kid is unproven, totally useless, and a fucking imbecile!"

I pleaded his case: "What are we supposed to do with him, just drop him off where we found him?"

Boxer replied with some thought, "Yeah … or put him through some tests and find out how crazy he can get, then maybe … maybe we'll let him in."

All of us looked at Norman, who for a split second cracked a smile on that lame-brained face of his.

Rather than run it up to Santino right away, we decided to take Boxer's instruction and put Norman through a series of measures to test his stamina as a knucklehead. First, we sent him on a simple beer run as a basic jumping-off point. Instead of snaking good beer, he ran out with some low-buck shit. His reasoning being "That's the stuff we always drink."

Next, he had to let us tattoo U.A.T. on his arm with a guitar string and some India ink. This stood for Us Against Them, who were another one of our favorite local bands on the backyard circuit. Norman became a little teary-eyed during the ordeal, but took the pain/fear combination pretty well.

Could Norman contribute to our woeful financial standing? Best way to find out, put him in a queer alley off Santa Monica Boulevard and see what he could generate. His instructions were simple: Bait someone his way, signal us with a whistle, we mug the trick before Norman has to pull his pants down. Poor Norman came out of the alley, less than ten minutes later, with less than he went in with. A Herculean boy-lover, somehow on to our grift, came up behind Norman, put him in a headlock, held a knife to his throat and removed his wallet.

"Why didn't you whistle like we told you to?"

Norman said, "I haven't been able to whistle since second grade."

"Why didn't you yell for us, then?"

"I didn't want to change the signal."

Chemo heard a bunch of heavy-metallers were lining up to get Scorpions tickets at the Ticketron in Downey, a perfect place to stir up trouble. The four of us drove by right before they opened and saw nearly one hundred dudes in a single-file line wearing every animal print imaginable, parachute pants, and cropped hair with too many bandanas. We sent Norman over with a lighter and a can of Aqua Net Extra Super Hold hairspray to set someone's long-ass hair on fire. Youngblood, Chemo, and I stayed in the car with a front-row seat to the action. Not exactly thinking it through, Norman walked right into a lion's den of rockers, shooting bursts of hairspray fire. The crowd's bloodshot eyes turned their attention toward the fire. Even the heavy burnouts woke up.

Someone in line incited the crowd, "Heavy metal rules! Punkers suck shit!!"

A number of riled hippies started to surround Norman, yelling threats, bobbing and weaving as they attempted to knock the cheap flamethrower from his grip.

Norman squeezed a couple good blasts of fire off, causing one of the head-bangers to stumble away shouting, "He got me—I can't see... Fuuuck!"

All of us in the car were impressed, almost compelled to clap, at Norman's demonstration of raw stupidity. None of us could believe he actually did it. Norman was too caught up to realize he was about to get clobbered.

Chemo started yelling at him, "Run for it! Run for it!!"

Norman hurled the hairspray can at the charging metallers and took off for the car. A few longhairs removed their shoes and started chucking them at him. Norman dove through the passenger window as Youngblood punched it out of the parking lot, leaving the rockers in a wake of foul tire smoke.

School was almost ready to start for Youngblood, Chemo, and me, along with the rest of LMP still in high school. Our young clique decided to rally the other chapters and affiliates for a party at Creek Park to kick off the school year. A rolling dolly with a stolen keg strapped to it supplied the beer. A number of punk rock girls infatuated with our gang showed up to provide what we needed the most: sex and money for drugs. Women really do love outlaws. Sickness, on the other hand, thought she was top outlaw. Being punk rock and in a band wasn't enough. Sailor brought a bottle of 151 that she promptly took control of. Sickness jumped on top of a picnic table and slurred at top volume.

"Wanna see something evil?!"

She guzzled some Bacardi, held a lit lighter out and exhaled a king-size ball of fire. All were impressed and craved for an encore. Sickness downed another huge amount to excite her audience, lit up the high-powered booze, but accidentally inhaled the flames, causing her to fall off the table and gag up fire. It was a first-rate start for our party, except Vitamin Ena and Donna the Dead had to take Sickness to the emergency room.

Unfazed, we went right back to partying, like it never happened. The girls were getting frisky; one seemed like she was leaning my way when from out of nowhere, Chemo spotted a dark shadow moving toward us. All of us got in position to hide if it was the cops or charge if it was the RCP gang. After a few minutes of nothing happening, our group cautiously moved in to investigate. Clouds had blanketed the moon, making it impossible to see ten feet in front of you. Each step raised your heart rate. As we got closer to the unexplained, the moving blur began to take shape. A sizable blob was jiggling on the grass—a monster not of this earth. Chills ran up my spine. I should've covered my eyes or fled, but something compelled me to move forward. What I finally saw has scarred me to this very day. A six-foot, 300-pound whopper of a girl with crude makeup, spiked green hair, and a dress pulled up to her chest was furiously grinding on the ground. It was Evette Corvette, enforcer for LMP's female division, having what appeared to be a grand mal seizure. Then I took a closer look and noticed a pair of scrawny legs with jeans pulled down to the ankles, barely sticking out from underneath her. Scary Sherry put the pieces of the puzzle together and cried out, "Oh my God, it's Evette fucking Norman!"

I detonated with laughter, "That monster's gonna eat you when it's done, Norman."

Evette rolled off and looked me dead in the eyes. "Shut up Frank, you're next!"

Norman casually pulled up his pants, tried to act cavalier for a second, then ran for it. For nearly two weeks he didn't show his face anywhere around La Mirada. When Norman resurfaced, he told us Evette Corvette overpowered and raped him. The whole gang scoffed at the notion, knowing his story was bullshit.

That weekend we took him to an LMP Dukes party in Norwalk. Sailor walked up and gave Norman a hard slap to the back of the neck.

"If it isn't the freak who took on Evette Corvette … Stormin' Normin. You can buy me beer anytime!"

From that point on, he was only referred to by his new name—Stormin' Normin.

STORMIN' NORMIN, 1982–83.

The first day of my sophomore year, something became perfectly clear. I was way beyond out of place in my school environment, surrounded by stale kids. It had nothing to do with how I looked and it had nothing to do with how they looked. I knew these ordinary teenagers had never witnessed a kid bleed to death from multiple stab wounds. I'll bet none of them ever kicked open a toilet stall to find a junkie mumbling the theme to *George of the Jungle* with a rig stuck in his neck. I promise not a single one's watched a prostitute get fucked up the ass in a dirty alley. There's nothing to talk about or say to any of them. Why bother? Getting to school was a tedious ordeal anyway. Youngblood and I depended on his beater Oldsmobile to get us there since our parents were already at work. That car always required some kind of tinkering to get it started in the morning or it didn't run at all. In the end, school was uninspiring and not worth the effort. It became easier and easier to just sleep in, then at some point make our way to Vitamin Ena's. When Youth Gone Mad wasn't practicing, Youngblood and I were drinking beer, smoking sess—school or no school. I never thought past who was playing that coming weekend. Why care about anything else? Ronald Reagan and Russia were going to bomb us into oblivion anyway, so getting a proper education or some kind of job was a laugher.

FRANK STRIKES A POSE ON YOUNGBLOOD'S '68 OLDSMOBILE. NOTICE THE UNION JACK PAINTED ON TOP.

Vitamin Ena's brother, Mark Kostabi, took off to New York City to make a name in the buzzing East Village art scene. With the house basically to himself, he found more time for his number one passion: photographing his dick. There was never a moment when he didn't have pictures of it with him or a Polaroid for some impromptu snapshots. Any time chicks were around, he always found a way to talk them into looking at his perverted photographs. Some girls went for it, completely intrigued. Others found it vile. It was a potluck leap in the dark with a bizarre outcome every time.

Ena and Sickness were spending a lot more time together, becoming pretty much inseparable. Sometimes they were unreachable for days. Nobody knew where they went or heard from them, including their own band members. The two were also very selective as to whom they allowed over to watch this new late-afternoon TV program called *MV3*. Ena and Sickness believed all our reputations as punk rockers were at stake if it leaked out we watched the show. It was basically an *American Bandstand* for local New Wavers and the fashion-obsessed. The format included live in-studio dancers who were L.A. locals dressed in every outfit we targeted, dancing to the latest New Wave videos or live bands like Berlin, the Bangles, and Wall of Voodoo. All their trendy fad clothes, paired with excessively theatrical dance moves, became more ridiculous with every episode. One of the two hosts was a hot alternative-style chick with poofed-up hair and Valley girl delivery named Karen Scott; the other was KROQ radio deejay Richard Blade, who we thought was a fag. At rehearsed moments, he would turn to the camera and politely holler in his Aussie accent…

"Let's go dance with our MV3 dancers!"

He looked like an old buffoon who tried too hard to be "with it" on the dance floor. Karen Scott danced pretty cool though. For one hour, Monday through Friday, we lost our water weight with laughter while pointing fingers at the television set. All the while, we secretly dreamt of New Wave sex fantasies. At the end of the show, all of us felt utterly superior. When Youngblood and I actually made it to school, we caught kids wearing the exact same apparel worn by the *MV3* dancers only a week before. What a bunch of no-risk followers.

CHAPTER 6
"SEASON'S BEATINGS"

FTER ONLY A MONTH OF SHOWING UP at school sometimes, I stopped showing up altogether. Letters were arriving in the mailbox every other day asking: Why am I missing class? Was I sick? Are there any family troubles going on? Of course none of these letters made it to my mother. I routinely burned them. Then phone calls reached her work, asking for a parent-teacher conference, which my mom was having no part of. She had her own solution in store. Knowing this day was coming, my mother took steps to enroll me at Frontier High, the continuation school for dropouts. Her brother had some juice in our school district, enabling me to register there at age 15 instead of the mandatory age of 16. Before you could blink, she signed the lease on an apartment in South Whittier right across the street from Frontier High. There would be no more excuses for me not showing up... smart woman! By happy chance, Youngblood had already enrolled there a month before, after truancy caught up with him. Degenerate found his way there a week later, same week he was jumped into LMP. Little did Mom know, she gave me a fresh start at arguably the most gang-infested school in all of Los Angeles County ... not so smart after all!

Frontier's student population was 88% gang members, 11% pregnant girls and heavy metal lowlifes, and 1% Youngblood, Degenerate, and now me. Being the only punk rockers there, all the hardcore cholos stayed away from us. We were purely too weird. They had no concept of punk—the clothes, the attitude, the music, or the message. Once in a while a cholo would ask us if we were devil-worshippers.

"Ay man, you pray to El Diablo?"

Frontier came with a hazardous student body and a rep that stretched way past East L.A. with representative lowrider gang members from Whittier Varrio Locos (WVL), Jim Town (JT), Quiet Village (QV), Brown Brotherhood (BBH), Eastside Whittier (ESW), Southside Whittier (SSW), Whittier 13, Park Boys (PKBS), East Side Dukes (ESD), Los Nietos (LN), Canta Ranas (CR), Peaceful Village Norwalk (PVN), Varrio Norwalk (VNWK), Pico Viejo (PV), Pico Nuevo (PN).

Now there were three LMP members to share space with. Continuation school was an easy adjustment when it came to the curriculum and what the teachers expected of you. Frontier High was an open campus with a shorter day. Students were allowed to smoke cigarettes and wear whatever clothes they wanted, without hassle from the administration. This was the end of the line, before you were kicked out of the system entirely. Teachers only required your ass in a seat if you wanted a passing grade. A cloud of apathy hung over the campus.

Eager to join Youngblood, Degenerate, and me, Stormin' Normin stopped showing up to school. When Stormin' Normin turned 16, his gift was a transfer from who knows where to Frontier High. Now there were four of us. At least once a week he inquired about the status of his application to join our crew.

All we could tell him was, "Hang in there, the higher-ups are still taking it into consideration."

Stormin' Normin wanted in bad.

Holiday season rolled around, ushering in all kinds of ill will. I refused for the last four years to participate in any kind of Christmas activity. The way I saw it, punks didn't do such things. Christmas meant sitting around with stupid relatives and listening to boring stories before you opened up some lame present you had no use for. Screw that. When Mom got around to decorating the tree on her day off, my indifference for the holidays peaked. Mom needed help topping the tree since she wasn't that tall. Putting the angel on top was considered a privilege, according to family tradition. Fuck tradition. Instead I took my rare prized 8x10 framed photograph of Sid Vicious and placed it above. Mom called it sacrilegious, but left it up there to make me happy. This became my tradition until I moved out from underneath her roof. Relatives who visited asked my mother, "What's the significance of this deranged druggie on top of the tree?" She always replied with a customary "He's going through a phase," knowing I had checked out.

Boxer and Youngblood's household also had an off-the-wall Yuletide tradition. Their mother baked gingerbread men cookies from scratch. Upon Mom leaving the kitchen, the brothers attached penises along with big tits before they went in the oven. She didn't notice the transsexual cookies until it was too late, but still had no qualms about serving them to her guests. Like my mother, she figured any Christmas participation from her disturbed punk rock children was better than none at all.

Christmas was a week away. Boxer, Youngblood, Magnum, Santino, Joker, and I were enjoying the fruits of Boxer's labor inside his bedroom, with the door locked. His mature pot plant budded, providing us with a lot of weed that gave you a head-change, then a headache. Why the fuck not, it was better than nothing. A bottle of peach-flavored schnapps Magnum boosted from his grandmother's purse got passed around the room. Youngblood got extra drunk and started reciting lines from *Quincy, M.E.*, the medical detective TV show starring Jack Klugman. Youngblood's particular monologue was from last week's episode where they dramatized a stabbing murder at a punk club.

"You're not blaming that girl's death on punk rock, are you?"

Youngblood paced around the room imitating a heartfelt Quincy.

"Don't underestimate that kind of music … It's a killer. A killer of hope!"

Bursts of hearty laughter and weed coughing overtook all of us except Joker.

"That show looked so fucking fake! That band and slam pit, all of 'em wearing a bunch of clown makeup. Old Quincy walking around sweating punks for leads—I'm not buying it. I would have stabbed him in front of everybody!"

Another round of Quincy monologues was interrupted by a pickup truck full of Christmas carolers who parked right outside. Young girls and boys, accompanied by adults, were holding candles, dressed in matching shiny white robes while singing "Silent Night." All walked up to the house together, then lined up across the lawn continuing their Noël serenade. Everyone in the room moved to the window. Magnum started undoing his belt, causing a chain reaction. Each of us took similar steps to pull down our pants. Some pressed their asses against the glass, some of us pressed our dicks against it. One by one, every caroler's face went pale. Their holiday spirit got bushwhacked, literally. The adults, without delay, herded the petrified youngsters who were getting an eyeful of anatomy. Instead of moving on to the next house, their spiritual director was practically throwing kids back in the pickup truck shouting, "Let's get the hell out of here!"

Our hijinks were put to a stop by a knock on the bedroom door. Everyone played it off like nothing unusual happened as Boxer opened up. His mother stood there smoking, with a puzzled face.

"Did any of you see what happened out front? That was so odd…."

She took a strong drag off her cigarette.

"The church group choir was on our lawn singing then all of a sudden they ran off … I know you guys did something!"

Our lack of concern wasn't helping our case when Youngblood spoke up, "Mom, we didn't hear anything, what are you talking about?"

She seemed to kind of buy our denial and slammed the door.

Any girl that fucked us for the way we looked had a pet name in our scene: the punk rock "pass-around." Our groupies weren't the same caliber as your typical rockstar's. Some couldn't get dates with the popular crowd. Some simply wanted a sample of scum. Degenerate and I scooped up a pair while we were high on acid at Florentine Gardens. We were known for this. Degenerate was a punk rock fashion plate: wore extra high boots, strategically ripped T-shirts, a spotless motorcycle jacket, and this silly Clark Gable moustache that wasn't punk rock in the least bit. We didn't get it, though he must have been doing something right, because the girlies ate it up. After taking turns on our pass-arounds at Motel Hell and in the car, they still wanted more. Instead of dumping them on the boulevard at dawn, we decided to feed them acid and take them home with us to pawn them off on the crew. Circumstance outmatched our ambition. Youngblood and Boxer's cars were gone. Santino only kept company with fine chicks. Sailor's booze intake left him useless till afternoon. Eddie lived in OC. Captain Out of Hand was too violent with women. Joker had his hands full with a divorcée he stayed with. Popeye was still in prison. Vitamin Ena and Sickness were pretty much a full-time relationship at this point. Chemo had a concussion from stage-diving. Magnum found his hand still more interesting than pussy, which left us with our only choice.

Degenerate and I arrived at Stormin' Normin's with these two drugged-up nymphos in melted makeup, begging us to give it to them extra hard. We knocked on his door and waited for the usual "Peanuts squawk" from the resident adult. Several minutes passed by, until we heard that voice say something sounding like "Norman locked himself in his room again, come back tomorrow."

Both of us were dumbfounded. This time we actually understood "The Voice." A mix of exhaustion accompanied by residual LSD hyperconsciousness must have decoded their complex speech intonations. Neither of us, however, was in any condition to drive the girls back to Hollywood. Needing to use a restroom, we brought the pass-arounds to a gas station and ditched them.

Christmas Eve finally arrived. I was with Boxer and Youngblood, watching the film *Phantasm* on Beta at their house. A rattle-boned old man had command over a demonic metal ball that hunted people down, then drilled holes into victims' skulls. Our fright-fest got put on pause when Stormin' Normin stepped into the room holding a long machete at his side. His face was void of all expression, except for a minute twitch at the corner of his mouth.

MOTEL HELL, HOLLYWOOD, CA, 1981–82.
PHOTO BY EDWARD COLVER.

Normin just stood there and said nothing for an uncomfortable amount of time with that menacing weapon at his side.

Boxer blurted out, "Why are you standing in my doorway with a Mexican sword?"

The kid was non-responsive.

Boxer looked over to us, "Handle your retarded little buddy. I will shoot a hole in his head no questions asked."

He reached underneath his mattress for his pistol when Youngblood spoke up, "You better wake up and drop that fuckin' thing now, Normin!"

I chucked an empty beer can at him bouncing it right off his chest, snapping him out of his state. Normin let the machete drop to the floor.

"I'm pretty sure I killed them."

Youngblood asked, "Who...? You killed who?"

"My house, I hacked it up."

I carefully escorted Normin to the couch and sat him down.

"Kick back and watch the movie, Normin, we'll be right back...."

Boxer quietly pulled Youngblood aside. "You and Frank are going to see what happened over there. I'll make sure he stays put."

The two of us took a short walk around the block to Stormin' Normin's, where everything appeared okay prior to arriving at his front door. There, a considerable-sized hole was chopped down the center; shards of wood littered the ground. We were actually able to step directly through the splintered opening into the living room. Debris from broken lamps and smashed collectibles were scattered about. Outside of the damage, his home was put together and decorated quite normal, almost too normal. Youngblood called out with slight apprehension.

"Hello ... Mr. and Mrs. Normin ... is anybody there...? Are you there...?"

No one responded. It was lifelessly quiet, too quiet. Youngblood and I ventured deeper, following the hack marks through the hallway. Arriving at the stairs, I solicited this time.

"Hello... Hello there ... is everybody okay?"

No answer again, nothing at all. Both of us started getting the willies. We knew something was up there past the stairs. Both of us shoved each other around to conjure up enough guts to go up to the second floor. Deep machete gouges lined the walls all the way to the top. Suddenly a muffled noise came from one of the bedrooms, stopping us like a red light. Without saying a word, we pulled out our knives, and then cautiously stepped into the master bedroom.

Surveying the area we noticed a pattern of gashes around the bathroom door.

Flooded with dread I strained out, "Hey ... who's in there? Is everything all right?"

Youngblood picked up a slipper from the carpet and threw it at the door. "Who's in there? Say something!"

After a couple of seconds, a woman's voice replied.

"We're fine. Everything's fine in here. Norman just acted out, he's a little upset."

Youngblood smirked, "Norman's sitting in my bedroom watching movies, we took his machete away ... do you need any help?"

A man's voice answered back, "Jehovah is taking care of us, he has protected us from harm. Thank you."

We took the reply with quizzical resignation and walked out. Stormin' Normin's parents gave us the impression that a machete attack was just good old-fashioned growing pains.

When we got back, we enlightened Boxer on what Stormin' Normin was clearly capable of.

"If we can get him to do that on the street, he'll make a good LMP."

Boxer shook his noggin, agreeing, "Oooh yeah, I'm sold."

New Year's Eve, Stormin' Normin finally received a nod from the higher-ups. Attempting to murder his parents surpassed any test we could put him through. Instead of going to some amateur night countdown party, Youngblood, Chemo, and I decided to take Stormin' Normin to Creek Park for his mandatory LMP ass-kicking. On the way there he knew something was afoot. His face was beaming with joy. I've never seen anybody so up to get beat down. After we polished off some Schlitz with a pint of the lowest gin, it was time.

I stood up, adjusted my red braces, tightened up the strings on my Doc Martens, and removed my beret. Youngblood and Chemo went through their similar rituals.

I ordered Normin, "Stand up; wipe that idiot smile off your face."

After he got right to his feet, it only took one direct shot to send him back down. Stormin' Normin had no offense and even more pathetic defense. He merely lay there fetal, instead of protecting himself. The kid only stared up at us with a watery-eyed look of betrayal, eating one boot after another. It was depressing. Normin's pitiful exhibition took all the fun out of it, forcing us to stop well before the required time.

"All right, all right ... get up," I uttered begrudgingly. "You've had enough. You're officially in."

He picked himself up, brushed off his clothes, and flashed his Lennie "Of Mice and Men" smile.

Youngblood took the initiative to shape him up.

"Now you're LMP, so stop locking yourself in your room like some kind of bed-wetter!"

His retort was instant: "Locking myself in my room?"

"Yeah, every other time we come over, your parents say Norman locked himself in his room again."

Stormin' Normin snapped back, "Lock myself in the room?! They lock me up in there days at a time, telling me the Devil's outside, the Devil's outside! Can't have any holidays—no Christmas, no birthdays, no TV! All they want to do is fucking pray! Get on your knees Norman, on your knees Norman! Same bunch of fucking garbage!!"

The three of us had nothing funny to say about that. Stormin' Normin certainly had great cause to be punk. His freedom to express himself got shut down more than anyone I knew. His chance to be any kind of kid was shot down with strange particular cruelty. Stormin' Normin was the true definition of a punk rocker.

On the following weekend the four of us decided to take down RCP at Creek Park. That gang of long-haired loadie rockers were throwing their weight around. Again. Every kid growing up around La Mirada for the last decade lived with taking their shit. I was LMP now, more matured, and ready to square off. They knew who I was ... they remembered. Tonight my crew was taking the park back to claim it as ours. Nothing was going to stop us.

Youngblood, Chemo, Stormin' Normin, and I charged them with chains, bats, and brass knuckles. The seven dirtbags never saw it coming; too busy camped out on a picnic bench taking turns blowing bong tokes down their poor dog's throat. Chemo whipped his bike chain down on the table with full force, causing an ear-shattering explosion of beer bottles. A tornado of desperate fists and frenetic kicks came right back at us. The zit-ridden fat guy came swinging at me in slow motion. I nailed him right in the ribcage with my bat, leaving him begging for air. Youngblood walked through a glancing stoner punch and connected with brass knuckles, putting his man to sleep. Stormin' Normin whaled away with his chain against two RCP burnouts in dirty flannels, doing their best to cover up.

STORMIN' NORMIN
AND LARRY PARKED
BELOW ERROL
FLYNN'S.

Three down, four to go.

A mean-ass shot tagged me square in the noodle, throwing my equilibrium off. Hands tingling, I dropped my hardwood bat to the ground. Now it's fists and boots the rest of the way. One of them picked up my bat and swung it at me with ferocious purpose. I lunged backwards and felt the wind swipe at the tip of my nose. Chemo chain-hacked my guy right across his legs, pulling the rug out, crashing him face first to the cement. The stoned Labrador tried to bark, but only coughed out sounds. "Arkkk! karrrk! arkkk!"

I turned to survey what was coming next, only to witness Youngblood catch a bottle right on top of the cranium, propelling broken glass far and wide. Adrenaline burn sent me full-speed at the hippie culprit, tackling him to the ground. I unloaded one punch to the face after another until my fists hurt.

Blood everywhere.

Stormin' Normin was still pummeling the same two guys who couldn't get up.

After watching berserk kids with weapons hand out a slaughter, the rest of RCP slipped away. The five left lay there, a groaning mess of blood and fractured bones. Youngblood and I rifled through their pockets and took their weed, pills, and anything else of value. They only had loose change, like true lowlifes. Chemo and Stormin' Normin destroyed their shitty bicycles by ghost-riding them into the creek. We poured the remaining beer all over them and shouted a careful reminder. Just like the movies.

"This is LMP territory now! RCP is fucking done; any of us see you long-haired pieces of shit again we'll kill you!"

LMP GANG: 3 – OPPOSING GANGS: 0

CHAPTER 7
"LIFE OF RIOT"

1983, THE SMALL GROUP OF LMPS I RAN with outside Youngblood, Chemo, and Stormin' Normin expanded. Silent was recruited out of La Habra High; we met when I briefly attended school there. He fought on our side against DYG when we wiped them out, earning his shot to get jumped in. Silent got his nickname because at selective instances he wouldn't say a word. Any time he got loaded on anything, he didn't speak to anyone. Not even girls. When cops questioned him, he would lean against something, smile, and say nothing. Not a peep. Silent came off like some kind of throwback greaser tough guy. As a result he took gut shots or got his Triumph motorcycle knocked over from angry pigs, but he just continued smiling. It took everything out of us not to laugh. Silent did a few months in juvie for attempting to steal a drum set from a neighborhood church to help our pal Mark Atkins' band, The Republic. Their drums were hijacked by some thieving immigrants at an East L.A. gig where anything that wasn't bolted down was ripe for the picking. I watched The Republic practice at Mark's house where his dad always bought beers for us and the La Habra LMP clique that hung out there. Mark went on to achieve notoriety as singer/leader of the band Guttermouth. Silent started putting in work, getting closer to lowrider Westside La Habra gang (WSLH), hoping to one day run our La Habra LMP chapter.

Bear became another common with us. He was unmistakably involved in some kind of murder near the South Bay where he lived, so he had to lay low and hide out. Boxer and Youngblood's parents let him stay at their house after we lied to them about how he was bullied at school and needed to enroll at Frontier High. Bear looked like a blond skinhead grizzly. Always wore long-sleeved shirts, carefully rolled up, and spit when he talked. Had the redeeming qualities of quick decision and absence of fear. Boxer constructed a flimsy bunk-bed setup, placing Bear down below next to his pot plant and kegerator.

Bear was inventive when it came to incorporating weaponry in your clothes. He came up with the idea of putting three-pronged fishing hooks with the points exposed in the lapels of our leather jackets. Any time someone grabbed onto us in the pit, or in a fight, their hands would be torn to shreds. The first time we applied this tactic, our crew stood out front of the Music

81.

Box after a show, counting the number of guys exiting with bloody bandanas wrapped around their hands. His other stroke of genius was taking a chainsaw chain and wrapping it around your engineer boots, sharp side out. Any fool that got kicked wound up going down with multiple abrasions and painful lacerations all over their legs.

Once Bear settled in, he confided in me about some suspect behavior that went on at Boxer and Youngblood's house, how their parents did questionable things. He claimed their mother had full conversations with him while she walked around the home stark naked. Or lurked outside their locked bedroom door fully disrobed. Bear could see her curling her toes in the carpet from under the door for minutes on end.

I didn't know what to make of it, until he called me up and told me to "get on over here as soon as possible."

When I arrived, Bear had that "get a load of this" look on his face, pointing to some noise down the hallway. I had to see for myself, so I strolled toward the bedroom. A few steps down the hallway, Youngblood's mom was giving it to her sons and shattering my ears in the process. I caught more than an eyeful of nakedness; I felt my gag reflexes kick in.

"You boys are good for nothing! You airheads drop out and do zilch!"

Bear and I slid right past her into his temporary room. I thought to myself, at least be in better than mom-shape if you're going to be on display like that.

Her noise trailed us, "Oh look, there goes two more nobodies. None of you better fall down on my property and try to sue me. I would line you all up together and shoot you dead if I could!"

I also noticed at times their father would wrap his arms around his sons' girlfriends, and get cozy with them on the couch. He even whispered into their unwary ears when Boxer and Youngblood left the room. The brothers operated like it was all regular child-rearing material, so I just shut my mouth. After witnessing this behavior, I was no longer envious of the fact that the family spent more money on their kids than anyone else I knew. Any time a new record came out, they had it. They wore printed punk T-shirts bought from the record stores. We had to make our own. Before their boots wore out, they had a shiny new pair. If we saw a band wearing custom studded belts or the ones made of bullet shell casings, they had them within a week. Middle-class income, plus low-class lifestyle, equaled Boxer and Youngblood.

ithin a week of being LMP, our new enlistee Casper got into a fight outside our zone in Huntington Beach. HB punks had a reputation for being hard-ons with top-notch fighting talent, but were also known for lacking the penchant to do whatever it took—i.e., kill. Casper wasn't ready to accept a swarming rat pack of surfers-turned-skinheads. Three caught him alone outside a venue and wanted to mark their territory.

"You're a long way from home faggot, you're gonna pay!"

Casper recounted to me how much fun it was pulling his knife and seeing wide eyes of disbelief, mingled with panic, before picking the closest one to him and going to work.

"One!"

"Two!"

"Three!"

Casper counted out loud with each stab, all the way to "Twenty!!"

He hopped a series of fences and sped out of Dodge unscathed. Word leaked around that LMP did the killing, but no one could prove shit; it was dark and they were drunk. Only Casper and the dead guy knew the details. Casper said the guy tried to cover each puncture with his hands while he was being stabbed, and he actually stuck the HB guy's hands to his body several times.

If the HB punks thought they could get some payback, we were easily found, but no OC gang was gonna come to L.A. without dying.

BOOTS,
BEER & BREAD.

made strong lowrider allies at Frontier High and ran around with them on occasion when nothing was happening in my scene. The more we hung out, the more we found out we shared things in common. All of us lived the gang life and worked at building our rep at every opportunity.

One night I was out with four lowrider brothers; two were with Quiet Village (QV) and two with Canta Ranas (CR) who needed tires for the Chevy Fleetline they were restoring. The first tire shop that didn't have a junkyard dog patrolling got raided. We hopped the fence, broke a window, and tossed the whitewalls over. Way too easy. The interior of our rundown Toyota Corolla was crammed. Each of us had a tire in our lap except the driver. The bouquet of B.O. and rubber was unfriendly to put it mildly. A patrol unit doing its evening rounds pulled next to us at a signal. Bad break. We knew we were busted, four lowriders with a shaved-head punk, sitting in a grocery-getter … come on. They hit their lights immediately. Two cops walked up with flashlights illuminating our interior.

"Well, lookey here—Pancho Villa and his band of revolutionaries are bringing tires back to the village. Get out of the car!"

The other cop pushed us down to the curb and put the stolen tires around our heads, one by one.

"Look at how that works—we don't even need cuffs for these idiots!"

There we were, sitting on the curb with whitewalls on our heads, for all passing traffic to see. I was outraged. The others fully accepted it with their faces down.

"Fuck this!"

I threw my tire across the boulevard.

Both cops put me to the ground with nightsticks and started kicking me.

"I know my rights and I don't have the right to wear a tire over my fucking head!"

The cops started laughing, surprised I spoke up.

"Then just put your hands in the air like a good boy so we can see them."

I couldn't believe my lowrider buddies weren't sticking up for themselves, still wearing tire necklaces.

"Where's your fucking balls at!" I yelled.

"Hey, pipe down freak, you're in big trouble here…."

We all spent the next week in juvie as our cases got sorted out. Who would have thought, one of the brothers caved in and rolled over on the rest of us. But the snitch brother screwed himself because he was already on probation. They gave him a maximum two-year sentence; we only got two weeks and proba-tion. Our cops and courts notoriously hated snitches, used them, then threw the book at them.

I found the juvenile hall situation at Los Padrinos to be no different than Youngblood described it, except for having to listen to all sorts of shitty miscel-laneous music. After recreation time, music from the radio was piped into your single-man room. One day it was funk for the black kids, another day oldies for the Mexicans, then loadie-rock for the white kids. It all depended on which race was the most well-behaved that day. During loadie-reward day, one of their representatives was playing air guitar in the room across from mine. The boy put everything he had into it, like a center-stage encore performance at Cal Jam. He went so far as to pretend to light his Stratocaster on fire, then pulled down his trousers for real, and pissed on it. That was the highlight of my boring incarceration. Nobody tried to get crazy on me. It was a cakewalk. Punks had a rep for being nutso and that's all gang kids respected.

'I am not a gang member'

When I was released, Dad was nowhere to be found as usual. Mom came down on me, trying to make me go to P.O.P.—Parents of Punkers—with her. P.O.P. was a support group located at a family therapy center on Lakewood Boulevard where punks had to go through lame counseling with their parents. I flat-out refused. Ironically, it was on the same street as Middle Earth Records, one of the few punk and import record spots in the L.A. area I could count on. Calling us punkers was the biggest irony of all. True punks hated that term, took it as disrespect and fucked you up if you said it. Only the media and squares used that idiom.

The Cathay de Grande consistently constructed a solid bill of hardcore bands. As customary, LMP crew was there one night getting smashed with some LADS before entering, polishing off as much booze as we could. A group of Valley punks smarted us and were smoothed over with a quick ass-thumping. Bouncers working security out front wanted a piece of the action. From time to time, they strayed away from their door duties to get involved in beefs that didn't concern them. Some were miscast knuckleheads who wanted to test their own toughness against us. This turned them into oppressive authority targets we otherwise would've left alone. One got his teeth kicked out; the other hobbled off, shouting for assistance. Next thing I knew, Argyle Street was columned with pigs in full riot gear, holding shields, ready to crack skulls. More police were pulling up in cars, lining the entire block. It was time to get out while the getting was still good.

Silent, along with the LADS co-leader, made a break for it and ran straight toward a parked cop car. The LADS member leaped headfirst, letting his momentum slide him across the hood. Sharp studs covering his leather jacket made an ear-piercing grinding noise, leaving behind thoughtful scratches. Silent, not to be outdone, pulled a sharpened screwdriver and gashed the entire length of the police cruiser's side panels as he ran by. Two officers stood witness, unable to believe their eyeballs. Down the block were countless unmanned law enforcement vehicles, abandoned by the riot squad. The LAPD was busy verifying our police state by clobbering punks out front of the Cathay de Grande. About a dozen LMP and LADS lined up on one side of a patrol cruiser, rocked it back and forth, and finally flipped it over, crushing the roof. A big hooligan cheer rang out amongst us as we ran away from the mob chaos. Within minutes a police helicopter was up and searching—gone, baby.

Celebrating our misdeeds at Oki-Dog was out of the question. Too many new punks and trendy posers were starting to ruin it; what's more, we were sick of paying for food and the sheriffs closing it down before we got it. Errol Flynn's was our true refuge, where we partied all night, replaying the events. Destroying a cop car was beyond asking for it; it was straight up egging them on.

Sailor, Magnum, and I were spending an easy Sunday on Santino's porch with his dad, The Godfather, soaking up some gangster wisdom. Stark-staring-mad Magnum was showing off his vintage three-piece pin-striped suit, complete with black-and-white wingtips, smoking a cigar, while reciting infamous James Cagney lines.

"I wish you was a wishing well, so I could tie a bucket to you and sink you."

A car pulled up in the driveway and out stepped The Godfather's nephew. He leaned against his car, troubled, glancing at us without eye contact. The Godfather drifted over and had a private conversation with him, then walked back to me with a humorless look on his face.

"Frank, that man over there is my nephew and a Los Angeles Assistant District Attorney. He can't speak to you directly. There's something we would like you to take care of in Whittier."

Clearing my throat, I was all ears.

"My nephew's son was beaten up pretty bad by three older cowards. He's okay now but took a real whipping … if you could find these guys and return the favor, he would consider himself in your debt."

I didn't think twice about it.

"Give me their names, I'll take care of the rest."

The Godfather walked back over to his nephew, who scribbled on a piece of paper and handed it over. The man looked directly to me, gave a subtle nod, and then drove off.

Santino's father handed me the list and pronounced, "Family is life and life is family…. Now we can finish our beers."

Déjà vu set in, back to my Little League days when my coach took me aside, educating me on the "big picture" of team play.

My dad's boss, Sam Sciortino, always said, "Remember your people and your people will remember you."

Next afternoon I went straight to Whittier High to hit up a friend from our punk rock community who attended school there. I showed him the names.

"I know who all three of those jock dickheads are. I'll find out where they hang out and get back to you, Frank."

I emphasized, "No one needs to know about this, I want it to be a surprise."

"Not a problem, Frank, it's my pleasure. Hate those football fucks."

SANTINO WITH MOM AND HIS DAD, THE GODFATHER.

983 marked the first deaths within LMP. Big Annie was permanently wrought with emotional issues. Any time our La Mirada crew was together, she frowned continually, wearing her depression like a tiara. Partying and getting loaded never made her happy like the rest of us. The crew eventually stopped paying any attention to Big Annie. Nothing cheered her up. We thought it was just an act, earning her the nickname "Dungeon Queen." When she threw parties at her apartment near Skate City, Annie essentially sat removed, not present. As a result, parties at her apartment got rowdier—why give a shit about decorum if she didn't? This naturally culminated in a "destroy the place!" bash where a band played in the living room. Punks put holes all the way through to the stucco outside, broke windows, vomited on the floors, and pissed in the corners. Definitely one of the best parties LMP ever participated in.

Her landlord lost it and filed a lawsuit demanding restitution estimated at $20,000 buckaroos. Big Annie answered the civil suit by blowing her brains out all over her apartment unit. X-man ended up having to scrape the mind chunks and splatter off the ceiling for her landlord a week after the incident. The entire La Mirada family attended her funeral. Some said they saw this coming, but didn't have the ability to do anything. It caught me off guard, forcing me to look at the possibility of suicide. If I was gonna off myself like that, I would take every single one of our enemies with me.

Not too long after the Dungeon Queen's demise, death struck again. Her name was Wendy, from the Norwalk Dukes LMP assemblage. She gradually slid down a pill-addicted slope of ruin. The girl ate ludes like candy, eventually adding a nasal mewl to her speech. She hated coke and speedy drugs; low and muted felt like home. Even worse, the poor girl prostituted herself sometimes just to get where she needed to be. No one thought Wendy's dosage could ever exceed her tolerance for the strongest of downers. We were wrong. She accidentally slowed her heart rate down to zero, and it stayed there.

PHOTO OF BIG ANNIE, *PENTHOUSE* MAGAZINE EXPOSÉ "SLAMDANCING IN A FAST CITY," 1982. PHOTO BY MARK SHAW.

Somebody needed to be blamed. Our crew focused on a has-been singer from the Masque days, turned mid-level pill-pusher to supplement his income. We heard he supposedly supplied the fatal dose. None of us confirmed this rumor as record though. No matter, we never liked him or his act anyway. His band went by a moniker taken from a true-life 1950s Puerto Rican street gang, featured in a 1970 film that launched the career of Erik Estrada. Asshole had the nerve to attend her funeral. During the eulogy Santino, Sailor, and I each murmured in his ear, "You're dead."

On multiple occasions the plot to kill him fell short. We showed up to where he lived, but didn't have the patience to wait him out. Other times, we had willing participants, except no working car to get there that night. He was a very lucky man, being that we never quite got our shit together to do him in.

When the Grim Reaper loiters among you, the weight of circumstance instills a fatal validity. His flak hits right when you think everything's business as usual. Another punk on the LMP waiting list, named Yoda, took a shortcut on his way home through the Candlewood Country Club golf course, only to find our pot dealer Goober swinging dead from a tree. Someone forcibly hung him, then pulled out his dick and gripped his hand around it for laughs. Yoda assumed suicide until he saw tons of motorcycle tracks in a circular formation around the lynch tree. Goober the hippie was our most reliable pot connection, who we thought had no enemies. Goober never shorted anyone, even though he was practically the only game in town, moving significant weight.

Turns out the tire tracks were no coincidence. Goober pushed his weed in a place called "The Acres," located in South Whittier. That place had a biker gang presence dating back to Vietnam. Everyone thought he was in league with them, kicking money back to the three-piece patch, up to the point of his unfortunate demise. Making a joke of his killing was some real classic biker shit for sure.

Gary Tovar of Goldenvoice brought big-name punk acts from the UK to play in Los Angeles, expanding the scene.

Anticipation surrounding the Exploited show at Mendiola's Ballroom in February was extraordinary. Wattie, the singer, was screaming "Maggie Thatcher's a CUNT!" all over the UK, getting him into hot water. She had become Ronald Reagan's puppet; punks on both sides of the Atlantic hated their guts. Pop culture analysts and bourgeois trendsetters were saying punk was dying, but not to us.

Most everybody from all four chapters of LMP made sure to show up. Various gangs were in attendance from all over L.A. The location was filled past capacity with wall-to-wall punks; tons were still out front hoping to get in. The pit was bona fide bedlam, a style and technique display, with kids flying off the stage every which way. All around the edges, fistfights were commencing between crews, and skirmishes were flaring up with the bouncers. Looking around the antiquated ballroom you saw the pit consume the entire floor. No escape. In between songs, I heard screams coming from the door, subsequently followed by scores of police batons swinging down on punks.

Within seconds, the place was brimming with cops wearing gas masks, fucking kids up, and spraying mace on anybody they saw. A street war had broken out inside. Unarmed punks trying to retaliate were slipping on spilled beer mixed with sweat and adrenaline. Those that fell took boots and batons until they stopped moving. Bottles started sailing en masse at the men in uniform, stirring up the melee. Kids beaten limp were getting tossed out the doors; I even saw girls getting the treatment. We somehow slithered outside with no crew casualties, just minor bumps and scrapes.

Outside, Huntington Park looked like World War II, a full-scale Blitzkrieg with punks playing the part of Poland. Stormtroopers clashing with our type was nothing new, but this was unlike anything in our past. Panicked kids scurried for their lives, bouncing off riot shields. Two cops got hold of a random skinhead girl and tossed her through the ticket booth window. Police made sure the punks they were working over weren't able to get back up. True sadism from the pigs caused us to take it out on the city. Our immediate retaliation was to shatter every window of every business along the street. I heaved a beer bottle at a cop when he wasn't looking my direction. One of my enemies from Suicidal ran by at the perfect time. The deputy mistakenly fingered him for it, and beat him senseless—two birds with one stone.

We hustled to our cars and split town, driving over to a familiar pizza joint. It was headline news on every local channel, blaming punks for the violence. The newscaster take was typical.

"Once again our brave police restore order after marauding punkers do their best to destroy property and terrorize the public. When will we see an end to this punk menace, when will the parents get control of these destructive kids…?"

CHAPTER 8
"NIGHT OF MY LIFE … NIGHT OF MY KNIFE"

I WAS TREKKING DOWN MELROSE AVENUE in Hollywood, midday, looking at new Doc Martens I couldn't afford, when Lady Luck struck. The woman I had met in front of the Chinese Theatre, who wouldn't give me her name, was walking on the opposite side of the street. Without thinking twice, I bolted across Melrose to try and start up where we left off.

"Hey, haven't seen you around in a while."

She kept walking coy, ignoring me.

"You don't remember me? We took a picture together standing in Frank Sinatra and Doris Day's footprints at the Chinese Theatre."

"Ha-ha. Dream on, Frank."

I was shocked she remembered.

"Wow, you remembered my name."

"How could I forget about Frank the entrepreneur from the Walk of Fame?"

Trying to put on the charm, I quipped, "You wouldn't hold that against me, would ya?"

She laughed, leaned in, and rubbed my hair: "Your shaved head is so cute."

"So are you gonna finally tell me your name, mystery girl?"

"Maybe… We'll see."

We walked and talked for a while on the avenue, ending it with her finally giving me a name, number, and a date the following week.

It was time to fulfill my contract with The Godfather. My buddy checked back with me, and gave up the location where the three marked jocks that beat up the D.A.'s kid hung out after school. I enlisted the help of Hulk and Shady from our La Mirada crew for the deed. The spot was an after-school burger joint, where only popular jocks and girls that fucked them congregated. We were definitely going to have an audience for our show of force.

I walked inside, no words said, and slammed one of their heads firmly into the arcade game he was playing, shattering his nose. In short order, I jumped on top and started tattooing his face with everything I had. When done, his face looked like ground beef with ketchup squirted all over it. Shady took apart another in similar fashion, splitting his nose open from bridge to tip. Hulk came with a barrage of weighty shots that put his guy down and dumb. A highly emotional clerk started throwing ice at us, threatening to call the police. The spectators had a nervous breakdown and did nothing but get the hell away fast. Hulk grabbed a half-eaten burger on the way out. All three meatheads were sent to the hospital and not seen at school for a while.

Next day, The Godfather notified me personally that his nephew at the District Attorney's office was pleased with the outcome, stating, "I will remember this if a case ever comes through the court."

Accounts settled in full.

Time passes in wondrous ways.... Dad was on deliveries and I was running around Sam's truck yard with his trusted guard dog, Frank the Shepherd. Oil-tainted puddles from last night's drenching layered the lot, giving us a new adventure. I, Blackbeard, the seafaring pirate and most feared captain of the seven seas, Frank my first mate and gun sergeant. We built our worthy ship out of an old rusted semi-fender and scraps left to rot. The sail was constructed from an old pair of stained coveralls.

Peering out of the cannon bay, I spotted three pairs of legs heading in our direction. I noticed Sam's loafers, work boots in the middle, and dress shoes on the end. They stepped inside a trailer shutting the doors behind them. We abandoned ship and got next to the trailer, pressing our ears to the side. I heard a scuffle of feet and a number of stiff thuds. After a brief quiet, the doors opened. Sam and another guy wearing a casual suit were holding up this crying man in a delivery uniform by his arms; he was bleeding from the nose. Sam spoke as they walked him toward the office.

"Everything's gonna be okay, anybody can make a mistake once...."

Both Sam and the suited man walked with a smooth gait, assured and powerful. Head down, the uniformed guy shuffled to keep up as he wiped his nose. I started to follow, walking like Sam, strolling like a man in charge. I was Sam, Frank the Shepherd my right-hand man.

"One mistake," I proclaimed when a forceful hand grabbed hold of my shirt and yanked me aside.

"You stay out of that man's business, you hear me!"

I looked up and answered my father with a confused nod. The three men went back inside the office as I waited for a good smack from Pop. It never came.

He released me and patted me on the shoulder.

"Go busy yourself over there with the dog."

oungblood, Chemo, and I drank beers with a small group of punks from Whittier that didn't enlist in gangs, but were cool enough with the right people to keep out of harm's way. They always had brews, and transportation that could make it to Hollywood. There was Benny, Opie, Matt, and Pete. Benny drove us around in a rusted old sedan left to him by his grandmother. He believed girlies really went for convertibles, so he sawed off the top and welded the doors shut. Benny convinced himself he was a "Cadillac Man," but the thing was a PT boat without its canopy.

"What about the rain tonight? Sky is cloudy, Benny..."

"Let's just go to Hollywood, Frank, I got some killer acid for cheap. If it rains, we sail the open seas. Fuck it!"

was frying out of my mind in front of the Seven Sleaze. Pooling showers were provoking me; noise from the city sickened me. Benny's hair started crawling with angry lice. Some chick with teased hair, wearing a spaghetti-western poncho, began taunting me. The hostile girl aggressively weaseled in my space. No elbow room. She spit disease-smelling alcohol all over me. I lightly tapped my half-empty beer bottle on her head, thinking she'd get the message. Shrill piercing laughter came out as she stumbled backward. The reaction enraged me. I grabbed on to her poncho before she hit the ground and booted her right into the gutter. Murky rainwater enveloped that confrontational bitch as she cackled away in the filthy sewage drain. Turning around, one hundred punks were smiling, giving me approval for removing the nuisance.

Time flashed ahead; I was bathed in hot green and red light, holding the corner of a wet white sheet above my head. Speeding southbound, I had a brief glimpse of clarity. We were using the sheet as a makeshift convertible top, shielding ourselves from the rain during the drive home. I got soaking wet; the rest of the night was a blur. Where did it go?

Next day, I found Chemo and asked him about last night's acid-induced confusion.

"What was the deal with that wild chick fucking with me? She would not stop laughing."

Chemo just listened.

"Wonder how much hairspray she needs to keep that look going, dumb-ass cowboy poncho ... I fucking hate New Wavers."

"Frank, you serious? That was no New Waver in some poncho. She was a homeless lady with ratted hair shivering in a blanket! She was asking for change, then begging for her life after you hit her. She wasn't laughing at you, she was screaming in pain after you broke a bottle over her head."

I searched my toxic brain for a memory.

"Really...? I hit her?"

"Yeah, Frank, and kicked her, blood was running down the gutter. You bummed everybody out—people couldn't believe what you did. They were all talking about how LMP are the cruelest guys on the face of the earth."

I pondered for a moment, taking all the possible facts into consideration.

"She lay in the gutter for an hour before the paramedics hauled her away. You fucked her up good. People said she was dead, but I didn't see any body bag."

I was still drawing a blank.

"Well, what can I say—she had no street smarts spitting on a loaded punk rocker. She got off easy."

The night I've been counting down for days had finally arrived. My big date with Madeline, the mystery girl. The money Degenerate was gonna loan me didn't happen. I needed another plan, fast. I started running through the possibilities, wracking my brain for a last-minute approach. I couldn't hustle tourists outside the Chinese Theatre, in case she saw me, and LMP discouraged it these days. Forget a shoplifting spree. Soon as a punk walked in any store, security was on your ass every step. How could I sell the merchandise quick enough anyway? Robbing a house or somebody for cash was way too big a chance during the day. BINGO—I got it! Sell my signed Dodger baseball cards of the starting 1977 World Series team to a pawnshop. My father had taken me to "Camera Day" that year where the organization let fans on the field to take pictures with the players. They were strict about not allowing autographs, but I was such a polite kid back then.

"Please, Mr. Garvey? Please, Mr. Cey, you're my favorite!" until I acquired all nine signatures.

That marked the last time my dad and me did anything together, when he loved his Dodger baseball more than beer or giving me an ass-kicking. Turned out that my kid politeness paid off though, as I got a decent bankroll from the pawnshop. I was more of a Baseball Furies guy now anyway.

Degenerate loaned me his junker for the evening as long as I returned it full of gas. I picked Madeline up at her Hollywood and Vine apartment, 8 p.m. sharp.

Madeline didn't invite me in, said she would rather go without delay to the movies, being she ate a late lunch. She was all smiles and didn't seem to mind riding in a bucket with torn-up seats and no reverse gear. Her easygoing laughter put me at ease when she had to help push my car out of the space. Our choices at the theater were *My Tutor* or *Bad Boys*. She chose Sean Penn's *Bad Boys*.

Soon as we walked out of the theater, Madeline grabbed my hand and suggested we go to her favorite café, the Onyx in East Hollywood. A place I had no familiarity with whatsoever. Inside, the place was full of beatnik artist types, weird old men reading books, and a smattering of punks. All she wanted to do was sip cappuccino and talk about the flick.

"I felt so bad for those kids, so much violence around them. Sean was so believable! I loved his hair..."

Whatever she said didn't matter. I just liked to watch her talk. I dug the sound of her voice even though I thought aspects of the film were a joke. No way would they allow unopened cans of soda in a prison, and that radio explosion was so fake. How the hell you gonna make a bomb in youth prison?

Driving back to her apartment I was so preoccupied. All I could think about was whether or not I could get a kiss and how was I going to get it? Everything she said sounded like a bunch of delightful noise smeared together. Naturally, I went along, chiming in with "That's great" and "No way" when needed. I walked Madeline to her front gate and patiently waited for my opportunity during the small talk. As I was trying to close the deal, she looked without blinking into my diffident eyes. Madeline's vampish smile made me go for it. I only planned on a small kiss but she laid into me tongue and all.

"Frank, thank you for the great movie. I'll see you around."

She smiled, licked her upper lip, and walked into her apartment building.

On my way home to drop off Degenerate's car, all I could think about was how different Madeline was from the girls I usually fooled around with. The LMP girls that ran with us—Sickness, Donna the Dead, Scary Sherry, Evette Corvette, Smelly C, Scrappa Marry, The Grimace, Push the Clutch, Tits, Kimba, Vaseline, and Jap Jenny—also didn't have what this one had ... the thrill of a real woman, full of twists and turns.

Two years after the death of Bob Marley, our ska-boy pals from Monterey Park invited us to a festival held at the Federal Building in Westwood, directly across from the UCLA campus. Their friends the Untouchables, a local ska/soul band that got on the map with a few KROQ hits, were playing at the event. Later, they would get featured in the punk cult movie *Repo Man*, as a scooter gang that beat the shit out of Emilio Estevez for attempting to repossess their family car.

Ska wasn't our thing at all, but Santino rallied a number of us for the show, seeing it as another chance to show force outside the punk scene. Degenerate drove his bucket, Youngblood piled the rest of us in the Union Jack Oldsmobile. Law enforcement had the entire place surrounded. Los Angeles was fast becoming a police state. Anything punks frequented, cops shook us down and clubbed us with nightsticks to show who's boss. What made this particular event unique was that local police had no jurisdiction on federal property, so the goon squad was forced to remain on the perimeter unless extreme violence broke out. Consequently, our whole gang stood at the edge of the grass only feet away from police, drinking beer, passing joints, and even making pig squeal noises at them. We left all our weapons in the cars so L.A.'s finest couldn't do a damn thing.

A SHARP-DRESSED
FRANK, 1983.

Stormin' Normin got hold of some potent California Sunshine LSD at the show. The acid had a couple of us frying heavily and more antisocial than usual. All the Krishna cult freaks, unbathed Rastafarians, old stinky flower children, homeless vagrants, nudists in loincloths, street performers, love enthusiasts, fake gurus, and self-proclaimed healers had me feeling a cut above. That's where I learned to hate the stench of patchouli. Funny thing was, so much seemed to happen that day, yet we never really moved from our corner spot the whole festival. Early evening we decided to get the hell out of there. Residual sharpness from the LSD still had me slightly playing tug-of-war with reality. Dissolving tracers.

I looked across the street and caught a number of heavy metal types walking step for step with our crew. They started to talk and point at us, puffing their chests and swinging their hair. Fortunately, our cars were on a block that forced us to cross paths. No way were we going to let Mötley Crüe point fingers at us, ever. All of them waited for us to approach, rolling sleeves, cracking knuckles, and nodding their heads. The biggest one, who appeared to be in charge, stepped up front and called out Santino. He insistently pointed to a tattoo of a muscled-up hippie chopping off a punk rocker's head on his forearm, and then motioned to Santino. The hippie and his tattoo were legend in Whittier. He was a well-known street fighter that hated punks and considered it a privilege to smash their faces in. Santino and Sailor often talked about him, hoping to one day go heads up. The big hippie knew exactly who Santino was.

"Don't do anything, I want him for myself, this is between us," our leader ordered.

Both sides had something at stake: the age-old question—who is tougher, punks or metallers? Everybody stepped back as the heavy metal heavyweight came forward, fists up, to meet Santino. They took measured steps until both got within reach and began exchanging blows. Nothing solid landed, causing the huge punk-hater to change his mode of attack. He skillfully got hold of Santino, picked him up, and body-slammed him to the ground. The hippie monster raised his arms high, taking a WWF moment to admire his work. This provided Santino with just enough time to get to his feet and counterattack. The opponent was stunned, like he had witnessed the dead come back to life. Santino dug deep and delivered four of the best blows he'd ever released. The hippie went down like a ton of bricks. He got lucky Santino didn't have a weapon. Now Santino stood over him, mocking, arms high in the air.

The metalheads were completely demoralized after watching their Bismarck get sunk. We started pushing the others around, telling them to hit the high road or die. Joker reached under his jacket, giving the impression he had a gun. The tattooed scrapper got to his feet and took off racing. Santino chased after him with Stormin' Normin and me in hot pursuit. The longhair crew knew not to follow. Weaving in and out of parked cars, our quarry started to get away from us. Santino felt the point was well made and stopped the chase altogether. Stormin' Normin just kept on after the guy at a torrid pace and eventually disappeared amongst the buildings.

We casually walked back to where the fight started. Youngblood let us know they kicked the shit out of the rest, along with putting huge dents in their car. After waiting for over a half-hour for Stormin' Normin to come back, it was time to leave. Later that night, about twelve o'clock, a car pulled up in front of Santino's. The door opened and out popped Stormin' Normin in a cloud of smoke.

"What the fuck happened to you, man?" I questioned.

"I hunted that hippie for a long time ... then I got lost—what happened to you guys?"

Santino explained to the boy that we had quit chasing right away, got tired of waiting, and split.

Stormin' Normin's story was, "I went back to the festival and met up with these cool reggae people; they gave me a ride right now."

Blood stoned eyes, Stormin' Normin pointed behind him to a car that had already left.

"One of those reggaes is gonna tattoo a heavy metal guy getting his head chopped off by me ... on my arm."

Mid-1983, the whole world was cracked venom running through my veins: nuclear meltdown, Lebanon terror, Thatcher controls, and Reagan's "Evil Empire." If you ain't with us you're against us. My private world was punk rock gangland, with a proliferation of new crews, along with old ones, that wanted to take a shot. Punk gangs randomly threw parties in their turf with bands, booze, and a basic invitation to come over ... if you dare.

Tonight's hosts were SGP South Gate Punks and Circle One. They somehow conjured up enough balls to have an event deep in our territory's warehouse district with Corpus Delicti playing, four worthless local bands, a keg, and a slam pit. Who the fuck do they think they are? We found out late in the day and only managed to put together a bare-bones war party with nine representatives.

We arrived simultaneously, in a show of force. Inside the warehouse, punks were collecting in clusters to protect themselves. Others surrounded what was left of a keg. When Corpus Delicti hit their first note, the whole place pivoted toward the band like coyotes at sundown—they wanted their food. Roughly 15 South Gate Punks, and about 20 from Circle One, scrutinized our every move. Regardless, LMP took possession of their pit—bashing, knocking down SGP and Circle One members slam dancing in the trenches. You could bet that the hundred additional partygoers felt something brewing between us. It was obvious we weren't there for the music.

One fistfight broke out, then two, and then all nine of us were each fighting a one-on-one brawl. LMP was in a heavy-handed frame of mind. Opponents lost heart within a minute and scattered away. We were seasoned street fighters at this point and knew how to stay composed, giving us a clear edge even when outnumbered. Wounded egos and fat lips were commiserating. Knowing an ambush was being planned, we went outside and waited for blood. Handing out an ass-kicking was not enough. The courage to out-brutalize any adversary continually put LMP on top.

A few of us retrieved weapons from our cars, brought readily for the occasion. Bear took to the task of calling SGP and Circle One outside.

"Come out and face the music, pieces of shit! You posers are gonna meet your maker!"

Backing down at your own party was unheard of. SGP and Circle One came out from the warehouse mustering their best psycho-killer faces. The small sinewy one whined, "You fuckin' LMP fuckers come to our fucking party and start shit?"

Santino let his fists do the talking and threw the first punch, dropping one quick, then right away fighting two more. Everyone rushed with a personalized method of attack. I crashed a bottle across the top of some bleached head. Shitdick fought axe handle against ball bat with a Sid Vicious wannabe as Youngblood took two guys into the fence. Gun-happy Cooper took out his Colt revolver and waved it around in the air for all to see.

So much was happening all at once.

Shitdick connected with his hard wood, reducing a phony to tears. Boxer followed that by breaking a nose. His challenger staggered away, trying to push it back into place. I went toe to toe versus a Circle One, taking plenty but dishing more. He finally went down after I landed a money shot to his temple.

Soon as one goes, another one jumps up to get crushed. Our two Norwalk soldiers were fiercely tackling adversaries into the ground, treating them like bugs. Shitdick caught an Easton aluminum dead in his ribcage, forcing him to take a knee. Santino responded, putting a whiz-bang high boot on the skinhead about to finish Shitdick. Boxer managed to get another SGP down and apply some steel-toe therapy. Cooper smacked a guy dead in the face with his gun and then pointed it at the next, promising, "I'll do it! I'll do it!"

We had evened the numbers at this point …

"CRACK!"

The field froze.

Bear had brought down his axe handle right on top of his target's forehead. Slow motion, eyes rolled back as blood came spouting out similar to an oil strike. He teetered a moment, then fell forward face-first onto the cement.

I saw a velvet red pool form around his lobe.

SGP and Circle One panicked, locking the warehouse door while the rest dispersed over the fences. Santino claimed victory. We jumped into our cars and split to celebrate. From out the windows, we watched the poor stiff drown in his own blood.

I reflected back to when I was young and naïve, still learning lessons. Many times trying to beat my dad at cards … I could never win. Even when cheating, I couldn't win, because the person I was trying to cheat was better at cheating than me. That punk deserved his lesson the hard way.

All of us met back at Santino's for a short-lived celebration. But he figured it wasn't a good idea for all accessories-to-the-crime to be together, gift-wrapped for the local dragnet. Boxer, Youngblood, Bear, Shitdick, and I took off heading north. Right when we made a turn down Boxer's dead-end street, it was law enforcement ballyhoo. Spotlights turned their attention precisely on us. Stupid cops surrounded our Chevy Blazer, looking like they just won a big stuffed animal prize. The helicopter noise was deafening as we filed out of our vehicle at gunpoint…

"Hands where we can see them or you will be shot!"

"Don't make any sudden moves!"

"Do as you are told—do not fuck with us!"

Rookie pigs shouted foul-mouthed *Police Story* dialogue at us left and right. Each of us got escorted facedown to the asphalt, then to our own private squad car to make sure we couldn't get our lies straight.

I was flabbergasted at how quickly the cops had Boxer's place staked out. After I assumed the position and got cuffed, Officer "By the Book" opened his car door to the biggest bombshell that night. Bear's girlfriend Sophie was lying in the back seat, startled, eyes unfastened like she just saw a ghost.

I exploded, "What the fuck? It's you! It was you!! You snitching bitch!!"

My arresting officer tried playing it off with a cheap "Ooooops, wrong car, sorry," but savored the moment like a true sadist pig.

He knew exactly what he was doing. Fuck her—Bear blew it bringing his chick to enemy territory, a real amateur move. Like dominos, she picked a fight with him, got dumped, abandoned, then topped it all off by ratting to get even. We avoided being booked, fingerprinted, and thrown into some rank holding cell by the skin of our teeth. I must have frightened the shit out of Bear's now ex-girlfriend since she ended up fingering him alone for the assault and leaving us out of it.

The next day, Bear's folks put their house up as collateral and bailed him out on the charge of attempted murder. Somehow the SGP buffoon lived, but wound up slow in the brain. His family didn't want to press charges, fearful of possible repercussions from LMP. That didn't matter to the D.A., who wanted Bear locked up for a long, long time. Within a week, sheriffs awakened Boxer, Youngblood, Shitdick, and me at 5 a.m., serving us with subpoenas for Bear's trial. That same week, sheriffs brought each of us in privately for questioning. Santino volunteered to testify on Bear's behalf. Cooper wanted no part of it. Afraid he was going to catch an open case while under the law's microscope, he took off to roadie for Joan Jett and the Blackhearts.

Our other collaborators from that night kept a low profile at home, waiting on possible subpoenas. Santino instructed all of us to grow our hair enough to part it on the side, so we could appear believable while committing perjury at Bear's hearing. Judges went for that kind of square grooming.

"Of course we didn't see who was responsible for hitting that kid with an axe handle, but it wasn't Bear for sure, because he was messing around with some girl he really liked in the car."

The case was put on hold so both sides could prepare.

"If you had a gun with only two bullets and you're in a room with Stalin, Hitler, and an LMP member, whom do you shoot?" The answer going around Hollywood was "Shoot the LMP twice and get the fuck out!"

Living life on my terms, not doing what they told me, was all I understood. For me it was truly an outstanding time to be an LMP. The amount of respect I got on the streets was hard to believe. From the beach to the Valley, we were known and feared, and our enemies kept a safe distance or got dealt with. The streets were ours. We didn't infringe on lowrider, black, or biker gangs' way of things, so they stayed away, letting us do what we wanted. For the most part, they only cared about profit. Our approach to the hardcore punk rock movement was working.

LMP GANG GRAFFITI.

Fingerbone, Joker, Stormin' Normin, and I were in Compton to watch SIN 34. The singer, Julie, a cute girl from the comfortable Westside, always showed up to gigs in a luxury-class sedan, driven by her mother—spoiled brat punk that ripped. Fingerbone was a new recruit I plucked from a small-time Whittier outfit called SBP, Suburban Punks. In order to properly expand our ranks, Santino directed me to monitor the local outfits and take on their craziest members. Incorporating them into LMP was a cinch, due to the recognizable rep we achieved that lured them to join us. Outside the restrooms, a small band of hardcore types and skins were gathering up to challenge us. They seemed like a gang, though nothing absolute about them stood out, until one started yelling in our direction.

"MID CITY! You guys ain't shit!!"

They jumped bad—time to leave scars. The four of us fought hard, taking on more than what's fair, but managed not to get overwhelmed. Security was all over it, breaking us up before we spun out of hand. I took a mental picture of all their faces for future reference.

Near the end of that month, I went to a Florentine Gardens show with my beer-drinking allies from Whittier, in Benny's no-top Cadillac. It was a last-minute journey to Hollywood, so no LMP crew came with me. The gig was pretty tame by punk rock standards. No rat packs, no one carried away from the pit, no one slumped in the corner bleeding. I exited alone since Benny and Opie were still generating time with chicks. I made my way to the car, turning up my hard-as-nails exterior. Everyone wants revenge when you're all by yourself. In my periphery, some standard shaved-head/leather jacket/Doc Martens guy was making his way toward me. His shoving people aside clearly defined the state of affairs. Soon as he got in my neighborhood, I estimated the tale of the tape: 60 pounds heavier, ten years older, six inches taller, and very familiar. Straight off I identified him as one of the punks I clashed with at the SIN 34 gig.

"Fuck LMP—MID CITY!!" he proclaimed.

Nothing left to speculate on. I spat in his face, catching him by surprise, then pulled my sure-to-be-trusted butterfly, and without nerve, stuck that mother right underneath his rib cage.

"Fuck LMP?" I baited. "No, FUCK YOU!"

Puzzled. Dead silence. Then after a moment, he looked down and saw his own blood. His eyes lost all spirit, his body misplaced its fortitude. The Mid City punk stumbled off, cursing for help.

Impulse took over and I fled the parking lot to the main drag, then realized there was nowhere to go. I had to clean my knife, get the blood off it. Quickly I surveyed Hollywood Boulevard and noticed the gutter was running water. My hands felt oddly strong, like they didn't belong to me. A hint of fear surfaced, but I shoved that feeling down and moved on. I feverishly cleaned the reddish-purple blood from my knife. Perfect—if the cops sweated me, I'd be in the clear. Now, I was just another punk with a blade, who would suspect I did anything wrong? My wheels kept on turning. If I get caught, or somebody puts the finger on me, it's an open-and-shut case of self-preservation against a grown man way bigger. If he dies, I split the city and relocate.

I was skyscraping from thrill, strength from achievement, top to toe. I bolted forward to Benny's Cadillac. Damn! No roof on the car ... I lay on the floor of the back seat and pulled the sheet over me. Ten minutes later, still no Benny and his cronies. Where the hell were they? Sirens everywhere, it was way too hot. Got to get out, pigs would eventually find me here. I took off my jacket, wrapped Benny's white sheet around my head like some street weirdy, and hightailed it out through the alley up toward Franklin Avenue.

More sirens—I hope he dies!

I went west down the street, turned on Vine Avenue and found myself in front of Madeline's apartment building. Heart still racing, I had to come down, compose myself.

Calm down.

I buzzed her tenth-story residence and waited, time without a curtain.

"Hello?"

I said nothing. Her voice bit into me.

"Hello? Who's there ... hello?"

CHAPTER 9
"CHAPTER HATE"

HOLLYWOOD BOULEVARD TO PERSHING SQUARE'S skid row, transferred buses to Whittier quad, then walked a mile, and at last arrived home at 3 a.m. Felt like two years and still I was wide awake. I couldn't sleep; instinct sent me straight to Santino's to be freed from the miasma of the streets. What a chickenshit I was for not seeing Madeline. Like grade school all over again: jelly-legged, dry-mouthed—all the pre-teen symptoms of inexperience. But, if she had come down, it would've have been over between us. Too much adrenaline with no game plan ... hope she didn't think someone was stalking her.

3:30 a.m., I quietly stepped up to Santino's porch. I was about to tap on the window when I heard a beer can fall from the roof. Cautiously, I hopped up on the wall to get a clear look, and there was The Godfather. Sound asleep, surrounded by beer cans, curled up with his faithful military-issue rifle. This had been his nightly routine lately. Camped out on the roof with a sleeping bag, 12-pack, and an M-1 carbine, ready to pick off invaders until the beer put him to sleep. Members of neighborhood rival VLM were vandalizing his cars in the middle of the night for several months. Throwing rocks through windows, shooting tires out, or denting them with baseball bats—it got so bad The Godfather was forced into buying crappier cars. His auto budget dropped from $800 to $80 in no time.

"How can I own a decent car if VLM is going to smash them up every time? They'll learn respect when I put one in their ass!"

I went inside and woke up Santino to help me lug him off the roof. After getting his father down, Santino got the full report of me stabbing the Mid City Punk. I edited out detouring to Madeline's.

"Good job, you did everything right, except you should have tossed the knife after you cleaned it."

"Why? It's my only butterfly knife and it's a real Bali-Song. I just got it."

Santino gave me a look of disdain and spoke to me straight.

"It's evidence, Frank, get rid of it quick. Never keep a knife after you shank someone with it. Ever. Even if he lives, it's still attempted murder. Toss it in the trash or the sewer somewhere."

fter a few pre-trials and sworn statements, Bear's court date was still pending. His attorney notified us that the victim suffered permanent brain damage.

"People will have to help care for him the rest of his life."

Now the D.A. wanted to crucify Bear, and busting LMP became a clear law enforcement objective.

The lawyer emphatically advised Bear, "Get a full-time job and lay low—stay out of any kind of trouble."

It went in one ear and made a break out the other. Bear continued to sleep on Boxer's floor and still go to shows, or Hollywood, any chance he got.

Tonight the plan was to go check out this new nightclub in Hollywood, a current hotspot for punks and scenesters. Santino, Joker, Thugsey, Bear, and I crammed like sardines into Boxer's Chevy Blazer to make the trip. It was necessary for LMP to represent anywhere things were jumping in Hollywood. The offbeat club wasn't noteworthy by any stretch, and none of us had any real success with the ladies. All they wanted to talk about was some place in London called the "Batcave." Must have been the wrong night. We stuck around the parking lot to finish our alcohol and hopefully find stray drunken sluts. Even that situation was bleak. The only thing grabbing our attention was this tall ska-dressed dude picking fights with the parking attendant. Boxer hated loudmouths. Some hated for style, some for color or religion, Boxer categorically despised braggarts and blowhards.

"Bring that shit over here, ska-mouth!"

The ska laughed Boxer off and went back to his vociferous rant.

"That's what I thought—all talk." Boxer sneered.

The ska gave a formidable stare in return and took off his cardigan sweater jacket.

"Okay, no weapons, just one on one. Let's do this!"

Boxer told us to lay back as the ska put up his dukes. I wish somebody wanted to put money down. I knew what was coming.

Our pal slipped left, and then began peppering the loudmouth with the old one-two, right through his guard. His opponent came back woozy with cheap swings that skimmed Boxer, then a haymaker that missed badly, putting him off balance.

Boxer took advantage. He set his feet and lowered the boom with a thundering right that collapsed the ska to his back. Boxer fired a quick smirk in our direction, took a seat on the ska's chest and dispatched more punishment. Left right left right left, picking his spots. One more shot and the guy was through.

Taking a page from our playbook, the ska pulled a sharpened steel rod and plunged it into Boxer's neck. Curveball. Boxer shut down.

The ska stuck him again through his upper lip.

Boxer rolled off, holding his wound, looking at us for the diagnosis and remedy. Bloody mess.

The ska jumped up and exerted all his energy as he escaped around the corner.

How did that just happen?

Joker took off first, Santino grabbed a hammer from the Chevy's toolbox, Bear got an axe handle, and both joined chase. Thugsey and I picked Boxer up, brought him to the car, and applied pressure to his wounds. Boxer didn't care at that moment about his wounds; he insistently pointed toward the action, beckoning us to join chase.

We rapidly drove to where Santino, Bear, and Joker had already cornered the ska boy and blocked the alley, cutting off any chance of escape. Payback's a bitch, time to ante up. He was trapped like a rat, sweating profusely, and scared shitless.

"Come on guys, please … I didn't mean it, I was just scared … please … please don't … I'm begging you please!"

Answering with great silence, revenge slowly sealed the gap.

Ska pleaded, "You don't need to do this!"

Joker replied with a switchblade "click" and six precise shanks to the ska's midsection. The ska fell to his knees, clenching his wounds as Santino and Bear moved in.

He gasped and screamed out, "Please, no—No more!"

Simultaneously, the hammer, the axe, and the blade struck from all sides. He bounced and flopped for a minute, trying to protect himself from the horrendous onslaught. Mesmerized from the sidelines, I kept lookout while Thugsey continued putting pressure to Boxer's neck. Sparks flew repeatedly from Santino's hammer after it would hit the concrete and ricochet into the ska's cranium. Bear walloped the axe handle off his torso while Joker kept stabbing away. All three took turns in tempo, until they ran out of energy.

The ska's body knew it was over. Time was ticking. He lay there with his face caved in and blood bubbled out his last remaining breaths. Transformed into a pulp of unrecognizable meat.

Boxer's injuries turned out to be small. The sharpened steel cleanly missed his vitals. Stroke of good luck, with a few stitches he was good as new.

Hollywood LADS gave us the lowdown straightaway on how everybody in our scene knew it was LMP. They told us, "DOA—cops couldn't even identify him ... nobody saw nothing."

That's how it was in 1980s Los Angeles. Anybody could get away with anything, so long as you were on the freeway before LAPD showed up.

Another man dies ... it wasn't hard to believe.

Some hippies were pushing a fresh batch of four-way windowpane acid at the La Mirada Regional Park.

They told Chemo, "It's the highest mic level you can get before you go legally insane!"

Right up our alley.

We made sure to eat the LSD near sundown, in order to peak at nighttime and maximize our illusions. Creek Park was still LMP terrain, providing us with a safe zone away from police in case things turned weird. Soon as nightfall came, the back and forth started.

"Are you frying yet?"

"No—are you?"

"No ... he –he –ah –ha –ha –ha!"

The uncontrollable laughs had begun, thus visuals were soon to follow. Instead, something odd happened to my breathing. The rasping noise of my lungs, expanding and contracting, became uncontrollably loud—but it wasn't me.

I looked to Chemo, "Are you hearing it? It's really creepy ... creeping me out, man."

The moon was cavernous black; the park I knew so well turned multilayered and unusual. I felt like I was solely responsible for losing the big game. Crystal-clear bright lights and familiar shouts broke my downhill spiral.

"Frank? What the fuck, man?"

Youngblood and Stormin' Normin stood in front of the car, with Chemo already in the back seat.

"Frank. Get in the damn car or we're leaving—you're taking forever!"

I broke to the car in double time and placed myself inside near Chemo.

They said I crawled.

Our vehicle lurched toward the 101 freeway as Youngblood grilled me.

"I was parked there for over ten minutes ... couldn't you hear me calling you?"

I thought about the answer long and hard before replying.

"What...?"

I looked over to Chemo, "What?"

Chemo handed me an already lit cigarette to pacify my stress.

Took one drag ... then another drag...

The smoke felt like mustard gas, killing me. The deathsticks had to go. I rolled the window a crack and flicked it. My cigarette hovered a foot outside the glass, floating, following along, keeping a vigilant eye on me. The cherry was radioactive.

"Chemo ... Chemo... can you see it?"

He laughed back, "No, I don't see any of it. There is no IT!"

We hit town vertical to Cathay de Grande, featuring Channel 3. The nightmare continued.

Sickness, Scary Sherry, and Donna the Dead looked gorgeous inside the club. Shitloads of scumbags were trying to buy them drinks. They could tell I was frying from across the room, commiserating, laughing, and cooking up some plan that hopefully didn't include me. Leave me out of it.

Scary Sherry sauntered across the room, purposeful, with one clenched fist.

"Hold out your hand, Frank."

"No way, Scary, get away from me!"

"Oh come on, Frank—pleeeease do me this one favor ... I'll never ask you for anything ever again."

Her polite delivery broke my steadfast opposition. With a ton of trepidation, I opened my hand.

She poured what must have been over 50 coins into my palm. "Hold this for me till later, Frank," then disappeared amongst the crowd.

Everything reached crucial. I could not let her down. My mind was operating out of character, asking questions, and being responsible. How long do I have to hold this? Should I put it in my pocket? If I do, will it get mixed up with my own money? What am I supposed to do? Where can I put it? Where did Scary Sherry go? Shit! Fuck! No! No! No!

I yelled at Youngblood, "What the fuck am I supposed to do with this?"

He mildly snickered and walked away.

No one would take it off my hands. I opened my fist to take another look at the change that sparkled with utmost importance. I couldn't handle it. I wasn't cut out for this kind of favor. Why me?

Two hours in the corner of the club and I was about to commit myself. Stormin' Normin threw me a rope, telling me Scary Sherry had gone outside. I hurried out to find her. Nowhere to be found, no nothing ... maybe the rope was to hang myself with. Some punk told me she went next door to the liquor store. I rushed over and found her.

"You have to take it back!" I barked.

She looked at me like the Secret Service.

"No, I told you to hold it for me, Frankie."

"Please please please...." I begged her.

"No, a promise is a promise."

Out the door she went, laughing.

Okay ... all I had to do was buy something and this episode would cease to be. Unfortunately my hand, along with my forearm, turned to copper—bleeding copper. Time was running out. I grabbed a 40 oz. bottle of malt liquor and brought it to the register. A dark swarthy type, underneath a giant genie hat, waited for his money. He knew I was a minor, had to make the purchase quick; it was part of the deal. I dumped my fistful of coinage all over the counter and began.

"One, one, one ... ten—one, one, one, five—ten...."

Silver change, combined with copper change, was confusing. Every time I thought I hit ten everything got erased, then I had to start over. A line of disgruntled customers filed in behind me.

The genie spoke.

"This is not cool dude, come on bro, I have many customer here."

I simply could not deal with it, couldn't count it, couldn't comprehend it, and had no idea how to use it, or what it was exactly for.

The genie pressured me.

"Mister, I have business to run perhaps...."

Money. The root of all evil. My patience ran out.

"Oh yeah, well I've got motherfuckin' money to count, so I guess we all have our problems!"

Customers behind me started hissing in mutiny as the genie clerk reasoned.

Another time perhaps you have enough money, this obviously is not enough for your purchase. Come back when you ready, bro, I will take care of you."

"Screw this—take it all!"

I tossed it on the counter and walked out.

"Sir—wait! You have given me much; please you come back perhaps..."

Shambling my way back to the parking lot, I shook off some of my madness. No beer and limited mind science once I reached everyone. The LMP crew was having their usual punk rock social, scamming on girls, slap boxing, shit-talking, and guzzling booze. My fellow acid tripper Chemo was content spitting loogies high in the air and catching them with his mouth. Shitdick and a newcomer recruit from Norwalk, called The Governor, came jogging up. Shitdick was first-generation American, his parents working-class Brits, but somehow, he adopted the soccer hooligan look. The Governor was six foot, Irish, 240 pounds, and already tattooed.

Youngblood asked where they've been and "How could you miss Channel 3?"

Shitdick recounted, "We were in the X-rated bookstore watchin' films in the booth."

The Governor proudly admitted, "Yeah, I took a huge shit on the floor and walked!"

Shitdick clarified, "Nah, he didn't take a shit, he left a shit! Hahahahhaa, it stank like fuckin' hell. Ahhh hahahahaha! When we came outside we ran into Peaches. You guys know her—she always works in front of Seven Seas ... anyway, her fuckin' pimp comes up to us sayin', 'What the fuck, dis bitch is workin' motherfuckahs, not socializinz! Buy sum pussy or get your crazy shaved heads da fuck away from her fat ass! Don't talk to none of my bitches unless you talk to me first, you broke ass fools!!' So the Governor and I look at each other and smile because we are thinking the exact same thing ... I hit him right smack in the face and Governor breaks an empty 40-ouncer right on his pimp hat!"

"He took off runnin' for his life. We caught up to him in the alley."

"Dumb fuck tripped over his own pimp stick."

"We beat the shit out of him!"

"He kept screaming about old-school this and old-school that...."

I noticed Shitdick and The Governor had blood on their fists and spatters all over their shirts.

"Did you kill him?" I asked.

"Well, when we threw him in the dumpster, he wasn't breathing," Shitdick established.

I became incensed.

"Why the fuck are you still in Hollywood, huh?"

"We didn't want to miss the show ... or you guys," The Governor foolishly answered back.

Now I was even more livid.

"Fuck the show. You are supposed to be on the freeway … long gone! Where's your bitch then? Why ain't you puttin' Peaches to work?"

The two just gave me a vapid look.

"You guys killed her pimp, now you own her—she should be payin' you, making you money!"

"Oh, we didn't think of that," Shitdick timidly put out there.

"You guys are two real amateurs—where's his jewelry and his big roll of cash?"

"Yeah … those two are fucking amateurs." Chemo confirmed in between catching loogies.

Both of them made me sick. I pulled rank and made the decision to get out of town, back south on the freeway, mad and still frying. My guys put us in jeopardy, caused me to slide further down my bum trip, and to boot didn't even get any money out of it. I was bugged out, silent, too deep inside my head the whole way home. Even if Youngblood, Chemo, or Stormin' Normin tried to talk to me, I wasn't hearing it.

Once we arrived at Santino's, I chose to leave my pals and go for a walk. My mind was zipping, couldn't sleep if I tried, a lot of speed in those tabs…

The screw turned, neurosis shook its finger at me. I didn't think I'd get home alive. Ever since the warehouse incident with SGP, things were burning hot for us. The avenues were exceptionally dark. Seemed like every streetlamp was busted. Cops kept driving by slow, staring at me, flashing their spotlight. Time passes in strange ways when you're alone on an island, and my isle was inhabited with head-shrinking cannibals. Felt like hours, long drawn-out, should have been home by now. My brain was thick, overly aware of the intimidating trees advising me to beware. I'm not stupid. Approaching each trunk I could hear them breathing louder and louder. Trees sounded like people suffering from asphyxiation, gasping for life. Remember, you're still frying, I told myself. I ran cautiously as the branches tried their best to get hold of me. They were toying with my soul, wanting me dead. A root tripped me—I fell face forward, shredding my chin on the sidewalk. More bottomless inhaling of agony and torment … I peeled myself off the ground and sprinted at high speed down the center of the street, darted across intersections, avoided suspicious sorts, and proceeded forward at all costs. What should have taken ten minutes at best, took over two hours. I finally reached my residence and slept 15 hours straight.

I ran the shower, splashed my face, and dampened my hair—hoping to give the impression of actual bathing. I tied my sneakers and ran for the door. Dad and I drove to the yard while I planned the day's events of finishing my fort with Frank the Shepherd, making it airtight for our attack on the swarming wasp nest. As we arrived, a few more men than usual were standing around, smoking, wearing cement faces. Dad told me to wait in the car.

"Fucking feds!" I said to myself, still not knowing what that meant.

One of the men in suits came over after a while and asked if I saw the clutch home run from Dusty last night. Of course I did, but something was wrong and the Dodgers didn't matter at this moment to me. Sam and Dad walked out of the office, Frank the Shepherd led the way. Sam waved me over. I hustled up and made sure not to slouch.

"I need a favor from you … it's a big responsibility, but you're a young man and it's time for these things. I'm going away for a little while … I need you to look after my dog, he loves you and I trust you'll take good care of him. You think you can handle this for me?"

Dad nudged my shoulder.

"Yes, Uncle Sam, I'll take care of Frank, I love him. When are you coming back?"

Sam gave me his unflappable smile,. "Soon enough boy, soon e-nough," and walked back inside his office.

Frank began licking my hand obsessively. I didn't know what exactly was happening or why.

My father went to his locker and returned with a few things. "That's all the work for today."

Driving home, my dad took a couple long sips from a brown bag, and then broke the silence.

"Frank, I'm gonna give it to you straight. Do you know what respect means?"

I thought I knew, but just shrugged instead.

"It means you do what you say and say what you do … always. It means when you give your word—you damn well better mean it."

He went on to explain what Sam's true line of work was, about "The Family," and what respect meant to the old gangsters. He opened up about Sam's rise to power and how he really made his money. He even reminisced about his own early days in Detroit and the hot water he wound up in. He left nothing out. I swear I didn't take one breath the whole ride home. He went on and on how the *different families operated, how they worked together, how they settled disputes within their own organizations, how the commission was formed, how money was divided, and how different families controlled certain unions and cities.*

"Sam is family ... and a fair man. He always did good by me, now he's going to prison for a while—so you do what he says and take care of his dog when we come to the yard."

I put the pieces together best I could and nodded.

"You got to be on top, Frank, or you end up on the bottom."

That was the last time I ever saw Uncle Sam Sciortino.

MY DAD, LEANING ON HIS GOOD FRIEND SAM SCIORTINO, UNDERBOSS OF THE LOS ANGELES CRIME FAMILY 1974–1979.

A phone call from Santino opened my eyes at dusk. Orders were to show up at Boxer and Youngblood's for a mandatory meeting. Our leader wanted a full report on Shitdick and The Governor's pimp incident. Since one of them was my recruit, all responsibility fell on me. Behaving in a correct manner when flare-ups occurred was paramount to Santino; he had zero tolerance for blowing it on the streets. Guarding LMP reputation was constant priority number one, not only in the punk scene, but also among all of Hollywood's street denizens. Pimps of Hollywood were in fact a seminal part of the punk rock landscape. Their prime territory was Sunset Boulevard, on the corners of Stanley and Genesee, including the area around Tiny Naylor's restaurant at Sunset and La Brea, where waitresses served customers on roller skates. All these locations of ill repute were right near dives we frequented, so LMP knew most of the hookers, along with their managers, either by face or in passing. Pimps still wore the quintessential garb of flamboyant colored suits with matching trench coats, furry hats, and pimp canes, like characters in some exploitation film. They all were known to be ruthless and possibly deadly, hence killing one of them could stir up serious unrest around our common territory. Protecting a cold-blooded reputation was essential to their existence as well.

Infamous funkster Rick James was as common to that part of our cityscape as the Hollywood sign. Every weekend, 8 p.m. sharp, Rick strolled down Sunset Boulevard along the stretch of hooker/pimp turf with a ladylove under each arm. Punks who infected the clubs on that strip found his presence irresistible. His methods were engaging to say the least. Rick acknowledged everybody, but only spoke to the streets—he knew the difference simply by looking at you, and Hollywood was his town. Oki-Dog also unloaded many a wiener to Mr. James and his late-night women. Each time I saw him, he gave me a handshake, followed by some street anecdote, before he sat with our table of outcasts. We must have added something to his life of cocaine, pussy, and moral pollution.

SHITDICK, HAVING A
SMOKE IN FRANK'S
BEDROOM

Santino laid into Shitdick and The Governor after getting the whole story on the pimp incident. Taking that pimp's money and whore in the name of LMP would have demonstrated to all just how on top of it we were. He never wanted us to come off as a ragtag collection of punk rock knuckleheads, but rather a disciplined group of street soldiers that acted accordingly. Santino ordered us to get answers from the independent contractors of the sex trade on what went down, without giving up any information.

THE GOVERNOR, CRUISING THE NEIGHBORHOOD.

After innumerable attempts at trying to get Madeline on the phone, we finally set a second date. I had to impress her. She was out of my league and looked to have many options. I scrounged together some cash, chilled some white wine, and lifted some strawberries from my mom—all stuff that worked on women in the movies. Degenerate let me use his car again to facilitate my plan. Give Madeline a taste of my Hollywood, something different than what the competition could come up with. Otherwise ... I really had nothing to offer.

My stomach simmered all the way to her front gate, right up to the moment I buzzed unit #1010. She came down with a delighted smile, wearing a pastel top and Sasson jeans.

"Okay Frank, where are you taking me ... what's the big mystery?"

Her lips were flamingo-pink.

I told her, "Sit tight, trust me, I have it all planned out."

I opened her passenger door, drove ten minutes, and then parked on a side street off the Sunset Strip. I grabbed my prepacked backpack of love, took her arm, and strolled down a dark alley. Every step, I felt her nerves as she hesitated, "Frankie ... what is this?"

I reassured her, "You're gonna totally dig it," as we approached the next step of trust.

Two levels of stairs took us to a rooftop and something more challenging. "Okay. Here we are, climb up. I'll be right behind you, spotting."

She looked up at the tall three-tier ladder, rife with anxiety.

"I don't know, are you sure? Where is this gonna take us?"

"All the way to the top...."

Slow and steady, one level at a time, no going back, we reached our destination. Standing four stories up on the ledge of a billboard high above the infamous Whisky a Go-Go, Madeline was awestruck. Her grip bruised my arm as she looked out across brilliant Sunset Boulevard. Burning lights of Hollywood, melting with moving traffic below, made it feel like you were levitating. Madeline's body started to lose tension, drifting into mine with the slowing of each heartbeat. We kissed, and lost track of time. Passing cars provided the jukebox. It was perfect ... our movie.

The boulevard started jumping. I figured it was time to make our way down. A number of police cars were approaching the Whisky as we came out of the alley. Madeline and I exchanged laughs as we noticed a helicopter shining its light on the roof. Hand in hand, we nonchalantly slipped past the cops and strolled pronto into the Roxy next door. No bands were on stage. It was a dance club night, right out of music television. New Wave mania ... my favorite. It looked kind of scary out on that disco-lit floor, but she dragged me right forward. Nobody I knew could have possibly been there. Besides, I really liked this girl—plus "Come on Eileen" was playing. I started mimicking the nerds next to me. Madeline was having a blast and didn't seem to detect me being full of shit. "At this moment you mean everything!" was what I was feeling and what was coming from the speakers. The more we danced, the more I felt a new kind of happiness that was altogether unfamiliar. It must have been her.

Closing time, drove back, got a few red lights, then the green light to come upstairs. Her place was well put together, very adult, like I imagined it would be. Guarantee no punk ever got past the doorman, let alone up here. So what if I didn't fit the bill, she was mine.

Two days later, back in La Mirada, Santino wanted answers. Was that pimp dead or did we need to watch our backs? Santino didn't like the unknown; LMP hit the streets, war-ready. Returning to a spot where our crew recently murdered somebody went against conventional wisdom. I was uneasy with the whole thing. The familiar collection of pimps and hookers didn't fraternize with us like they usually did. No one had seen Peaches or her pimp and no one acted like they cared, but someone knew something. Santino was satisfied for now and broke it down for us:

"Killing the competition is always good for business."

Flipside had been semi-regularly writing about the exploits of LMP and other punk gangs in the scene. One of the writers seemed to be interested in us and our opinion. Different quotes or pictures would show up in their issues, attached to some type of show review. But then *Flipside*, as well as a local La Mirada newspaper, started complaining about violence from punks in the scene, whereas before it was complaints about violence from cops and security. Apparently, an associate of *Flipside* got pushed around at a show and may or may not have taken a fall, hurting his eye. Blame was attributed to "one" of the numerous long-standing crews, which we did not appreciate in the least bit. Shit … give credit to somebody.

Bear's pre-trial hearing kicked into Serious with a capital S. All of us took an oath to tell the truth, God as our witness. Hair was grown out clean-cut-ish at this point and we were all excited to do our best Brando on the stand. First day of depositions, Bear's attorney tried to convince him to take a plea bargain and put it all behind him. But Bear wanted to act—thought it was gonna be fun to convince 12 people he was a good boy and said "No deal."

For a number of days we gave statements, wearing whatever dork clothes we had left for family functions and the like, even parted our hair on the side. It was an exhausting amount of trips to the courthouse, telling the same fabricated story while they waited for us to slip up and say something different. We were solid throughout. The court reporter was a 20-something blonde with enormous tits and tight sweaters. When she made eyes at us, her nipples would jut out real nice. Bear finally had to comment, "Sure is cold in here," which elicited a monumental smile from her and a pronounced throat-clearing from the judge. Hot court reporter or not, the charade wore out quick. After several weeks it became readily apparent we were over this and no longer had the constitution for it.

BEAR, "BIC" BALD BEFORE SENTENCING.

The following day, it was a row of oxblood Doc Martens, fresh-shaved heads, tapered Dickies, and flight jackets at the courthouse. Sneers and victory smiles from the prosecution followed faster than you could whistle Dixie. Next day, right before the actual trial started, Bear took a deal. No jail, no sweat; a long probation and financial restitution to the victim. Bear's parents, having risked their house, saved his ass. His saga was pure LMP. Bear left Manhattan Beach, narrowly escaping an accessory to murder charge. He hid in Whittier, joined our gang, and ended up accused of attempted murder. While that case was pending, Bear helped kill another man ... an exceptional LMP résumé for the time being.

Doing nothing but scoring pills and loitering with hustler kids at the corner of Sunset and Western was not out of my ordinary. These kids were all runaways and did what they had to do for survival. Not only would they sell stolen pharmaceuticals, they also peddled their mouths and other openings. All of them looked like they just had their brains fucked out. I never considered the boys honest homosexuals, just kids put in a bad spot once they fell on the streets. Nobody gave a shit either way. Even the girls hustled both ways.

119.

Cheek'o was kind of their father figure. He always looked out for them and could typically be found supplying drugs at punk shows, wearing the "droog" look obsessively—black bowler, cane, false eyelash, oversized codpiece and all. When comfortably drunk, he leaked inside information about who the hustlers' return clients were and made us promise never to pass it on.

My favorite was the notable actor who played a private eye that drove a European sports car, and had the best moustache on TV. He came biweekly to pick up the most muscular boy on the boulevard, each time in a different disguise. Another celebrity that should have contained her perversions was the redheaded whirlybird comedian who starred in a black-and-white sitcom with her husband. Her strong appetite for youthful girls was quite peculiar. The comedian's driver was directed to bring home underdeveloped redheads. If none were accessible, she had wigs standing by at her swank mansion in the hills. Juveniles, going down on her while she chain-smoked, tickled her fancy. Cheek'o had no reason to lie.

Some of these kids would be around for a while, where others quietly disappeared without a sign. We just assumed their folks came and scooped them up, tried to counsel them or did some type of intervention ... Who cares?

Same location different night, Shitdick, Stormin' Normin, and I were all very drunk and doped up. Out of the urban mirage came this rotund black man, high-stepping in front of us, wearing a marching band uniform laden with tassels and epaulets. His attire was two sizes too small and filthy, but he was dedicated, down to his imaginary baton high in the air.

Feeling venturesome, Cheek'o started to walk behind him, imitating his every move, followed by Stormin' Normin with that dumb smile of his, then the hustler kids, Shitdick, and finally me. We all rallied behind him, playing make-believe instruments, and marched down Sunset Boulevard's sidewalk like it was the Rose Parade. With each step, our sullied drum major intensified his spins and twirls. The moves actually began to appear rather skilled and well rehearsed for a street vagrant. Our contingent naturally played along with it, as absolute joy glowed from his face.

As we passed a parking garage, a shadowy figure hurled a bottle that bounced right off our bandleader's uniform, stopping him dead in his tracks. Before we had a chance to laugh at the improvisational slapstick, he began wailing at the top of his lungs like an injured child. Our brows lowered in harmony as we naturally inched forward to attack the showstopper. He didn't even try to run, instead stood his bum ground, swinging his tattered jacket and cursing. The bum slapped at Shitdick who closed in pulling his shiv. Stormin' Normin and I followed suit as all three of us pincushioned him with our knives. During the attack, he just teetered and bled, showing no real pain or emotion until we backed off.

His body started to tremble, exhibiting some bizarre state of shock, before falling to the ground sideways and closing shop.

Our hustler pals looked a little traumatized at our sudden aggression, but knew the rules and kept watchful eyes. We all just walked away in different directions, ditching the evidence. Stabbing was becoming as easy as hitting a pitch.

CHAPTER 10
"TOO MUCH MONKEY BUSINESS"

CARY SHERRY WANTED PAYBACK. She broke into her old work with Sickness and a few others, and ripped off some unknown anesthetics. The office was just your garden-variety neighborhood dental clinic—nothing special. She used to make appointments there for an elderly dentist who yelled at her all day long, even when she did things right. She busted her ass despite being constantly told "Tone down your look" and "Watch your language." On top of that, the old dentist used to "accidentally" brush up against her breasts, and put his hand on her thigh. Sherry only lasted a month or so, and this was her compensation. No alarms—any amateur could have gotten away clean.

Unsure of what she ripped off, Scary Sherry made phone calls to all known dopers. She invited a collection of fiends to her house in La Habra for a taste test. Those who could get it together showed up to the door jonesing. According to Animal, our pal from Hollywood, time was wasting.

"Fuck this shit—give it to me!"

He grabbed the rig, paced back and forth, then slammed the needle into his vein with medieval flair. Animal smiled a moment before slumping into the couch, drooling. The guy was a circus act and very well-known in the scene, famous for a tattoo on his cranium that read LOBOTOMY. Animal was just one of those guys that everybody knew. I originally met him at one of those artsy-fartsy nights at Hollywood's C.A.S.H. Club. He kept calling me "Rank" instead of Frank.

Scary Sherry looked away while Sickness did the honors. She took the spike like a champ, and then fell right out of her seat, hitting the linoleum with a thud—a knockout shot. Sickness set me up with a low dose since it was my first time. She had become a full-fledged hype, so I knew I was in trustable hands. After some slaps to find my main vein, she eased the needle in.

"Bye-bye my friend."

From head to heel, warm flooded through me, and my eyes gently rolled back into my skull. It took over fifteen minutes to come back from Willy Wonka's dope factory. Flowing rivers of candy ... snozzberry, nodberry ... I could hardly move. Still to this day, nothing has ever felt so good.

Animal rose from his sofa casket demanding a fresh fix.

"More—I want more!"

He attempted to walk, but started urinating in his pants, and decided to abandon his dope quest and return to his resting place. Scary Sherry awoke next, not understanding how she ended up flat on the floor. I gave her the details on how she collapsed face-first. Scary Sherry frowned out loud.

"So what."

Three days later we're at Thugsey's house, drinking, talking about new punk bands on the scene, chicks we violated, crews we smashed, and guys we eliminated. Not even an hour later, beer started running short. I tapped Youngblood's shoulder and pointed to the driveway. Our fellow man-of-war, Sailor, staggered to his Ford Falcon and grabbed two beers from a 12-pack he was obviously withholding.

Youngblood's mood changed on a dime, but he greeted Sailor's return with a reasonably polite "Can I get a beer?"

Sailor shook his head no as he walked on past us.

"Frank, I'm not asking anymore, fuck his bogarting bullshit, I'm taking one."

I egged him on, "Just take the rest of 'em, he can't remember details anymore."

Without further ado, Youngblood snatched Sailor's stockpile and we started pounding the rest.

Ten minutes later, a pickled Sailor came back out, found his beers missing, and snapped. He accused us rightfully, then picked Youngblood up high in the air and slammed him to the ground, before I could react. Sailor got on top of Youngblood, ready to bring down the motherlode, when I charged and effectively knocked him over. The enraged beast rose up, refocused his wrath, and piledrove me to the lawn.

Both Youngblood and I were scattered about the yard, out of breath, searching for answers. No way were we gonna give up and let him beat us to his heart's content. Each of us picked up a beer bottle and began to circle Sailor.

He surveyed and spoke, "Now you want to make this difficult? Should've stayed down."

Before we could try and fix things, he came right at us like a juiced-up linebacker. Youngblood heaved a bottle at the fuming gorilla, missing wildly. I braced myself for the guaranteed monsoon about to arrive. For a split second, I wondered what medical facility I was about to wind up at, when—WHAM!—

from the blindside, Santino had body-checked Sailor to the ground, righteously bailing out the both of us. Sailor lumbered to his feet and started mad-dogging everyone in sight.

Santino walked right up to the legend and shoved him. "What the fuck, Sailor?"

Stimulated by the uproar, all LMP members came out of the party, looking to take care of business. They had no idea the dustup was internal. Neighbors across the street could be seen peeking out their windows at all the ready boots, bald heads, and anti-fashion.

Sailor huffed, "They ransacked my private beer stash right from my car," and puffed, "Hell no am I going to let that slide!"

Santino quickly surmised, "Let me get this right: you are gonna fight your friends over two fucking beers?"

"Threeeee! It was three beers!!"

Ha-Ha's burst out from the crowd. Sailor got so mad he socked the tree next to him and started bleeding.

Santino was not amused. "Okay, three beers. If you are going to fight over three beers ... then let's do it!"

Sailor knew he could take him, but the result would be his death down the road, and a horrible one at that. Santino didn't tolerate dissension within our ranks, or, more importantly, losing.

Our beer-hoarding enforcer knew the stakes and answered back, "Let's forget the whole thing ever happened ... should've hid my beer a lot better from those grubby hands anyway."

Santino nodded to Sailor's tenuous capitulation, thus letting him off the hook. Santino was at all times fair, his word law, and decision final.

After another wasted Saturday morning discussion with Mom about "my future," the rest of the afternoon was spent easing at Santino's, getting real-life instruction. Older veterans of LMP had been frequenting the scene less and less. Original members were now holding down full-time jobs to pay rent, having children, dealing with substance abuse, or, more unfortunately, getting locked up. For LMP to survive this shift, Santino continued schooling Youngblood and me in the ways of gang leadership. Time with him at The Godfather's was never wasted.

A phone call that same day from one of our vets reshaped everything for the time being. Renowned LMP Popeye was out of prison and on his way over. Bellyaches of pure amusement would be an understatement when he came pedaling up on a girl's purple Huffy, complete with basket, sissy bar, streamers and all.

"What's up, wood!" were his first words uttered to us in a couple years. Took us a minute to realize it was him. He had long hair in a ponytail and random Viking tattoos highlighting his extra 40 pounds of prison-starch muscle.

Santino grinned, "Wood? I'm Mexican!"

Popeye chuckled back, "Whatever, brother ... it's good to be home." He looked over to me, "Hey little brother, where's all the fun at?"

Santino snorted, "Forget that right now. You need to cut that hippie hair before you go anywhere with us."

Our leader was always business first.

Popeye tossed aside his five-finger-discount transportation.

"Who's got the clippers?"

That night, we took him to a gig at Santa Monica Civic Auditorium, where the Misfits were headlining. Popeye's shaved dome only accentuated his "Scared Straight" attire: stiff white T-shirt over a wifebeater tank top, some off-brand faded work jeans, and canvas prison sneakers. When we met up with our other LMP crews at the show, Popeye grimaced.

"My clothes look fuckin' stupid here."

I answered quickly, "You're no poser, don't even worry about it."

He nodded, "Watch and learn, little brother."

As Popeye made his way through to the edge of the slam pit, he calculated, and predatorily stalked every punk like a starved animal. I brimmed with anticipation, well aware that something unconventional was about to go down. He reached in and yanked this punk out of the whirlpool by the back of his leather motorcycle jacket.

"That jacket is mine—where did you find it?"

Popeye peeled the leather right off him. Stunned, the sucker simply let it go, realizing this guy would hurt him substantially if he resisted ... top of the food chain. The new cycle jacket fit tight, since he stood 6'2" and weighed a ready 220 pounds. Popeye surveyed the area till he fixated on a few tall punks standing near the stage. He sidled up, pressing his sneaker against an engineer boot, then to the next guy's boot and ... bingo.

"Those are nice fucking boots—hand 'em over or I'll kill you!"

The narrow punk took one look at a painful outcome and offered them up. After that Popeye climbed on stage and yelled "LMP, motherfuckers!", threw up our gang sign, then front-flipped into the unlucky first rows. Popeye was back on the scene with a vengeance.

We took Popeye's "home from prison" celebration over to Errol Flynn's after the show. He was on cloud nine. New clothes, plus a matching set of infatuated preppy chicks that came along to make things downright perfect. Our pal was getting first-rate attention from one of the drunken girls, who clearly wanted to fuck a freshly paroled convict. Five minutes later they snuck away into the bushes. What followed sounded like a cobra vs. mongoose struggle—shadows bounced and rolled, trees shook spastically. Convict lust filled the air. I could tell the other girl was a little jealous.

When the moans subsided, out popped Popeye's girl, limping, trying to fix her dress.

"Shit. I'm bleeding. Oh my God, I stepped on glass!"

Her friend immediately ran over to help. Popeye appeared next, pants around his ankles, arms folded like an Indian chief.

"Why does paleface come, bring garbage to our sacred land, cutting our women's feet?"

Degenerate and Youngblood cracked up at his lack of sensitivity; the girl friend was not amused.

"Why doesn't one of you comedians do something? She's bleeding bad!"

I helped wrap her glass-sliced foot with a bandana. Popeye picked her up and we all walked back down the trail to our car.

We drove directly to Oki-Dog for a cheap late-night snack. All of us sat with our condiment-soaked dogs and goofed at our fun-filled night.

"Hold on, I can't let this slide."

Popeye got up and walked over to another table of late-night patrons, adding an inch of height and width to his body with every step. He was back on the yard.

"Who the fuck you eyeballing, you better catch a square, punk!"

The pimple-faced rocker sat mute and confused. I almost felt sorry for him, though he never should have looked in Popeye's direction.

"You better walk before I pop every zit on your face with one shot!"

The rocker and his two pals ran off, leaving their food behind. Popeye claimed the guy's chow tray and brought it to our table. Degenerate, Youngblood, and I were smiling, but our two girls were noticeably disturbed by his display. Their criminal infatuation had evaporated. I took a look around and noticed trouble across the street. The scared rocker was talking to a pair of uniformed police officers, who were looking right at us. We casually stood up and walked to our car, thinking they wouldn't give a rat's ass ... how wrong I was.

The patrol unit came speeding around the block, skidding pinpoint in front of our car. Lights flooded us as they got out and started their badge-happy walk over. Sunburnt skin with matching moustaches looked us over.

"Who here is the big badass convict...?"

Popeye knew the routine and raised his hand up.

"Where did you do your time, tough guy?"

Popeye hesitated, and then spoke under his breath.

"California Men's Colony."

The two cops were unimpressed.

"CMC, huh? Oh boy ... don't they dress you up in pink pajamas there?"

Popeye bit into his lip.

"Sold your cigarettes and candy to big bad niggers, didn't you?"

Popeye shook his head slowly, "No sir."

"Yeah sure, you're a real heavyweight—let's have a look in the car."

Being Degenerate had already opened his door it gave them consent to search. The cop in charge sat us all down on the curb while his partner handcuffed Popeye.

"Trash like you gives me a reason to get up in the morning."

The lead cop started digging through Degenerate's vehicle with his Maglite, throwing stuff everywhere.

"What do we have here?"

He pulled two bloody baseball bats from the floor of our back seat. Cop number two grabbed his .38 and pointed it at us while pushing Popeye to the cement.

"Freeze, shitheads—we got ya!"

The girls started sobbing as Youngblood and I tried to explain the situation.

"Officer, that's not what it looks like, she cut her foot on some glass and the blood got on the bats."

"Look at the cut on her foot, look at her foot!" offered Youngblood.

The lead cop shined his light on the girls. The other dug his heel into Popeye's back, keeping his gun trained on us. Some sidewalk straggler came walking by us, not paying attention. Cop number two routinely turned his gun, cocking the hammer.

"Wrong turn, scumbag—beat it!"

The situation got defused after our story checked out; the girls confirmed our defense and Popeye was clean.

"Lucky you had some baseball gloves in the car. You caught a break tonight. You assholes will not be so lucky next time and you will be leaving without the bats, and these girls."

The punk rock deity must have intervened.

Frontier High's schedule was now half-days for eleventh grade. The L.A. school system kept working to my advantage. Teachers couldn't teach me shit and they knew it. They just went along, a pat on the back for merely showing up. I ran my own show.

Popeye, Youngblood, Stormin' Normin, and I were out at Cathay de Grande for amateur night. Bands were usually just bearable; it was more about getting girls and flexing LMP muscle. Popeye was pumped up. Amateur night started while he was doing time, so any kind of punk rock was good music to him. The lobby was packed as usual, with kids whose parents had no idea where they were, or didn't care about their health. We shoved through to the bottom of the Cathay's stairs, passing the booths, before a striking young thing stopped my walk. She sat on a table, all tarted up in bleached denim, white butched hair, and Blade Runner eye makeup. Madeline was all I wanted, but hot is hot. I caught a hint of a smile, so invited myself over to chit-chat. Noticing she wore

FRANK, RUNNING
HIS OWN SHOW.

a peace sign pinned to her torn-up blouse, I started a conversation.

"So why the hippie symbol?"

She explained her brother was brutally beat up at a punk show and suf-fered brain damage, never to be the same again. I pretended to sympathize, wondering if we were the ones who brought this upon her unfortunate brother. Was he the guy from South Gate Punks?

I played along.

"I'm a peace punk too. Violence is totally ruining our scene."

She started showing actual signs of interest, when something in the pit shifted her attention.

"Leave him alone, you mean jerk—stop it!" she cried out.

My gut tipped me off as to who could be causing the ruckus. I was almost afraid to look. Popeye had this guy headlocked and at the same time was sock-ing him in the kidney.

"Quit it, you bully!"

I tried to calm her.

"Don't worry. It's all part of the dance, he'll be okay."

Popeye was there only five minutes and already a fuss. He stomped onto the stage, snatched the microphone, and started shouting, "LMP! LMP! LMP!" until some born-fool sucker punched him accurately in the jaw. Before the dry-gulcher could run for safety, Popeye shook it off and kicked his feet out from under him. He came crashing down smack dab in front of me and my new gorgeous peace-punk friend. Popeye seized the guy in a chokehold then dragged him over.

"Hey little brother, let's take this dead motherfucker upstairs and show him who LMP is!"

STALAG 13
AT CATHAY DE GRANDE, 1983.
PHOTO BY ALISON BRAUN.

I was busted, red-flagged, found out, and could do nothing but shrug my shoulders as she ran off threatening to get security. Didn't she know that the Cathay had been dubbed the most dangerous club in the United States?

Popeye hauled the slobbering fool upstairs to the lobby. It was like watching the old-time sailor-man cartoon after he ate his spinach in the final act. Everyone in the Cathay's foyer circled the two of them, anticipating violence. Even the bouncers, who happened to be LADS, took a sideline position.

Popeye let go and let him know, "Here's your chance, punk—time for you to fight."

The sucker-puncher's face lost all color.

"Man ... I don't want to fight you."

My partner's eyes bulged, "So? You should've considered that before you took a free shot!"

The guy cheesed, putting his hands up in a pity plea. Popeye cocked his head, mystified, then followed swiftly with a huge backhand slap.

No punches back, nothing; he froze up and stuttered out, "I ... I ... d-d-don't—I'm not gonna fight you."

Popeye's face twisted up in disgust.

"Really? You're just gonna let me slap you like a lame and do nothing?"

He stepped away, except a tough crowd shoved him right back to Popeye, who decided to make a deal.

"Hey, I'll let you off the hook, but you have to suck my cock here in front of everybody."

Blood thirst from the Hollywood vampires burst out, "Do it! Do it!!"

Popeye started to unzip his fly, then changed his mind and threw a savage upper cut, knocking the guy out cold.

The LADS, who worked security at Cathay de Grande, were so impressed with Popeye's ferocity they hired him on the spot. Typical ex-con, he only lasted a couple weeks, respectfully fired due to his inability to show up. Popeye didn't really need the money anyway now that he was making his own hours "punking" people for their leathers.

"This is about me—not you," was one line he often spouted when grabbing someone's throat, before helping himself to their jacket.

Another was "You had your 15 minutes, now hand it over."

He always delivered the bad news empty of emotion, like he was reading it from a note. For around 30 bucks, leather jackets were easy to move in well under an hour at any punk club parking lot. They retailed close to $200 new or used, which in those times was a serious amount of money. At first I found it perplexing that no one fought for them. Sure, Popeye was intimidating, but at least the victim should have put up some kind of struggle. It never happened. The outcome was always the same: they couldn't give up their jackets quick enough. Popeye sure knew how to pick 'em. He went off to prison not so sharp in the brain—and came back one of the keenest judges of a man's character I had ever met. Nobody ever ratted him out or called the cops either. Maybe it was a rite of passage or some kind of honor to get your leather snaked by a crazy fucker ... who knows?

Again, after umpteen tries on my part to get in touch, almost giving up for good, Madeline finally rang me, explaining how she had to leave town because a close aunt passed away. I was entirely relieved without going overboard, thought I did everything right. We set another rendezvous immediately and went out on the town. This time, Madeline wore a sheer black number with matching tights and heels. She cancelled our plans before I hit the gas.

"Let's forget dinner, Frankie, take me to where you would normally go."

Madeline had put me in a precarious position. I wanted to introduce her to all my pals, show her my life, my truth ... but that was asking for it. She could get caught in the middle of some violent plot gone wrong, a rival or disgruntled victim finally getting his chance at revenge. Alone, I was never worried—my knife had my back. Madeline pleaded, wouldn't take no for an answer. She smelled remarkable and looked even finer. What could I do?

Seven Seas was perfect; punks knew better than to act up inside one of Eddie Nash's clubs. Besides, he knew me by face and would treat us well. Walking us toward a back booth, Mr. Nash gave me a subtle look of acknowledgment. After more than a few highly flavored drinks, Madeline became antsy and requested we move on to a more interesting location.

We parked on Fuller, then headed up to Errol Flynn's—maybe not the best choice in my drunken state. As we passed the entrance, I noticed our spray-painted LMP on the wall, still intact, greeting us, reassuring me. Voices of people already partying there echoed a corrosive serenade along the walk. The environment's looming danger was evident to Madeline, squeezing my hand tight up the footpath.

"What is this place, Frankie? Where are we going?"

I told her of its history and the things that happened there. Her eyes lit up with fascination at the tales of sex and mayhem. That was all she wanted to hear about from that point on. Revealing my life to a woman sincerely interested in my well-being was cathartic to say the least.

Reaching my secret spot at the top, Madeline was set in motion. Unable to wait any longer, she went down on me right there under the stars. We rolled around on an old wood fence, padded with my leather jacket. She couldn't get enough.

All smiles and soaked in sweat, we started our downward trek to where we parked. Halfway down, six or more out-of-line bigmouths started talking shit.

"Hey lover boy, hope you had fun with her—we did!"

"Is it our turn yet?"

My teeth clenched, grinding into the enamel. I couldn't let it go. I went for my knife—but Madeline grabbed my arm. The funnymen saw the move, saw I was not one to play with.

"Aw c'mon man, take it easy, it's cool...."

It was anything but. I took a mind photo of every single one of them for future reference.

"Don't listen to it, Frankie," Madeline pleaded. "Those boys are a waste of our time."

I waved my finger at them, gesturing how that was a major no-no, as we made our way down the trail.

A hundred yards or so from the car I heard one of them yell, "Pussy, you better leave!" off in the distance.

It took all my resolve to keep going, pretending Madeline didn't hear it, even though I knew she did. God, please let me see these guys again. I beg of you. Please help me to destroy my enemy. Please Lord, grant me this wish of death.

ANDRE THE GIANT,
"BATTLE ROYALE,"
THE GRAND OLYMPIC
AUDITORIUM, 1976.
PHOTO BY THEO EHRET.

CHAPTER 11
"SOTTO CAPO"

THE GRAND OLYMPIC AUDITORIUM in downtown Los Angeles had become the epicenter of something unique in hardcore. Gary Tovar, of Goldenvoice Productions, brought a new vision to solve the problems that commonly wrought havoc at shows. Kicking in the walls, trashing bathrooms, and attacking security was epidemic. Punk rock needed a venue that couldn't be wrecked by kids getting hopped up on our music's energy and wanton violence. The Olympic was a historic sports auditorium and prior home to professional boxing, wrestling, and roller derby. Goldenvoice hosted scaled-down, arena-rock-style shows there nearly every month, with big-time headliners like PiL, GBH, Exploited, Fear, Dead Kennedys, the Adicts, backed up by another high-caliber So Cal band like T.S.O.L., Circle Jerks, MIA, Vandals, Dickies, and then a few more up-and-comers to round out the bill.

Crowds at shows, formerly in the hundreds, ballooned to the thousands. Olympic Auditorium's floor area hosted a slam pit so massive it created a new phenomenon coined "The Multi-pit." Three separate concentric circles, spiraling out of control, sometimes merging together then breaking off again. It was a poisonous mixture of collisions and impacts, added tension, a twist of disregard, topped off with contempt. I still have my scars to prove this.

Punk gangs from all over made sure not only to represent, but also attend at full strength. Back in the old days of pro wrestling, a mural of "Andre the Giant, 8th Wonder of the World" stood high above where you entered. Now all you saw were decaying walls that reeked of urine, and trash cans filled with weapons. Security personally pocketed the good stuff. Staff didn't frisk everyone, but had a keen eye and knew who was probably carrying.

BLACK FLAG,
THE OLYMPIC
AUDITORIUM, LOS
ANGELES CALIFORNIA,
1983. PHOTO BY
EDWARD COLVER.

alking from your car to the venue, as well as returning to where you parked after the show, was a whole other ballgame. Underneath the length of Interstate 10 freeway, down to L.A. Trade Tech and McDonald's, was a series of open streets and alleyways where you parked. Under the cover of darkness, punk gangs from all over our city hid in the gaps and waited for you ... or us for them, waiting to randomly attack anyone who looked weak. Weakness no longer had any business in punk rock. If you were shaky, you got picked on or picked off. Expression was periphery, power was principal.

Olympic's stage safety measures were handled by punk rock's 9th Wonder of the World, Big Frank. Gone were the days of young toughs taking free shots at talent or going heads-up with the stage crew. Big Frank stood well over 6'5", lineman-muscled, dyed Mohawk, covered in tattoos, with two fists full of rings that functioned as impromptu brass knuckles. I saw him leave dents in many faces. More importantly, he had cred in the scene that dated back to the first wave of punk. Big Frank also ran one of punk rock's first record stores, called Zed Records, located in Long Beach. People journeyed there from all over to acquire the new cutting-edge records he gladly informed you on. If he knew you well, you called him "Uncle Frank." Uncle Frank never took free shots; problem was though, guys always wanted to test the big fella. They always flunked.

One evening, before an Olympic show started, a few of us were drinking outside the venue when Mike Muir, singer of Suicidal Tendencies, wandered away from his cronies and stepped out of line. Mike got dropped with one swift punch by my new LMP recruit Pineapple Head. Oddly enough, Mike wasn't a good fighter, but loved the action. What made this moment notably sweet was Mike usually didn't put himself out in no man's land to get knocked out. Being

SANTINO, THE
BOSS (FOREGROUND),
FRANK, UNDERBOSS
(BACKGROUND).

the face of the Suicidal movement, everyone wanted to take a shot at that guy and he knew it. Mixing words with Mike usually meant dealing with enforcers from Suicidal gang, who were no picnic, an entourage that beat you silly if you called him out ... or him you. More often than not, he baited guys into a Suey rat-packing. Now a low-level celebrity, with his "Institutionalized" single and MTV music video, we referred to them only as "The Pepsi Generation" because of his crybaby rant:

> *"Mom just get me a Pepsi, please*
> *All I want is a Pepsi, and she wouldn't give it to me*
> *All I wanted was a Pepsi, just one Pepsi, and she wouldn't give it to me.*
> *Just a Pepsi."*

What a momma's boy. Pineapple Head's good fortune that night was just Mike's rotten luck. We let him pick himself up, dust off his clothes, and walk away.

On a flat Saturday afternoon, waiting for the sun to get lost, Santino decided to officially name me Underboss of LMP. "You're now second in command, Frank, time for you to have your own crew. Frank the Shank, Underboss of LMP."

Not only did I get my own crew, but also the duty of being Santino's right arm. He never really said why. I figured it came down to trust. Number two in command came with more respect, brought new responsibility as a go-be-tween for other LMPs, and messenger when orders needed to be carried out. Sole charge and overseeing of recruits was also handed down to me. Attending Frontier High made this job almost too easy, being L.A. County's final stop for worst of the worst punks in our district. The second they stepped on school grounds, I measured 'em up for the task of bona fide psycho.

An influx of kids from minor league outfits were icing on the cake—guys from "Suburban Punks" and "T-Street" in Whittier, "Belcher Street Punks" and "United Brigade" from La Mirada, plus "LWP" in Lakewood, all wanted in the big leagues. I kept tabs on the newcomers, supervised their progress, and educated them on the politics of punk rock gang life as Santino had done for me. Being second in charge, I knew better than to abuse my new authority. Long-standing members wouldn't respect me, nor carry out orders crucial to maintaining our edge.

LMP "Easy Street" was the name chosen for my crew, in honor of Santino, the street he lived on and I learned on. A few original members were incorporated into my lineup; the rest I recruited personally: Me "The Shank," Popeye, Barney, Bumper, Captain Out of Hand, Joker, Shadow, Bubbles, Chemo, Stormin' Normin, Shitdick, The Governor, Pineapple Head, Mongo, Pissed Chris, Happy, Lil Skin, Fingerbone, Degenerate, Yoda, Dutch, Mikey, Shakes, Grinch, Yarnball, Jason, Matmoe, Pee Wee, Bones, Elmer, and last, Check.

Youngblood was also given his own crew, and Silent, who I brought in, was appointed leader of La Habra chapter. Additionally, I incorporated a new enforcer into Easy Street who became an overnight sensation. Sailor, the living legend, didn't care about LMP the way he used to. Booze and narcotics were landing him in jail all too often. Mongo took Sailor's place as the star sledge-hammer of LMP. Sailor's out … Mongo's in!

A genetic aberration at 16, Mongo stood 6'5", weighed roughly 260 pounds, and was already in adult shape from years of football, on top of seven years studying karate. His brawling talents were akin to Hoss Cartwright's of the TV western *Bonanza*, except Hoss was a gentle giant, always pushed into fights. Mongo, on the other hand, pushed you into fights. He relished going toe-to-toe against multiple guys simultaneously and never bothered with guys smaller than him. Mongo was a one-man gang who lived for the challenge. He honestly loved it.

Underneath the 10 freeway, outside Olympic Auditorium, Joker, Stormin' Normin, Barney, Mongo, and I were getting our sonic fix to the debut Subhumans release *The Day the Country Died* while we waited for other crewmembers to show up. The moon was suspiciously running late. Right when Mongo started getting restless, out of the darkness came eight members of Circle One. You would've thought they had learned their lesson by now.

Straightforward Mongo announced, "This is our spot, you white niggers. Take a fucking hike!"

Three of their biggest guys encircled our one, just the way he liked it. Desperately, I wanted to watch Mongo work his magic, but instincts took over. Four of them were not accounted for. I evaluated quickly and locked up with the one that looked the most dangerous. At that same time, Joker, Stormin' Normin, and Barney joined the action. Talk about a shot in the dark, Mongo was dropping foes without even seeing their faces. Our opponents promptly backed off and vanished beneath the overpass after their best got outclassed … again. A bottle-crash to the head felled Barney on the last assailant's way out. He always took the worst of it, a real magnet for punishment.

FRANK (LEFT), BARNEY WITH SIGNATURE FLATTOP (RIGHT).

ongo wasn't my only bright new star. He shared the bill with Pissed Chris, who came from our farm team, LWP. His penchant for madcap violence was a tad much for that crew. They were glad to send him up to the pros. Pissed Chris was nearly six feet tall, rangy like a prized welterweight, and shaved his eyebrows clean off to match his head. I never met anyone who came with as many enemies, or took more pleasure in making them. Passing time with Pissed Chris around our local neighborhoods was an activity like no other.

137.

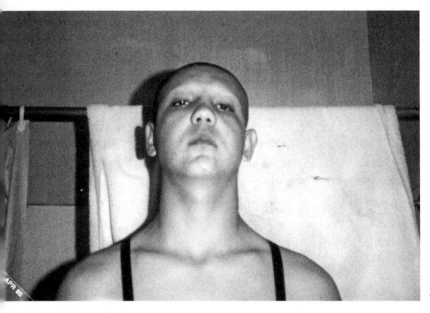

PISSED CHRIS.
EYEBROWS/
WHYBROWS?

Cruising around L.A., you had to frequently pull over so Pissed Chris could confront any unfamiliar punk rocker. The craze was now so contagious you could find punk rockers lurking around most So Cal neighborhoods. Pissed Chris' routine went something like this...

"Hey where you from?"

Reply, "Um ... nowhere."

"LMP fuck you!"

Reply, "Why...?"

"LMP motherfucker—you poser!"

At that point, they would droop their head, look befuddled, or most likely run away.

Pissed Chris' approach to punk life was no different than basic neighborhood-style gang banging. Whenever he couldn't find punks to intimidate, another routine unfolded. You stopped the car in front of someone's house, always around dinnertime. Pissed Chris calmly exited the car with a crowbar, tire iron, or a piece of pipe, and launched it through their front window, exploding glass throughout the house. He coolly climbed back in and we drove off. Pissed Chris never explained who these enemies were, or why the retribution. None of us ever found out.

Pissed Chris was dedicated to his former LWP gang, but moving him up to LMP became a win-win situation for everyone involved. Mike McIntosh, leader and founder of LWP, was also a sizable cocaine dealer with already enough heat. Turned out, he hooked his weight from a brother in Compton named Eric Wright, who later became distinguished N.W.A gangster-rapper Eazy-E. I used to see him at Mike's often. He seemed to enjoy our rogues' gallery.

"Y'all some crazy muthafuckas. Last of the true whiteboyz...."

Mike McIntosh knew everyone and had so much magnetism, not to mention classic movie-star good looks, he attracted all walks of life. Call it personality, call it what you want, but Mike McIntosh deserves much more than a few paragraphs. He ought to have his own book.

MUGGING IN MIKE'S BEDROOM. FROM LEFT TO RIGHT, FRANK, MIKE MCINTOSH AND TWO LWPS.

Mike ran a quasi punk rock gang clubhouse/social scene from his parents' house in Lakewood. When there was nothing to do, you went over to Mike's, where members of our gangs and suitable affiliates from the scene gathered. His folks were retired and loved the company of their son's peculiar friends. Mike's father Max would share his war sagas, drink you under the table, and chuckle as he sent you off to replenish his beer. His mother Vicky was sweetness personified; the two commonly vacationed at the Colorado River on weekends, turning their home over to their son's vice. Mike drove a champagne convertible Porsche 911 that looked too sharp for words, wore hybrid punk/greaser attire, with crimped hair teased up in spikes—truly too cool for school. Mike had the Porsche stolen for him and the VIN numbers switched, making it street-legal.

Mike was one of the first people I knew who had many tattoos, back when you had to earn them. He used to host tattoo parties at his house in Lakewood for underage punks. Fine-line artiste extraordinaire Mark Mahoney would give you the best black-and-grey work around, for half the going rate. Mark was an original-style East Coast greaser from New York's Chelsea Hotel scene of Sid

& Nancy, Johnny Thunders, dope fiends, and freaks. In '80s L.A., his customer base switched to hoodlums, bikers, and hardcore punk rockers.

Mahoney and McIntosh both had so much charisma, made you feel so good about yourself, somebody once said, "I've known those guys a long time and they are so cool to me ... but I wonder if they actually even like me?"

Suburban punk house parties that showcased local bands, playing hard and serious as they did at real venues, became a weekly thing. Around three or four dollars entry for guys, two for girls, was the going rate. That price included all you could drink, until the keg dried up. For a share of the money, bands played right smack in the living room, backyard, or garage when kids' parents left town, needed the cash, or were too stupid to care. All kinds came to these gatherings in search of sex, booze, music, or all the above. No matter what scene you belonged to—jock, New Wave, poppers & breakers, mods, transitional posers, surfers, cholos, even heavy metal hippies were given a pass, so long as you didn't act like an asshole. It was the first time most of these people were exposed to live punk rock. You often saw those types watching bands and slam pits with a measured mix of fascination and repugnance.

Having Mongo along turned the event into an opportunity for profit.

"Hey dude, I'm the new door guy. Go have yourself a beer."

Usually, the sitting duck understood pretty quickly they were being hijacked, after staring into Mongo's manic eyes. Mongo grabbed the coffee can of ones and fives, sometimes splitting it, sometimes not, then made people wait a little longer to get in.

"More they wait, more they think they are missing something—creates a buzz."

Whatever band was playing got stiffed out of their slice. We figured they had it coming.

"Charging us to get in ain't punk rock at all. Taking the money is!" Mongo rationalized.

Who could argue against such sound logic?

LMP Easy Street's arrival at a party was signaled by a special horn on Mongo's Toyota pickup, which sounded "Duh-Duh-Duh-Dunt, Duh-Dunn ... CHARGE!"

The gimmick, although ridiculous, made partygoers excited, like something had arrived. However, enthusiastic smiles vanished quickly from the lips of most everyone there as we came aboard. We absolutely took over everything and transferred temporary ownership to LMP till the party died out or the cops shut it down. Through the eyes of non-punk gang youth, our crew must have come off as Viking or Mongol hordes. Guys just started to back away from their girlfriends or their love prospects like they all of a sudden had some bad disease. Fellas put two and two together right away. If you want to defend her honor, a cold ass-kicking will be the end result. It's easy making time with chicks when your competition meekly slips out and never comes back. Dudes would honestly jump the back wall to get away.

Inside the house, it was open season. Rifle through the fridge and cupboards, make sandwiches or eat the leftovers, find the family liquor cabinet then drain it, break into the parents' bedroom, fuck drunken sluts on their bed, locate the telephones, make prank long-distance phone calls, find the medicine cabinets, and snake all the pills. Mongo, working as enforcer for our scheme, eventually became known in local punk circles. Our charge horn started tipping people off and had to be phased out.

Even Santino's dad wanted in on the action. The Godfather threw "rent parties," and made us get bands to play, then called the cops to shut it down after he got his easy money. Police took delight in the task of breaking up punk parties. Noise complaints eventually brought multiple squad cars, sometimes a helicopter, and always a confrontation. If none of us threw bottles or bricks, cops remained fairly calm, until the crowd started chanting "Blue by day! White by night!" and we always did. This chant of blue uniformed cop by day, white uniformed Klansman by night, perpetually pushed them over the edge. Police hated having the proverbial finger pointed at them, loaded with accusations of their fascist and racist behavior. Ironically, they always proved our case in point by putting on a little police theatre. Bullhorns with orders to depart or else, in the first act, followed up by billy clubs to the legs or ribs, and for a curtain call, punks leaving in back seats of black-and-whites.

Two hundred and forty-one United States Marines killed by suicide bombs in Beirut, Reagan attacks Grenada, there's a "Musical Revolution" and we don't care. The world as I'm seeing it, through TV and confusing mumbling from teachers whose names I can't remember, is pointless. I've become so far withdrawn from "normal" crap, living the lyrics being fed to me. I just turned 16—but nobody's listening. A cake and kiss on the cheek from Mom, no phone call from Dad. That same month, I got another tattoo for my upper-arm collage of skulls, women, and monsters.

CHAPTER 12
"MONGOLOOSE"

ONGO WAS A VERY, VERY SCARY PUNK. Even though he permanently wore comical smiles that said it was okay to approach, natural impulse told you stay away, or better yet, run. He wasn't up to date as far as the look happening at the start of 1984. Mongo still wore the clothes of 1980, whereas most of us in LMP were doing more personalized tweaks with our look. L.A.-area punks in general were either doing the British street thing or a hodgepodge of the cholo, Pendleton, plaid, bandana, and tapered Dickies vibe. Others wore the skate, surf punk, wino, Vans look. Suburban, beach, and inner-city youth had all established their own identities by way of style.

Mongo was no-frills when I found him wandering Frontier High in jeans, engineer boots, and droopy Mohawk. He was downright quirky, except his quirks translated into lengthy hospital stays for some. No matter where we were when Michael Jackson's "Thriller" song came on, Mongo got excessively keyed up and started dancing his own version of the music video, weird moonwalk and all. He took this Thriller thing very seriously and would fuck anybody up who laughed, pointed, or got in his way during his rendition. How do you keep a straight face when some Godzilla-sized punk rocker is doing a mutated version of the Thriller dance? I always believed it was a trap born from his distorted psyche. He loved wrecking shop with his fists, but always needed a semi-legitimate reason to do so.

➤ DAY 1

Mongo's mother left town for a week. No surprise, we decided to throw a small party for LMP and our tight-knit friends. I mean come on, what do you expect? As I approached his house on foot, there was Mongo leaning out of his upstairs window, butt naked.

"Mongo, what the hell are you doin'?" I yelled as two girls walked past, blushing at his snowman-like build.

"Hey Frank, I totally fucked the shit out of this blow-up doll for 20 minutes straight!"

The underage girls ran off, disgusted with excitement, and right then I realized Mongo was a god. He begrudgingly put his clothes on and we took a walk across the street to 7-11.

Working behind the counter was an oily-haired cashier, staring at his own security cam image on a little monitor. Grabbing a couple snacks, we noticed him fixating on the image, waving slowly to the camera while he watched himself wave back on TV. Mongo took one look and offered some assistance.

"It's cool watching yourself, I do it all the time. We saw you have a lot of trash piling up ... we could help you throw it out if you want?"

The cashier took a moment to understand, then warmly acknowledged Mongo's philanthropy.

"Sure, that would really help me. Very nice of you two guys."

I went along, knowing Mongo had some kind of off-the-wall plan going through his mind's eye. We stacked two cases of beer in our arms from the back storeroom, put a trash bag on top, and walked outside. Soon as 7-11's door shut behind us, we mad-dashed across the street, dropped the beers on Mongo's porch, and then ran back.

"Thanks again guys, my boss will be really happy...."

"Don't mention it, dude—we got your back." Mongo went on, "My church says this kind of stuff will help me get to heaven."

Twenty cases and five trips later, we were out of garbage. Mongo never understood the meaning of moderation. He walked every aisle, loading his leather jacket, underwear, and pants with every type of snack available to mankind. When Mongo reached the counter, he asked the cashier for a free carton of Marlboros for his paraplegic mother.

Whittier man stabbed to death at party

A Whittier man was stabbed to death after he helped chase away several men who tried to force their way into a party early Sunday morning.

John Araiza, 25, was pronounced dead at La Mirada Community Hospital at 1:50 a.m.

Sheriff's deputies said Araiza was at a party in the 11100 block of Santa Gertrudes Avenue in South Whittier when several uninvited men arrived.

An altercation ensued. Araiza and an unidentified second male victim chased the other men to

Mills Avenue and Glengyle Street in South Whittier, where they were confronted by still others.

Araiza was stabbed and the other man was hit over the head with a beer bottle, according to deputies. No suspects were in custody.

"Oh yeah. Glad to help out, I hope she gets better!" said the half-witted clerk as he handed over two cartons.

Back at Mongo's, we divvied up all the ill-gotten gain from 7-11, and started calling everyone to show up.

After two hours we had a full party with me, Mongo, Youngblood, Stormin' Normin, Joker, Shitdick, Pineapple Head, Lil Skin, Fingerbone, Shakes, Grinch, and a few random punks from Frontier High. In addition were some assorted punk rock sluts, including my two favorites, Vaseline and Jap Jenny. Vaseline had one half of her head shaved, the other half long, and married her makeup to match each side. It looked like you were fucking two different girls at the same time. Jap Jenny was an easy good sport, answering to her Japanese nickname, even though she was Filipino. Both were in stiff competition with each other for LMP's punk "slut of the year" award.

Once our people settled in with their beer, hard liquor, and weed, Mongo quieted everyone down to announce the evening flick.

"I want to first inform you that tonight's feature will be shown on my new state-of-the-art VHS player. The picture is better than anything you deserve to see!"

The room was reasonably intrigued with his pitch and started firing back questions.

"What state are you talking about?"

"How'd you buy that?"

"Ain't Laserdisc better?"

"What's the movie?"

Mongo grinned sharply, holding the mystery movie behind his back.

"Whoever guesses gets beef jerky and a free pack of smokes."

Shouting erupted.

"*Clockwork Orange?*"

"*Mad Max?*"

"*Caligula?*"

"*Taxi Driver?*"

Mongo laughed back like a dictator, "N-n-n-n-n-n-n-n-n-No—You're all wrong! Tonight's special presentation is ... *FOOTLOOSE!*"

Silence struck the room like a stocking from Santa Claus filled with rocks.

"Boooooooooooooo...."

"Fuck that!"

"Yeah right!"

"Weirdo dance fag movies suck!"

Mongo was disappointed with the reaction, sincerely caught off guard, and bummed.

144.

"What do you mean? This is a big deal … it's still in the theaters."

He frowned, pushed in the pirated copy, and pressed play.

➤ DAY 2

The next day brought a bigger cast of characters over to Mongo's. It rapidly became a revolving door of LMPs from neighboring cities, punks from around the area, indiscriminate oddballs, aimless cholos, easy girls from our scene, and others, all dropping by to smoke weed, drink, take pills, and fuck.

Mid-afternoon, we got seriously hungry, but didn't have the will or knowledge to cook anything. Apparently, Pissed Chris ordered a handful of pizzas and passed out before they arrived, leaving me to deal with it. Thirty minutes later I opened Mongo's door to a deliveryman. The smell of fresh pepperoni and cheese wafted into the living room, awakening the punk zombies from their graves.

"That'll be 70 dollars, sir."

Everyone inside looked desperately around the room for someone with cash, then back to me, then transformed into angry meat-eating psychotics. Our pizza man's eyes and body language registered, "Not again.…"

I walked out onto the porch, shutting the door behind me.

"Here's what's gonna happen, man—you gonna tell your boss that you got ripped off while stopping for cigarettes."

His mouth opened to question the situation but I cut him off…

"You saw those guys, believe me you don't want them after you, so here's ten bucks for your trouble. Be smart, go along, and everybody wins."

He started to understand, but changed his heart.

"I need this job and my boss is a jerk … you guys need to pay."

I raised my voice and took the warm boxes from his clutches.

"I asked you nicely the first time!"

The pizza man understood the gravity of his situation, took my $10, and walked away. Sure I had the cash to pay for everybody's hunger hangovers, but fuck them, I was saving for a car.

This small graft actually inspired a bigger scheme. My plan was to make use of all the full stomachs vegetating in front of *Footloose*, which hadn't stopped playing since last night. The plan required manpower, Mongo's truck, and me fucking some girl that bored the shit out of me. The girl called herself "Veronica from Santa Monica," even though she lived in Downey. Veronica pushed her phone number on me whenever I saw her, and constantly begged me to come over while her parents were out of town.

I called her up and arrived at her house at about 8 p.m. Inside, candles were lit and a romantic dinner already prepared. Veronica was a New Wave princess and as hot as they came, but my affection lay with Madeline. *A Kiss in the Dreamhouse* by Siouxsie and the Banshees played lightly in the background. I tried to scarf my food down and get on with it, but a second course followed, then dessert, and much wine. Finally, she disappeared for about five minutes, and then called for me to come to her room, where she stood completely naked. As soon as I walked in she attacked me and we were rolling in the hay. I didn't really formulate a plan as for when Mongo and the others were to come in. I did what I could by opening a curtain and unlocking a window so they could see inside and time it right.

The great Burglar Savior Lord of Theft must have gotten involved, because Veronica from Santa Monica turned out to be an especially loud screamer. Mongo and the crew heard her and understood this as their cue to enter. First, it was all the big stuff—couches, coffee table, La-Z-Boy recliner, dining set, TV, VCR, and entertainment console. I held up my end, occupying Veronica like a stud for hire. Mongo and my henchmen came back for a second truckload—lamps, wall art, records, videocassettes, fish tank, microwave, and kitchen appliances. They turned sloppy the second time around and started making a conspicuous racket. I covered both her ears with my hands while hammering away, hoping to compensate for Mongo's careless execution of the job. Making matters worse, I caught him cracking the door, and taking peeks at us from time to time.

Later, I found out those guys actually all sat down and ate our passion-prepared leftovers before cleaning out the joint. I waited all the way till 3 a.m., when she was deep asleep from sex and wine, slowly peeled myself off her soaked sheets, and quietly saw myself out. Mongo was waiting across the street in the furniture-loaded truck with that famous grin of his. Veronica from Santa Monica had nothing on me. No address, no real name, not even a phone number. When she eventually woke up, I would be long gone.

I laughed when Mongo pointed out, "Even if she wanted to call the cops, she can't ... I took all the phones!"

On the way back to our temporary crash pad, I wondered ... if and when she eventually ran into me, what would I say? What could she say? Would she eventually go to the police?

"Officer, I was getting it on like a total slut and didn't hear them ripping me off."

Maybe she'd have the need to express her feelings?

"Mom … Dad … he was making love to me and I really liked him."

Dumb bitch.

➤ DAY 3

We woke up next morning and found Mongo sitting in a folding chair outside, sipping a cold one, with our entire treasure from Veronica's house carefully arranged on his mother's driveway. Mongo's presentation was high-level, all the small stuff properly sitting on tables, and big furniture set up like it would naturally be in any home. Everything was priced fair with a carefully written sticker.

"Gentlemen, welcome to Mongo's LMP garage sale. All the proceeds are going to a worthy cause … staying loaded!"

By early afternoon, we had pretty much all of it sold, and a profit of $400 cash money, not to mention the handjob Mike McIntosh received from a lonely housewife for helping move her new couch. Beer was flowing. There was plenty of weed left and money for more beer, so we made sure LMP invited every girl available. Mongo and I had a feeling this would be a substantial event going into the wee hours. Keeping that in mind, McIntosh tightened us up with an eight-ball of coke at a brotherly discount.

Every one of our affiliates did their part to make it happen. Before I knew it, good friends and good times were overcrowding the house and our gathering was going off—even that hooch-hound Sailor made an appearance. I wandered through the mass, soaring high on primo nose candy, gravity pulling me toward the bedrooms. Inside the first room, Magnum was jerking off full-speed in front of a dresser lined with Mongo's family portraits.

I yelled, "Hurry, Mongo's on his way up!" then left that immoral scenario to check out the next.

I swung open the next door—a collection of peace-punk junkies were nodding out next to a syringe, spoon, and eyedropper. Harmless dopers. I figured why lecture them, it's too late anyway, and slammed the shooting gallery door shut for kicks.

Madeline was heavy on my mind. Where was she? Why wasn't she here with me? Downstairs, I intertwined my way outside for a smoke. I knew Madeline dug me, she told me so. Wonder if I did something wrong? Lighting up out front, I thought for a moment and calmed myself. Madeline was really busy, had a full-time career, and constantly spent time with her parents. We had something strangely special, so special, yet the only thing that kept us together was the undeniable fact we had nothing in common.

I was overthinking this, just three mainsails to the wind, and flying high. Mongo came barreling on by, holding Jap Jenny's wrist. He walked to his dad's work van, opened the back door, and climbed in.

Joker came scorching up saying, "Asshole Mongo—she wanted to do me, not him!"

The van got rocking eight different ways, trailed by sounds of ecstatic frenzy.

Joker knocked hard on the rear door, yanked it open, and hollered "I'm next!" laughing his drunken ass off.

"What the fuck you guys want?" Mongo pronounced.

His hand was clasped firmly over Jap Jenny's mouth. Her eyes were blinking S.O.S., and her clothes were flung about.

I fired back, "We want to watch."

Mongo growled his retort, "You two can go to hell—get lost!"

Joker pleaded, "Come on Mongo, why don't you play nice? You always watch us."

Jap Jenny's eyes got wider as she squirmed for help. Mongo reached into his pocket and tossed back a 20-dollar bill.

"Treat yourselves to dinner. Both of you."

I picked up the bill, looked at it, looked at Joker's "You decide" face, Mongo's scowl, Jap Jenny's wrathful glare, and gave it little thought....

"Have fun, kids!" and slammed the door shut.

Joker held out his hand, expecting half; I gave him the middle finger with a king's grin. I contemplated whether to steal somebody's car and go see Madeline, or stay put. Cocaine won that night.

➤ DAY 4

"Look at Chris Penn, he's getting pretty good, huh? It's like he's been dancing his whole life," Youngblood pointed out.

Mongo jumped up, "How's Bacon supposed to do anything, the whole town's against him—it's terrible there!"

Shitdick, The Governor, and Pissed Chris nodded in unison. *Footloose* had them riveted.

From the kitchen, Jap Jenny shouted, "How many times are you gonna watch that gay movie?"

She was answered by being ignored. I found it odd that she was cooking breakfast after what happened to her. Guess Mongo bought her flowers or something?

Mongo's father, Stinky Ed, made an unexpected appearance. He showed up mid-afternoon to pick up his tools and work van. Even though Mongo's parents were divorced, Stinky Ed kept some of his belongings there for safekeeping. The whole gang enjoyed Stinky Ed's company. Among LMP, Mongo's dad was eternally known as "Papa Smurf," an ivory-haired fusion of Kenny Rogers and Satan himself. Stinky Ed was a first-generation hard-ass that used to ride as Sergeant-at-Arms for one of the "Big 5" outlaw motorcycle clubs; *translatum*: Don't look his way unless you want death. Tattooed on his chest were three faded letters reading B.B.B., which stood for Bad Bastards of Baltimore, the gang he ran with as a youth. Stinky Ed always had a new piece of street advice for us.

"Don't let me catch you idiots with your pants sagging. It's a signal in the joint to tip off fellow inmates that you're in the mood for a little convict love. Parolees on the street will think you're a faggot."

Another time he told us, when the guards want to "make your life hell" in solitary, they take everything on your food tray and scrunch it together like a huge meatball, then throw it at you: "Here's dinner, scumsucker!"

More wayward girls found out about LMP's weeklong soirée at Mongo's, finally putting numbers in our favor. Even Stormin' Normin had some female attention. Mongo still had *Footloose* running in constant rotation. He hid the remote control and pulled off all the TV dials—just in case someone thought about changing channels on him. A cluster of wasteoids were camped out on the sofa, focused intently on Chris Penn, arguing whether or not Bad Boy brother Sean was okay with him taking such a wimpy role.

Mongo struck gold with a blonde that was too good for him, somehow managing to coax her to his lair. Stuck in the hallway line for the toilet, I could hear some impassioned back-and-forth coming from Mongo's bedroom.

"That's enough ... stop it! I'm not doing any of that!"

"C'mon Shelly, THIS IS MY PARTY!!"

It went this way for minutes, until I discerned the sound of a giant hand muffling her protests. Here we go again—Mongo was a certified date rapist who didn't understand the words "No, asshole" and "Stop!" I knocked on the door a few times to give this girl a fair shake at escape, but all I got in return was...

"Turn on some fucking music, let's get this party going!"

I pressed my ear to the door as somebody from the party cranked up angry thrash from Chaos UK or something along those lines. I heard more struggling, and then a long orgasm, surprisingly from her, followed by a "Get off me!" and finally, a long disgusting man-grunt. An instant later, his door flew open, and out came a smiling Mongo saying "Thank you," pursued by the girl called Shelly, fixing her dress.

"You're welcome, asshole!"

I'll be damned if she didn't go right back to partying like nothing happened. Even odder still was Shelly sharing a bottle of wine and having a blast with Mongo's prior conquest, Jap Jenny.

After midnight came an obnoxious pounding on the door.

Bam! Bam! Bam!

Everyone froze.

Bam! Bam! Bam!

In a flash, nearly 40 punks, including party favors, scattered to any possible hiding place—behind couches, down the hallway, or the backside of doors. I slithered under the easy chair recliner and pulled its footrest down to cover me, perfect vantage point. Mongo surveyed his living room for unhidden stragglers and drug paraphernalia, then opened up.

Two local sheriffs, one man and one woman, stood at the threshold, gripping their flashlights, looking up at Mongo.

"Neighbors phoned us complaining about noise from a party here. Who's in here with you? Where are your parents?"

Mongo answered too politely, "Only me, sir, watching a film. Guess I got carried away with the volume. Soundtrack's loaded with hits!"

I struggled to contain my merriment. The puzzled cops shined lights into the living room, looking for anything suspicious.

"You officers need to see *Footloose*, it'll change your life."

The two not-so-amused pigs clicked their lights off. "Look, young man, keep it down or we'll be back."

The female cop added, "—and you don't want *that!*"

Satisfied with carrying out their civic duty, the two headed out to their patrol car.

150.

Mongo called out sincerely, "Thank you officers ... be careful out there ... don't get shot or anything!"

➤ DAY 5

I finally contacted Madeline, arranged to borrow Mongo's truck, for a little cash of course, and was gearing up for a stimulating night on the town or back at her place. That afternoon, I got forced into helping Mongo paint his dad's garage a few miles away, along with some other menial bullshit.

Sundown, I was getting ready at Mongo's house while LMPs were arriving for another wingding. Just as I was about to walk out the door, two unknown burnouts from the 1970s came knocking.

"Hey, I heard you dudes a-partyin' hard."

One looked like burnt Burt Reynolds, but uglier, and fatter. The other was a broken-down and dirty version of Doug Henning.

Mongo rumbled, "What's it to you?"

Dirty Doug broke out a cellophane bag of treats and put it to Mongo's nose.

"How about a trade for this hash ... in exchange for some ice-cold beer?"

The aroma was irresistible. Mongo politely escorted them in and handed each one a cold Coors.

Once inside, their "Hey bud, let's party" demeanor petered out. Mongo's living room was filled with a diverse palette of punk rock's worst, wearing contemptible clothes, and shameful hair-don'ts ... homegrown hate.

Burnt Reynolds accidentally dropped his beer on the shag rug.

Dirty Doug opened his mouth, "If my boy came home with hair like you guys, I'd slap it right off his head."

I saw this coming as soon as they walked in. He then turned his attention to the TV.

"Figures you're watching this retard movie...."

All of us coiled to strike. Mongo took it personal and reacted with a mammoth open-hand SLAP! The Doug Henning lookalike went rigor mortis, lost control of his body, and dropped the hash. Blood trickled from his lower lip.

"Get out of my house now or die!" Mongo snarled.

The rest of us surrounded them with scare faces. Both Dirty Doug and Burnt Reynolds slowly backpedaled out the door as instructed. One muttered something under his breath.

Mongo roared back from the doorway, "What? Speak up!"

151.

"You'll learn ... you'll learn...." the Doug Henning double promised.

Everyone heard him compulsively say it over and over, as he walked backwards down the block.

"You'll learn ... you'll learn..." Dirty Doug's voice faded away as we lost sight of them.

Free hash! What an impressive start for the night. Mellow, tar-flavored smoke filled my lungs as I said my goodbyes for the night. I knew I was going to miss something by leaving, but on the other hand, so would they. Mongo begrudgingly handed over his truck keys and I was off.

Click-Click-Click.

A strong burning rubber smell took over, ruining my calm high. I slammed the door shut and stomped back to Mongo.

"What the fuck? Your car just took a major-class shit!"

Half puzzled, half premeditated looks gave him away.

"I told you it was on borrowed time," then came that fucking smile of his.

Hmmm, did he sabotage his own car just to get me to stay? Mongo was my loyal pal and recruit, but considerably selfish. Though I never could prove it, my instincts told me he crossed up some electrical wires just so I'd have to stay. Madeline understood, and even offered to come out. No way was I gonna subject her to Mongo's house of horrors. I made new plans for the following week.

Mongo's mother would be home tomorrow, so this was our last night of debauchery. It went off as usual, with several standout loaded performances, then faded only to LMP members, following Mongo's descent into beer oblivion.

About ten to midnight, a polite knock-knock-knock on the door broke our collective spell. I got up for door duties and looked through the peekie hole.

"Shit. He's back ... and he's armed!" I whispered loud, with earnest strength, so all could understand the level of danger facing us on the other side of the door.

Mongo knew what time it was and told us to ready up. Pineapple Head secured the Uzi from the hall closet, tossed Mongo his pump shotgun, who then handed it to me. Everybody else grabbed what they could and took positions around the room that eliminated elements of chance.

Mongo held the doorknob tight and mouthed in a low voice "on three," then fingered the countdown "1–2–3" and boldly opened his door.

A defiant Doug Henning stood there, holding a semi-automatic shotgun. Mongo put two hands on it and cunningly yanked him inside. I cocked my 12-gauge at

Burnt Reynolds, causing him to flee. Falling back inside, Mongo wrestled for gun control, while everyone else hectically scurried away from the barrel's end...

"I been working so hard
Keep punching my card
Eight hours, for what?
Oh, tell me what I got
I get this feeling
That time's just holding me down
I'll hit the ceiling
Or else I'll tear up this town
Tonight I gotta cut"

BAM!! *"LOOSE—FOOTLOOSE!"*

The shotgun blasted Mongo's sofa, spurting imitation down all through the air, and narrowly missed Pineapple Head's head by a quarter-inch. Everybody jumped or ducked, as attention centered on the struggle and where the barrel was pointing...

"Kick off your Sunday shoes
Please, Louise
Pull me offa my knees
Jack, get back
C'mon before we crack
Lose your blues"

KA-BLAM!! *"EVERYBODY CUT FOOTLOOSE!"*

The second shell shot fired point-blank into the wall and took out the lamp. Debris was everywhere. All LMP members who didn't flee the room were jumping around couch to couch, coffee table to chair, floor to ceiling. The spotlight shotgun dance, a blur...

"You're playing so cool
Obeying every rule
Dig way down in your heart
You're yearning, burning for some
Somebody to tell you
It will if you don't even try
You can fly If you'd only cut"

BOOM!! *"LOOSE —FOOTLOOSE!"*

The third discharge fired into Mongo's cottage-cheese roof and spread white dust far and wide. Pineapple Head and I were bobbing and weaving, pointing our weapons, stomping side to side in tandem with the movie music, trying to get a clean shot.

"Kick off your Sunday shoes
Oo-whee, Marie
Shake it, shake it for me
Whoa, Milo
C'mon, c'mon let go
Lose your blues
Everybody cut footloose
FIRST — We got to turn you around
SECOND — You put your feet on the ground
THIRD — Now take a hold of your soul
FOUR — Whooooooooa, I'm turning it"

KA-BOOM!! *"LOOSE —FOOTLOOSE!"*

Fourth shell exploded the TV and VCR to outer space. Mongo, after great lengths, finally shook the loadie's gun free from his retaliatory clutches. Exact same time I found my opening—SMACK!

I sledgehammered my shotgun butt hard into the loadie's head. He crumbled to a seated position on the buckshot-shredded couch. Mongo replenished the missing oxygen to his lungs, raised his just-captured 12-gauge, and swung for the guy's ribs. I followed in rhythm with my Mossberg on the opposite side. We both began smashing his collarbone, and worked our way down...

SNAP! CRACK!!

We walloped him countless times. The loadie's breathing labored noticeably from our merciless assault. We stepped away, fatigued and astounded by the threat that gurgled out of his mouth.

"You'll learn ... you'll learn...."

Joker replied back jubilantly, "He still has his teeth."

Pissed Chris teed off, landing one big shot after another, closing the loadie's eyes, breaking his nose, bruising and bloodying every spot on what used to be his face. Joker, along with some others, took to practicing facial hits—they were purely pounding meat at that point.

From out of left field Mongo shrieked, "Hey guys, be careful, don't get blood on my mom's sofa!"—proof positive he was out of his mind.

I fished through the guy's pockets and found nothing but a cheap lighter and a rubber, then rolled him off Mongo's mother's couch onto the carpet. Truth be told, he was still alive, and none of us had anything left in our tanks.

"What do we do now?" was the question at hand.

Half said, "Kill him! He'll come back if we don't!"

Mongo and the rest were headed in a different direction. We debated for what felt like an eternity, until Mongo finally concluded "We cannot kill Doug Henning in my mom's living room!"

The broken man was sprawled out cold, taking tiny inaudible breaths, feebly clinging to life. Our crew was caught in a genuine, true-to-the-letter Catch-22, unsure what should be done. We at least agreed not to carry out any of the wrong things people do, including:

(1) Roll the body up in a rug, stuff it in the trunk and get caught on the way to dump it.

(2) Chop it up into pieces and dispose of it slowly over time, where the blood and smell always give you up.

(3) Try to bury it deep in the backyard, where a snoopy neighbor always reports your digging to the police.

Ultimately, the decision was made for us as red and blue police lights came pouring through the windows. A number of sheriffs filed out of their cars, guns ready, led by the same deputies who showed up last night. Mongo met them at the door.

"He's inside—came in shooting up the place, nearly killed us!"

The two officers, plus a couple backups, surveyed Mongo's living room: a bunch of punks with their hands raised high, visible shotgun damage to walls and couch, broken lamps, and one pulverized loadie splayed on the floor. Protocol took over instantaneously.

The male lead cop broke out his service revolver and commanded, "Everybody on the ground. Hands where I can see them!"

They made sure the house was clear, read us our Miranda rights, and handcuffed us to one another, being cops don't regularly carry 30 sets of cuffs.

"First off, what in God's name happened here?" the lead cop pressured. Mongo gave a brief synopsis from his prone position. "We tried making a citizen's arrest, sir … he resisted."

They ordered us to shut the fuck up, called an ambulance, then confiscated Mongo's Uzi and Mossberg. The lead deputy took Mongo, a few others, and me outside and started questioning us to see how smart we were. Mongo explained, as did the rest of us, that this strange guy came in popping off shots, and that we were within our rights to defend ourselves.

Mongo's act of "My mom's gonna kill me!" and "I want to press charges—he's gonna pay for the shit he ruined," etc., etc. seemed to work on the pigs.

As the paramedics rolled the loadie out on a gurney, the cops removed a wallet from his back pocket. They ran his record and found out he had a long list of assaults and drug priors. Still, the lead officer continued to squeeze.

"You guys are not telling me everything. Why would this guy just come in shooting?"

"How would I know, maybe he hates punk rockers?" Mongo surmised.

The officer knew he had nothing after running Mongo's guns and coming up empty; both were flawlessly registered and legal. After another hour of third-degree questioning, they gave up. They told us if the Uzi and Mossberg were not fired, Mongo's parents could legally pick them up from the station next week. Mongo said his goodbyes to our valiant public servants, right before they hopped into their cars.

"Thanks again officers, and be careful out there. Don't get shot or anything!"

Very next day, Mongo's mother returned home furious. She told her ex-husband, "Survey the damage and get answers!" Stinky Ed was especially displeased with the destroyed interior. "More work for you dimwits. Can't leave you alone for a goddamn minute."

Since Mongo was a minor, Stinky Ed received the full rundown from the police and gave it to us. "You boys worked him over real good … severe concussion, broken eye sockets, shattered nose, four missing teeth, broke both his collarbones, managed to break every rib except one … you fucking idiot kids—now they want YOU to press charges against HIM, so he's probably going to try and sue ME! And they got MY guns! Could've avoided all of this—You know that, right?"

Mongo protested, "How, Pop? It was self-defense.…"

Stinky Ed gave us an all-knowing black look, right into our eyes.

"Should've killed him."

CHAPTER 13
"EAT MY FUCK"

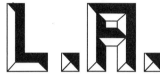 was, and always will be, its own animal. We rode that beast and sometimes she looked out for us. Other times she cut us. Deep.

Profits from our leather jacket sales "business," along with punk party takeovers, finally provided me enough money for a car. My new beater was no thing of beauty, but that '69 Chevy screamed Frank the Shank, and I didn't have to share her with anybody. Madeline was overjoyed that I could now come and see her whenever she wanted. We went out back-to-back nights, had so much fun walking, eating, drinking, and making love. I had definitely rubbed off on Madeline because her new outfits were more provocative than ever. She dragged me into the back bathroom of a pizza joint we called "Cockroach Pizza" on Hollywood Boulevard, where she inscribed "Frank loves Madeline," with a heart around it, in red ink. We made it right there in the stall without a care in the universe. She told me how much I meant to her and, in fact, that I was the only guy for a really long time. I reciprocated, going so far as blurting out words I had never said before: "I love you, Madeline."

Three days later, I was at Pasadena's Perkins Palace, watching a show, feeling terrific, when I ran into my pal Snickers. Snickers knew everybody in the punk scene and never missed a show, unless his band was playing a different show. He sang for a number of notable bands: the Cheifs, who were actually Darby Crash's favorite, the Simpletones of *Beach Blvd* fame, along with the Stains and the Klan. Snickers consistently dressed and looked different every time you saw him, like the true boulevard punk he was. He had either spiked, slicked, or mohawked hair, depending on his mood. He wore numerous outfits that included Viking helmets, sombrero hats, and even Fascist officer's caps that matched his leather jackets—always flamboyant to the hilt. Coincidentally, we had matching tattoos Mark Mahoney put on us: dancing can-can girl bracelets that wrapped around our wrists. Tatted on his other arm was Count Dracula drinking a Bloody Mary, the Wolf Man wearing a Pendleton buttoned to the top, and Frankenstein drinking beer from a stein—totally ahead of his time.

Snickers, in casual conversation, asked me, "How long you been messing with that girlie?"

"What girl?" I questioned.

Snickers responded indifferently, "Maddie, I think?"

"How do you know her and how'd you know I'm datin' her?"

"Saw you leavin' Frolic Room with her other day."

He hit a nerve, and he knew it by the face I gave.

Snickers kept on, "No big deal ... but thought you should know, my man Tommy Toilet's been diddling her for months and, from what I hear, he ain't the only one either...."

I turned ice-cold.

Snickers was no idiot, he knew what I was capable of, and had no reason to piss me off. Must have her confused—No fucking way!

"Who's this toilet dude?" I interrogated.

"Ah, some kid used to live in DC, he's mellow...."

Bullshit—somebody's gonna die.

I walked away, stupefied. I pulled my knife, held it close to me, and then turned back.

Snickers was gone.

Did this just happen? What just happened? Where the fuck did he go?

Toilet's dead meat!

Right away, I started inquiring about Tommy Toilet. Nobody from LMP had heard about him, but the bouncer from Gino's shared some info over a few cigarettes.

He said, "Toilet's a small-time pill pusher," nothing to be concerned about and actually a real "kosher dude."

Upon further investigation, I found out Madeline was allegedly a regular at Club 321, Odyssey1, Dillon's Westwood, and the underground dance scene in general. It was intimated that maybe she even did a bit of go-go dancing under the alias "Heaven Sent." I had to make sure before someone got hurt bad, so I phoned Madeline and made a date for the following night.

She jumped into my arms soon as she saw me, excited as always. I took her to a semi-decent coffee shop on Cahuenga Boulevard. She sat next to me rather than across. I intended to nail her to the wall with questions, harass the "truth" from her immediately. However, Madeline's voice did something to me I couldn't fight off. She talked about her career, movies, and how upset she was that they canceled *Little House on the Prairie* and *Square Pegs*; that nothing on TV was worth watching anymore; the new designer jeans she needed; and did I think those teachers at McMartin preschool in Manhattan Beach were really Satanic creeps, etc., etc.

This girl would never date anybody with Toilet in their name or shake her ass for cash. People were getting mixed up, impossible, no fucking way possible! But I had to put it out there.

"Are you dating a guy named Tom?"

Without hesitation she came back with "Tom? I'm only with you, Frankie." She looked down, saddened, and let go of my hand. "Why would you say that?"

Oh no ... what did I do? I'm such a dickhead for believing those jealous assholes, but I could no longer help myself. I'm no sucker...

"Does Toilet ring a bell? What about all those dance fag clubs and go-go dancing? Huh!?"

She looked at me like I just killed her cat, rose up, and walked out of the coffee shop.

FUCK! I threw some money down and ran after her through a crowd of religious wack jobs picketing some bullshit—I stopped her, grabbed her.

"I'm sorry, Madeline. I don't know what I'm talking about—heard some gossip and I believed it, like an ass...."

Madeline shook loose and told me to "Grow the hell up already!"

I chased her down the street and tried to make amends, explaining my side and how much she meant to me. Some sidewalk roller-skater bumped Madeline by accident, knocking her off balance to the ground. I snapped and pummeled the roller-skater to the pavement.

"Leave me alone, Frank!" is all I heard as she walked out of my life.

Was Madeline a liar and just another pass-around? Or was everybody else full of shit? She really never denied it. Was she playing me the whole time? For days on end, I tried calling and hanging out in front of her building. She completely avoided me.

Fortunately a war was brewing. Perfect distraction. 1984, music and style were changing at a ferocious velocity. New offshoots of what was, were hard to keep track of. Dumb alternatives to punk, heavy metal, and New Wave. Clever titles like speed thrash, trash rock, Paisley Underground, with their loud shirts, and something called post-punk, which didn't make any sense to me. Hardcore

WAR IS HELL. THE GRAND OLYMPIC AUDI-TORIUM, LOS ANGELES, CA, 1983. PHOTO BY EDWARD COLVER.

hit its peak with giant capacity venues serving the entire L.A. area. Olympic Auditorium was still strong in downtown L.A., and Fender's Ballroom got going in Long Beach. You could see a hardcore show with an immense crowd every week, if someone was willing to drive, and almost everyone from everywhere did.

More posers were coming in, flooding the scene with jocks and hippies who yelled "punk sucks!" the year before. Our music and message didn't matter. To them, it was about a look and a reason to join a clique or, stupider yet, start your own. Most needed protection at shows regardless. Venues were too big for their own good, with so many gangs from so many communities showing up, you had to have backup or else. Results were often life-ending. Back in the days when a fight broke out, I charged, knowing it somehow involved LMP. Nowadays, everyone was charging. Countless times I saw wanderers get swallowed up for good. Occurrences like the stray punk who fled from Circle One outside the Olympic, only to get hung up on a chain-link fence, where six of them fatally stabbed him in the back, and the jock posers who ran their mouths then ended up beaten to death at places they didn't belong, had become a weekly happening.

Our LMP network grew so huge that making and keeping new friends became problematic. One week you're sharing beers and good times with a new comrade, next week someone from LMP breaks a bottle over their head or threatens their life. Sure it sucked, but all you could do was offer a halfhearted apology. I didn't even know all the guys in my own gang anymore. But, fortunately for them, they knew me.

FRANK AND HAPPY,
SOUTH WHITTIER, CA.

Punk gangs had formed all over the country, and we were busy taking in more new recruits from Norwalk Village housing off Imperial Highway: Thing, Happy, Hulk, Dog Bite, and Phil Collins (because he looked identical to Phil Collins) were ready to be a part of our apocalypse. Entertainingly, they came with problems from a new gang in their area called N.I.P., Norwalk Insane Punks. Sure enough, they wanted a shot at our title, and decided to call us out all over town.

"LMP who?"

"It's a NIP world!"

Big mistake....

We did our usual research: found out how many they had, where they hung out, and who they knew, then went to work. First, I sent in my new recruits for an initial look-see at a party/meeting we fell privy to. Dog Bite gave an account of roughly 15 guys drinking beer inside a Norwalk house, which offered easy access through a side-yard door to the kitchen. We came with three carloads, including Mongo, Shakes, Pissed Chris, Lil Skin, Pineapple Head, some vets, and the new guys. We brought axe handles, knives, and a couple guns for good measure.

Our crew fanned out in front of their house; fat Pee Wee was on lookout.

161.

Mongo and I called them out, "LMP's here to huff and puff and blowwww your house down!"

"Come outside and get some!"

Four of their possible best came outside, weaponless, and rushed us. Our new recruits fought it out in record time, sending them running back inside, and bolting the doors behind them. Their neighbors came out during the commotion and were very quick to gossip, rumor, and point fingers. I didn't even get to hurt anybody.

We split, knowing The Man was on his way. Off to the park to hide out and drink was my command. Orders got followed without procrastination; LMP were well known to have considerable potential in this area of waywardness. Although, as I knew, the sweet taste of success was utterly lacking. Without true thrill of victory, my crew went about stewing bitterly on the wooden benches, waiting for me to give the word to return and finish the job.

After an hour or so, I figured NIP gang drifted back into false confidence. We returned, parked our cars a block away, put Pee Wee on lookout again, and creep-walked our way into the side yard. Mongo waited for a cluster of us to form behind him. LMP's big bad wolf Mongo raised his boot and crash-kicked the kitchen door right off its hinges. We poured in ten strong, knocking over chairs, paintings, end tables, and one irate cat. NIP tried their best to fight off our invasion, but were fully inundated by our intensity. From my viewpoint, watching three separate fights take place in a narrow hallway was something special. Cinematic even.

Pineapple Head cracked an axe handle over a wannabe skinhead's shoulder, causing him to domino into another, rip down and get buried under the oversized curtain. Mongo took a long floor lamp and commenced breaking every window in sight. A hider tucked himself between an open door and a wall. I took advantage and overhand-stabbed my knife an easy 20 times through the hollow door. All I needed was another quarter-inch to get him good, though I still caught him in the arm enough to make him bleed.

My knife got stuck and he made a break for it, scrambling out back and scaling the fence for freedom. One crafty NIP swung a vacuum that nailed Phil Collins in the ribs and sent him through a glass coffee table. News came from their TV, reporting Pete Rose reaching 4,000 hits, the most in National League history—"Fuck Charlie Hustle!"

Pee Wee alerted us with a warning whistle. Time to get out. We hurried away, leaving the place in shambles, and what was left of NIP running for the hills.

My crew motored over to Easy Street for a cooling-off period, in case some-one in Norwalk snitched. A sopping wet Pee Wee explained why he whistled for the getaway.

"You guys were loud and shit, some old bat came out threatening and said she called Neighborhood Watch and shit ... and started squirting me with her hose and shit."

I sent our new recruits home after a well-deserved pat on the back. Most everyone else split afterward, drained from the NIP ruckus. Only Mongo, Shakes, and I remained. Idle hands are the devil's plaything for sure. The three of us came to the conclusion, after ingesting numberless belts of disgusting Kessler, that those NIP guys got off easy. Neither the cops, nor that so-called gang, would ever expect a third wave of attack.

"Fuck it," was the consensus, "Let's do it!"

An hour later we hopped into my car and traveled back to Norwalk. The lights were still on in the house and all was quiet outside. Shakes leaned out my passenger-side window and squeezed off a few rounds from his newly ac-quired .44 Mag, hitting the NIP residence with every shot. I stepped on the gas, letting my V8/4-barrel combo handle our getaway. Soon as I spotted a freeway on-ramp, we were off to Hollywood. The best place to blend in and disappear after a local flare-up.

NIP remained defiant and continued shit-talking. These scumbags couldn't take a hint. Over the following weeks, the incessant windings of that prickling creeper vine of grapes finally ripened. It started with excuses.

"We weren't ready for them" and "they had us way outnumbered" then progressed to "LMP's gotta pay!"

Trusted people from the punk gang community let us know that NIP were getting guns of their own. They also proactively tried to find out who our high-er-ups were and where we lived. It wasn't just lip service either. Someone we knew from the scene actually sold them two pistols, a .380 Deluxe and a .22 single action, unaware just who they were intending to use them on.

It became our personal quest to take care of Norwalk Insane Punks for good. Santino was excited, and reminded me how to handle such a problem.

"Kill the leader!"

I found out where their number one guy went to school from our "eyes on the street" affiliate, and L.A. sophisticate, Slippers. Slippers was as dependable as death and taxes. Turned out Pissed Chris knew the guy's face, being he lived near their turf. A perfect two-man operation—one of us spots the victim ... the other gets the privilege.

We chose end of the week since campus security was lax on Fridays. Less than a block away, I felt the familiar warmth of murder growing near. Pissed Chris got dropped off at the back parking lot, right when school was letting out. His job was to spot the NIP leader, while I parked my car in a nearby neighborhood. I strategically placed my Chevy on a side street, facing two quick getaways, if need be. As I walked around the corner, Pissed Chris was walking toward me with a little extra something in his step. He gave the retreat sign, waving for me to turn around.

I bolted to my car, twisted the ignition, backed up, and simultaneously opened the passenger door. Pissed Chris dove in and off we went. I hot-footed away, purposely made as many turns as possible through several housing tracts, then zoomed onto the freeway and headed north.

Pissed Chris pulled a wadded-up rag from his jacket pocket, unfolding it as he spoke.

"Ever seen anything like this?"

Sitting on his palm was a bloodstained Buck knife, the blade horribly bent. I was amazed, wondering what bones were struck hard enough to twist steel.

"That's nuts, Bucks are guaranteed for life—It's a fake, huh?"

Pissed Chris cut me off. "Nah man, that's 100% American-made ... I think it bent on the third time I stuck him."

Yeah right, I said to myself, that blade had La Mirada Swap Meet special written all over it.

NIP was finished, taken off the map for good. Their leader lay in ICU with a slim chance of making it. Everyone connected to NIP said the rest of the gang returned to normal-guy looks and gave up on punk rock altogether. Starting any kind of clique, crew, or gang in L.A.'s hardcore scene was risky business. Old established crews wouldn't tolerate it; best to stay away.

Mike McIntosh landed a fine-looking failed actress turned street artist. She came with a room at the infamous Landmark Motor Hotel for the weekend. The same place Janis Joplin choked on her own vomit in 1970. Mike invited us all over to party, an ideal spot for us to lay low after the NIP thing. Perfect timing.

After being there an hour or so, in strolled Stormin' Normin with his new

PISSED CHRIS AND HIS
BROTHERS-IN-ARMS,
1984.

buddy H.R., lead singer of the immortal Bad Brains. Known philanderer and
substance *habitué,* H.R. was always looking for a place to crash when in town.
Frequently, he wound up staying somewhere in our loop to avoid the countless
"Bumbaclot bitchiz!" around L.A. who thought H.R. fathered their kids. Stormin'
Normin explained how, at pre-dusk, he rang Mike's doorbell looking for us, only
to find H.R. hiding in the bushes, and figured why not bring him along. Entering
Mike's hotel room, H.R. sat down in the middle of the floor, Indian-style, and re-
fused to get up. Throughout the night he would go off on some Yardie tangent.

"Bwaay! Mi ina big choble!"

"Cuyah, she gwan like she nice eee?"

"She tek mi money dem teif!"

No one knew what any of it meant, but from time to time I saw Stormin'
Normin engage him in conversation.

I finally had to ask, "Hey, do you really know what he's saying—what the
hell does he keep talking about?"

Normin unveiled, "I've kept my ties in the Rastafarian community. I totally
speak dread. H.R. is having girl problems, and they're really getting to him."

I laughed to myself ... who isn't?

T he next night brought us a new anomaly: a man in complete denial. Co-
pious amounts of cocaine will cloud your perception for sure, but there
are moments of hyper-clarity within a binge. Mike's new cast of invited

oddities featured a reddish-haired, freckly gent, dressed like a narc—Hawaiian shirt, faded tight jeans, and white Reeboks. He made everyone nervous except Mike. I felt beyond a shadow of doubt we had history together, but looking at him, the thought seemed absurd.

He lapped up Mike's cocaine, along with the rest of us, so he had to be okay—or at least not a cop. After several hours of staring at his Bozo face and trying to get him to talk, I figured it out.

"You're fuckin' Eddie fucking Munster!"

He went on doing lines without even batting an eyelash.

I pressed on.

"Butch Patrick, Eddie fuckin' Munster...."

Confusion from the partiers was apparent. All were looking at me, trying to catch up, and get on my playing field.

"What, what are you talking about?" challenged the mystery man.

"It took me a while, but you're Butch Patrick from *The Munsters*," I re-established.

Everybody in the suite locked attention and waited for his reply.

"No I'm not. Butch Patrick's not a real name, it's a surname."

I was taken aback.

"What do you mean not a real name—a surname?"

He carefully set aside his nose straw.

"Patrick's a surname, and no one is ever named Butch at birth ... so Butch Patrick's not a real name."

I didn't buy it.

"So what—you're still Eddie Munster."

Mystery man coolly shrugged.

"How can I be Eddie Munster if nobody can be Butch Patrick?"

Silence and deduction had their moment, then Mongo got overtly bent out of shape.

"Who the hell are you sitting here snorting all the coke if you're not Eddie fuckin' Munster? I don't like it!"

Mike McIntosh, being the diplomat, took us all aside one by one, and let us in on how "Butch" didn't want anybody to know his true identity. I was honored to be doing blow with Eddie Munster. Why won't he admit it?

Mike reasoned in a hushed tone. "He's ashamed, and waging a huge come-back in Hollywood, just play along...."

166.

"At least he left his mark in acting," Mongo pointed out.

More like a stain.

Oki-Dog was burned-out poser central. Being seen there was not part of LMP's master plan for 1984, but fuck it, we were starving. Our whole party, including "Mr. Patrick," caravanned over to Santa Monica Boulevard for a late-night snack. We filled the absence by devouring hot dog burritos, soggy fries, and chasing them down with paper-bagged beer.

My Oki Days of old, the nights of Sailor pushing Darby around in a shopping cart, ghost-riding him into walls until he cried "Push me out in traffic why don't you! Who you gonna hassle when I'm gone?" were history.

Feels like eons ago.... So much has changed, so many new faces. What would Darby say? A fitting chill made me smile. I know what Sailor would have done.

After hefting my drunken ass off the bench, I almost tripped over my pal Snickers, who was hobnobbing with a number of punk scene types I vaguely recognized. Both of our crowds shared people in common and went about taking over all the seating while trading banter. Snickers pulled me aside and walked us slightly away from the clamor.

"Hey Shank, how they hangin' man?"

"Just is bro and that's helluva nuff for me ... what's up Snick?"

"Ahhh ... my boy Tommy Toilet's here with me and no need for any trouble."

I was feeling a bit shagged and fagged and fashed by now, but here we go...

"Where?"

"That's why I took you aside man, he don't want any shit. Matter of fact, he has info about that one girlie you know. Toilet's an easy dude, try hearing him out first and please don't do what you always do."

I went along with it, being in my state of exhaustion and sober nostalgia.

"Hey TT, this is Frank the Shank, it's cool man...."

Tommy Toilet was a Billy Idol clone, add a broken nose, and subtract the salon haircut. I could tell Toilet had been thoroughly educated on who I was, and what I ran with, by the discomfort in his eyes.

"Hey F-Frank, heard great things a-a-about you from so many people ... want to let you know that I had n-no idea you were d-dating Maddie. If I did, it wouldn't have happened, m-m-man...."

The guy was stuttering scared. I had no desire to talk to him, but I needed answers. My mind circled to a story my dad told me years ago on the day Uncle Sam went to jail: about the time my dad hid out in boxcars, while heading west from Detroit to start a new life.

"I was alone and tired somewhere between Kansas City and Albuquerque, living on canned food and cigarettes. Caught some bug. I was sick as a dog. Resting in a corner, I got woke up by a grimy hobo, riflin' through my pockets. I prepared for this exact bit of circumstance, sleeping with a long knife in my hand. I waited until the hobo's hot breath got near my face, kept playin' possum for a moment, then attacked. I grabbed the bum's collar and dug the blade into his throat, pushing it up to the jaw line until it stuck. Then yanked the knife out. He hit the floor, arms flappin', trying whatever he could do to hold his squirting neck together. I went through the hobo's pockets, taking back my dollars and smokes. Blood was gettin' all over the boxcar. So before it got too messy, I mopped up the bum's blood with his own coat, dragged his sorry carcass over, and booted him off the moving train."

Dad got even, dead even. Now it was my turn.

"How long did you hang with her?" I questioned.

"Ah mannnn, she broke my heart after a f-few m-months, figured out she was doing a f-few friends of mine on the s-s-side."

I started to believe the sap.

"Hard to see that shit comin."

"Yeah-yeah, I mean n-no-no Frank, I had no idea. I thought she was cool, I thought I was It ... ya know?"

For a split second, I felt I had to stick Tommy Toilet and put him out of his misery. No ... that's an amateur reaction, unless you've come home from a hard day's work and find 'em both in the act. Any reaction at this point would be a declaration of weakness.

My final words to him were "Easy come, easy go. She's a whore, man, you'll get over it."

I said my goodnights to Snickers and headed back to McIntosh's hotel room for first dibs on the foldout bed.

Truth is, Madeline was the only girl, to this day, I ever trusted with my secrets. I told her how my dad used to beat me and how lousy I felt about myself, that if he didn't care, then why should I. I let her in. I spoke my heart and didn't hold back. I loved her. Thought she was the answer.... That cunt actress slut, hope she gets gang-raped and set on fire.

168.

CHAPTER 14
"LOW CLASS OF 1984"

Punk was now being exploited to its fullest potential in arenas, sitcoms, and movies. *Suburbia*, directed by Penelope Spheeris, was actually tolerable, even though it came out years too late. They shot most of it only a couple miles from my house, off the 605 freeway where it meets the I-5. The film spotlighted punk squatters, dealing with everyday hate from older generations. Casting actual punks and bands from our scene made it sort of watchable. Redneck harassment and hippies who beat punks up while they minded their own business felt corny though. Stuff like that happened when I was a kid, but not anymore. Tables turned years back. Now we tortured them.

Something I had only seen on inner-city boulevards for years was beginning to happen in the suburbs. B-boy and popping crews were up-starting all over. Guys in tracksuits would be head spinning, or doing some swirling maneuver on top of cardboard, while another rapped and held a huge radio. White kids that jumped on the bandwagon for their chance at "street" was like watching Looney Tunes. Fancy graffiti pieces were even appearing more regularly up at Errol Flynn's, but outside of that, the place remained the same. Same ole LMP tag, still untouched at the front wall, same ole Hollywood scuzz, along with the same ole squares who lacked the street smarts to know they shouldn't be there. Maybe there is a God.

Being in a particularly lousy mood, I decided to drag myself over to Errol Flynn's with Pineapple Head. Nothing to do but drink booze in the dark and see what kind of dipshit was poolside at our decrepit estate. Sure enough there was a sprinkling of wannabe B-boy misfits, and trendy whatever-guys adventuring in separate, small groups. Without any other punk rockers or homeless dirtballs floating about, Pineapple Head and I felt watched, like zoo animals. Curiosity drifted our onlookers toward us in no time at all. We exhibited a necessity for space through our demeanor, but these greens didn't get it. I chucked my empty bottle of gin on the concrete to make them understand. It did the opposite. A counterfeit B-boy came over, asking us smartass stereotypical questions about punk rock.

"Do you really hate your mom and dad?"

"Do you have a pet rat?"

CRACK!

Pineapple Head beat me to the punch, connecting his homemade cane, topped with an 8-ball, right to the guy's dome. Humdinger was, that shot to the head made the exact same sound a cue ball does when it hits the apex ball during a perfect pool-hall break. Second shot sent everybody in the vicinity tearing ass out of Errol Flynn's, with no thought of assistance. This guy was alone in the worst way. Third shot put him in a state of shock and shut down his faculties. The guy's yellow-bellied shit-friends had no balls and thoughtlessly abandoned him. Either way, he was gonna die. Pineapple Head kept swinging, further crippling the guy as he lay hemorrhaging, half conscious, and mumbling.

"Why ... why... why are you doing this to me?"

All Pineapple said in return as he dealt the fatal blow was, "Because."

I felt nothing. That idiot should have listened to the lyrics.

PINEAPPLE HEAD, SELF-
EXPLANATORY.

L os Angeles Summer Olympics of 1984 were about to get underway. The eyes of the globe would soon be upon us even though USSR was boycotting, more Reagan Cold War fallout—what an asshole.

LAPD chief Daryl Gates proclaimed, "City of Los Angeles will be the safest place in the world!"

Soon after the proclamation, homeless bums began roaming our suburbs like an undead plague. Chief Gates had herded his nuisance onto buses and dumped them off without anyone's knowledge. Gates also implemented his Olympic gang sweep, jailing thousands of young black men across L.A., and sent our SWAT team to Israel for special training. Extra helicopters, on lease from the military, zigzagged our skies relentlessly. If it were up to our fascist regime, Charles Bronson would be lighting the torch at the Memorial Coliseum.

Simultaneously, punks that wandered Hollywood were being swept up in a dragnet as a direct result of Pineapple Head's incident up at Errol Flynn's.

Friends from LADS, schlepped in for questioning, said the definitive nothing, clueing us in to "lay even lower and cover your asses by stayin' out of Hollywood till it cools down."

On top of that, *Flipside* Magazine was on our ass—writing something about punk rock gangs like LMP ruining the scene. Cops were closing ranks and the critics turned their back on us.

Our habitat had shrunk even more. The situation confined us to our homes exclusively. Five-ring fever was all they were playing on the tube, night and day. The running of the Olympic torch was set to make its way down Whittier Boulevard, only blocks from my pad. Like most Angelenos, we couldn't help but get swept up in the spirit of the games. Me, along with Mongo, Joker, Shitdick, Pissed Chris, Degenerate, Pineapple Head, Lil Skin, plus maybe nine more lined up on Whittier Boulevard, and waited for the relay to pass by. For the first time in years I felt small. Seeing the torch in person, after following it on TV from New York, and its journey through 33 states, I felt like a kid again. Like when my Little League ball club was about to play for the championship.

After the opening ceremonies, gold was all that mattered, and we took it personal when USA lost any event. We even traveled a few cities over to Cerritos for the cycling competition. Somehow, we ended up at a block party somebody put together in honor of the occasion. The house party was located right next to the 91 freeway, which functioned as a 16-mile stretch of the Olympic course. The party hosts figured we must have belonged to somebody or why would we be there? They were very welcoming.

LIKE A KID AGAIN. L.A. OLYMPIC PRIDE, 1984. MONGO (MIDDLE) STARS & STRIPES, FRANK (TO HIS LEFT) IN WIFEBEATER.

Barbecue sauce covered our faces as we sat on the tall back wall, overlooking the Olympians pedaling by en masse.

Shitdick remarked how he wanted to throw full beer cans at those "Cheating fucking Führer-following Nazi Germans!"

He was convinced everybody except Americans injected steroids. The United States ended up winning top spot on the platform for that race.

We stayed long after the event ended, taking full advantage of free food and beer, while trying to scam on housewives. Their drunken husbands were busy talking about future home additions and new state-of-the-art lawn mowers, when Joker did the unthinkable. One "invited" guest, who happened to be from Denmark, slurred into an alcohol-infused patriotic discussion with Joker and Shitdick.

"No, no, Cuba and Soviet Union always best at boxing, no, no, no...."

Shitdick disagreed, "What are you saying there, Sven? Everyone knows USA might have the greatest boxing team of all time this year!"

Sven got bullheaded and his accent thickened.

"Look punkar ... Look ... You don't know! USSR and Cuba are not here because your hysterical American attitude—you are afraid to fight them!"

Joker got out of his seat. "We ain't afraid to fight anybody anywhere in the world!"

Sven kept pushing it: "No, no ... that's why YOU boycott last Moscow games ... Afraid to compete ... Afraid to FIGHT!"

Shitdick came unglued, "No one's afraid—it's Reagan! It's all Ronald Reagan!!"

Shitdick sat back down, Joker walked off, in what appeared to be an attempt to let cooler heads prevail. I was actually real proud of my guys for keeping it above the belt and letting that wacky foreigner run his foolish mouth. Despite the nationalism on display, their devotion to goodwill triumphed.

Not a minute later, I saw Joker shot-put something in Sven's direction. The dark brown fudge substance coated the European's entire face and neck.

"Eat shit! America rules!!"

The stench was overwhelming and unmistakable. Sven froze, realizing a turd bomb of human feces just exploded all over him. Blue anxiety. A pause like no other blanketed the party. Joker casually walked over to the condiment table, and started cleaning his hand with a pile of stars-and-stripes napkins. Feminine screams erupted, followed by stumbling middle-aged breadwinners trying to show they still had control. We wore out—putting a flamethrower to our welcome. It was time to vacate, and fast. All of us took off running, through a maze of party furniture, and angry geezers, all the way to our car.

What was that foreigner thinking about, insulting our country and boxing team? Not to mention our local fighter from East L.A., Paul Gonzales. We were downright proud of Paul, and no way was some Euro-trash going to disgrace our guy. Paul ended up winning the gold.

Once the Olympics finished, L.A. didn't simply pick up where it left off—it blasted off. Vice hibernated during the Summer Games cleanup. Now, the streets were gushing with homelessness, theft, robbery, gang warfare, addiction, and some new form of cocaine called crack. Los Angeles didn't have the money or manpower to sustain police-state tranquility.

Punk rock was no exception, and in fact rose to embrace the spike in local depravity with a global hardcore extravaganza at the Grand Olympic Auditorium—flagrantly fitting. The venue that held L.A.'s first Olympic boxing bloodsport competition in 1932 became ground zero for one of the most violent shows LMP ever participated in.

In the true spirit of the games, Goldenvoice put together a lineup of bands from foreign countries, including Holland's B.G.K., Italy's Raw Power, Finland's Riistetyt, Mexico's Solucion Mortal, headlined by our very own Dead Kennedys, and NYC's Reagan Youth.

Right before entering, I saw a Guardian Angel get the shit kicked out of him for trying to play peacemaker at the wrong venue. Come on hero, go chase a rapist—you can't stop this. Twenty-five of us met up at the upper seating area, and took inventory on what gangs chose to gamble in tonight's violence game. Every major participant from the Valley, to Hollywood, to the L.A. beach cities was clad in garb respective to their crew. Even guys from Hollywood Rat Patrol, Mikey Mouse Club, The League, NSF, and South Bay Skins were standing strong. No one was trying to blend in whatsoever; if you wound up a casualty, you would know which gang to blame.

The slam pit was full-on berserk; all cliques present were holding down different sides of the pit areas, sending in their young soldiers for blood and prizes—hats, leathers, ripped-out earrings, weapons, and shoes. LMP saw the task and got ready, wrapping studded belts around our fists, attaching more fishhooks to jacket lapels, tightening boot chains, and putting large sockets inside our hands for a brass knuckle effect.

We walked through a thick crowd, across a floor that reeked of vomit, booze, smoke, and piss, then stopped at a central point between Suicidal and Circle One. Our numbers were pretty even. Both gangs knew if they made a move against us, they would die. They seemed to relax their stance by looking away, not wanting to provoke us. I wanted them to make a move so bad—I was sick and tired of sharing the spotlight with those motherfuckers.

Punks were flying all kinds of ways off the high stage and landing on the crowd with too much style to describe. We sent our own young bucks forward for a little appetizer. Phil Collins and Pee Wee went in tandem, swinging at anything that moved. After a few times around, they came back with an inflated confidence you can only arrive at through adrenaline and blood.

Pissed Chris decided to show the young LMPs how it was done. Approximately two minutes in, Pissed Chris came back with a hat that read "FFF," an abbreviation for the Fight for Freedom gang. We geared up for their counteraction. It never came. That was the difference between us and them. If that was our hat, you know what would have happened.

Aggressionists at the edge of the slam pit were no longer content with routinely shoving those who wanted out of the human undertow back in. A smattering of brawls began to flare up; they had turned on each other. Some gargantuan girl, who dwarfed even Evette Corvette, was putting on a clinic in that part of the ring. She grabbed the two most egregious culprits, and blistered them with Ne-

EL DUCE 1982–83, THE
MOST OBSCENE DILDO
IN AMERICA. PHOTO
BY EDWARD COLVER.

anderthal fists until they waved the white flag. Anybody that skanked by us got socked, elbowed, or tripped. I lost count of how many Mongo sent kissing good-bye. We were the flippers in a punk rock pinball machine, propelling kids into more obstacles to score points, or knocking them out of the playfield for good.

During the last song, I took a break and walked off to the pisser. The outer hallway resembled a trauma center from some low-budget disaster movie. Resting on the wall and floor, kids tended wounds and caught their breath; some were reliving their ordeal out loud, others quietly plotted punitive measures. As the show ended, we walked outside and were given a special treat of the lowest level. El Duce, singer/drummer of the Mentors and acclaimed rape-rocker, was addressing faithful fans that wanted their celebrity moment with him. After a small group gathered, he unzipped his fly, whipped out his schlong, and started beating off to everyone's delight. The gathering cheered El Duce's vulgarity until he lost interest, and put his dick back in its cave. Joker lined up with the other junior deviants to shake hands with arguably the most obscene man in America.

"Joker, you just shook the hand he jacked off with...."

"No shit, I'm never washing this hand again—El Duce's a maniac!"

What could I say to that? Joker had a valid point.

El Duce's local celebrity went well beyond his band and lewd behavior at shows. He managed the Ivar Theater, one of our favorite after-midnight haunts in Hollywood. The old neglected playhouse hosted burlesque for the bottom rung of the warped social ladder: sick teens, base-value foreigners, sex tourists, and dirty old men. El Duce allowed booze, drugs, food, even picture-taking, as down-and-out women stripped naked for a few bucks. He was eventually fired, for allegedly forcing female employees to blow him after hours while he wore his black executioner hood. Shortly thereafter, the Ivar Theater got shut down; cops were apparently getting greedy, sampling the merchandise as well. I guess the best way to elude a news scandal was to close the place.

El Duce was also labeled "One of the most disgusting perverts ever put on television!" by Wally George, "Father of Combat TV," who predated both Geraldo Rivera and Jerry Springer. Wally, a devout Reagan supporter and right-wing hardliner, titled his show, on network alternative KDOC, *Hot Seat*. From that pulpit, he lambasted limitless radicals, drug advocates, pacifists, and bimbos. Wally sported a towhead-blond combover wig as he sat behind a desk and launched verbal attacks on his guests. His young audience would yell out and point fingers throughout the show. Classic photos of John Wayne, Richard Nixon, and a NASA space shuttle launch graced his set. Guests always lost the battle of wits and Wally would have them escorted off his show by security.

"Shut up! Get off my stage, you sick moron—the interview's over!"

Equal parts rabble-rouser and carnival barker, Wally George only invited outspoken idiots on, so he could throw them off. Who would have thought Rebecca De Mornay, the actress every kid jacked off to, the hooker from the movie *Risky Business* ... was his daughter.

Some faker, vacationing in poverty, had been recently fucking this hot little Latin number I had my eye on. She lived spitting distance from my pad. I would watch the faker roll by, playing the role in his new mini-truck, blazing oldies from his Alpine, with no regard for who might be taking notice. Joker and I knew we could get good money for his flashy rims and decided to borrow them permanently. If this clown was gonna flaunt his shit like some kind of playboy, then leave it on the street, he deserved to get took.

One evening, he parked about four houses down from his part-time lover's apartment, being there were no spaces available in front. He got out and hurried along, almost reaching the front of her building. We shook his truck, setting off its alarm, and then quickly hid. He turned around, walked halfway back to his vehicle, saw all was copacetic, chirped the alarm off, and then chirped it back on. As soon as he got near her complex we shook it once more and hid. He came jogging back all the way to his truck, gave it another look, and then reset his security system. Again he walked away and again we shook it, setting off the siren. This time he came back within range and turned it off for good, assuming it broke. Once the guy stepped inside his chick's place to get some ass, Joker and I swarmed. We loosened the lugs and jacked up each side, set the truck on cinder blocks, pulled off his rim/tire package, put them in my trunk, and bailed. As we drove away, I imagined in delight the "Why me?" look on that guy's face when he came to realizing who really got fucked.

Bear figured enough time had passed since fleeing from his hometown murder incident in the South Bay, and knew a Filipino kid there who was interested in buying our new rims. The Flip kid paid hard cash as soon as he saw those shiny laces and even invited us to smoke out in his back garage. Turned out he was a ranking member of one of the deadliest Filipino gangs in Los Angeles, and had their initials tattooed on his stomach. He wore spiky black hair, a long tail, Ton Sur Ton tapered pants, and Jap-slaps. Giant fish tanks were bubbling everywhere, and a variety of martial arts weapons lined the walls—swords, three-sectional staffs, sais, tonfas, nunchucks, and throwing stars. Obnoxious scratch music, with robot voices, was booming from his DJ turntable setup.

"I'm gonna get dose presh rims gold-dipped, roll my Supra hard and get pamous all over Westwood!"

He reached underneath his couch, pulled out a mini submachine gun and removed the clip.

"See this pucking Tech-Niner, man? See this pipty-shot clip? Better respect … I show dose pake gansters what time it is—Believer it!"

He was a very happy guy and kept making us smoke more of his "pucking best weed" that looked like it belonged on the cover of *High Times*. It kicked our ass.

I drove us home while Joker divvied out our money, and cut Bear in for brokering the deal. Bear was all amped up and wanted to return. Wanting to rip the rims back off from the Filipino and take his gun.

"Come on! Let's go back, he'd never see it comin'!"

Joker joined in, also wanting to double up.

I stopped at a red light and thought out loud, "He's waiting at the door with a sword—get it out of your head. They all think they're Master of the Flying Guillotine."

A tiny old lady crossing the street broke our debate. She gradually inched along with her walker, until she reached my car. My Chevy was nearly all the way in the crosswalk, blocking a clear path.

BAM! BAM! BAM!

The old lady began bashing my driver-side fender with her walker, all piss and vinegar. We were dumbstruck by the balls on this old lady. She certainly didn't give a shit who was inside the car, we might have been mass murderers … oh wait, we were.

What could I do but laugh and give the old lady her due? Bear snapped and jumped out of my car. She saw him coming, turned around and sped up her movement. Bear easily caught up, and side-kicked the walker out from under her. The old woman's refusal to let go, coupled with momentum, sent her gliding hard to the blacktop. Still gripping her walker, flat on the ground, she smiled and openly mocked us.

"You're all going to HELL, hahahahaaa HELL HELL, you'll burn in HELLLL!!"

None of us cared. We always said we were going to hell. Fuck it.

CHAPTER 15
"GENERATIONAL SCARS"

y senior year arrived with summer of '84 still hanging on me like a crummy song you can't stop singing. First day showed up ... I didn't show up. Second day arrived ... I didn't arrive. Third day clocked in ... I'm clocked out. A phone call woke me up at 10 a.m., two hours after my school day started without me ... again.

"Frank? Hello? Hello? Frank?"

Why in God's name did I pick up the phone?

"Frank, is that you on the line?"

Hmm ... might as well say something to this slob.

"This is Frank, may I ask who the hell are you?"

"Hello Frank, this is Principal Bloom from Frontier High School. My records show you have not attended any of your classes this year, thus far."

I put my blanket over the receiver and purposely mumbled out something unrecognizable, then hung up the phone. The phone rang back within seconds—and didn't stop. Ahhh ... this dirty bastard's gonna play this game, huh? I picked the phone up on his fourth attempt, with my same disguised voice, and added static from my radio alarm clock.

"H~ello~^~^~must~^~^~be~^~^~^~bad~^~con~n~ec~^~tio~n"

Click.

Too easy, teachers are a worthless lot. I positioned myself back down for a comfortable post-morning nap. Then there it was again, ringing, two, three, four, five, sixth ring I picked it up, listened, and said nothing.

"Frank ... Please, take what I have to say seriously. Your whole future could depend on it."

His diligence intrigued me. "Yes, Mr. Bloom, what can I do you for today?"

"Frank, my records also indicate that this is your senior year and you only need two hours a day, only ten hours a week, to graduate from high school. A diploma is crucial to not winding up on the fringes of society. You've made it too far for me to just stand by and watch you flounder. I am personally seeing to it that you graduate."

I never heard anything so ridiculous.

"Okay ... so you're busting me?"

"No, Frank, I am going to call you Monday through Friday, 7 a.m. on the dot—until you graduate. Got that?"

This tall fat man was determined. Wonder if he got paid more when the seats were filled?

"So expect my call bright and early tomorrow, son. I will be waiting in front of your classroom for you to arrive and start your senior year."

Click.

Same afternoon, Mongo, Pissed Chris, and I made a half-drunk stop at Albertsons. We gathered up plain-wrap beer, cheese, lunchmeat, and bread. Got in line, then emptied out our pockets. I was doing the math, counting up all crumpled bills mixed with change, when right up front were the king and queen of punk rock criticism—Al and Hudley Flipside. You gotta be kiddin me, the nerve of them to call us out in their fanzine, when they ran that rag out of our territory in Whittier. No way was I about let it go.

"I think you two best watch what you say about LMP."

Al and Hudley looked right at us, and their carefree dispositions deviated to worry.

"We don't like you," charged Pissed Chris.

Hudley handed her old man Al their grocery bags and they hastily scampered out of the store. We left Mongo to pay the checker for our afternoon supplies, while Pissed Chris and I followed them outside.

"Hey Flipside! What you got against violence?"

The couple hurried to their parking space.

"Yeah, how's violence bad?" Pissed Chris asked for an answer. "It's punk rock—somebody has to get hurt!"

I put it to them direct as Hudley fumbled for her keys.

"Stick to the music if you want to keep being neighbors."

Mongo came out of Albertsons, already drinking beer.

"Did we make Flipside give up free tickets for the next Olympic show?"

Everybody was pointing fingers at the kids who lived brutally. Bands were upset over losing friends to the crusade, but still kept feeding it with their lyrics and sound, then wanted to cry about it? Every single band wound us up like *A Clockwork Orange*, yelling something violent and negative on every single record. Was there one happy punk record? I don't think so. Everyone in the scene dealt with some type of bloodshed. Most didn't have a choice if they wanted to survive the hardcore punk scene in Los Angeles.

"Be an individual, don't be a follower!"

Easy for you to say when you were protected on stage, or behind a typewriter, but the trenches were another story. And bottom line, we were the majority of the kids who bought tickets. Nearly all of you so-called musicians and punk rock scholars wouldn't have lasted a minute.

If violence is art, then LMP was the Jackson Pollock of punk. Our victims, more often than not, wound up looking like one of his paintings ... abstract expressions of red splatter on black cement. We definitely shared Pollock's inability to take criticism with any sort of reasonable acceptance. How dare they! The audacity of fools, they had no idea of what we'd accomplished.

Next day, my phone rang at 7 a.m. sharp, as promised.

"Good morning Frank, this is Principal Bloom, what a great day to learn something!"

This guy was militant, some kind of General Patton.

I thought I heard him say under his breath, "School is hell, don't be a coward, soldier."

Barely awake from a bad dream anyway, I decided to play along. I fell out of bed, put my boots on, and walked across the street to school. As expected, there's Bloom, standing out front of my classroom in his brown corduroy $50 suit. He forced me to shake his hand.

"Glad you followed through on your promise, Frank, have a great day and expect my call tomorrow morning, 7 a.m. sharp."

School sucked, but Bloom really wanted me to graduate. Fuck it. What were ten or eight hours a week? I decided to give it a go. It would make my mom happy and piss my dad off, knowing I followed through when he couldn't.

Friday night. Joker, Fingerbone, and I were at a club in Hollywood, making short work of a pint we smuggled inside, buying dollar soda chasers. It didn't take long for Joker to spot a guy he swore jumped him, with two accomplices, at Errol Flynn's last year. He always spoke about what he would do if he found them. Minutes dragged as we kept an eye on him, until he had his fill and walked out the door.

The three of us stalked after him. When he paused to light up a smoke on a dark corner, Joker made his move from behind. He pulled the empty pint bottle out from his leather and busted it over the guy's head. Joker expeditiously went to work with the jagged bottle edge, sinking it into his abdominal region. The guy got rubbery and difficult to get a clean shot on.

"Stay still!" Joker complained, being the evil entertainer he was.

Fingerbone and I kept critical surveillance so Joker could take full advantage. He had one hand on the captive's collar throughout the onrush, same time glass sharding his stomach. Blood began to flow. Screams followed. Joker changed positions, wrapped him in a headlock, and cupped his hand over the guy's mouth. No more screaming. Two more to the side was all it took. Spiritless, his legs gave out, and Joker let him fall to the ground. He plucked the fallen guy's wallet from his pants pocket and we walked away pleased, knowing Joker got his retribution, and us a bit wealthier. The supposed-to-be-dead guy somehow conjured enough strength to pick himself up and start shouting down help with what was left of his lungs. No time to confer, we cleared out as fast as our boots could move. Police siren noise started overtaking the din of weekend nightlife, signaling get off the street. Running on max for five or so blocks led us to the chain-link fence surrounding Hollywood High. We scaled it no problem, went straight across the athletic field, and followed faint sounds of music emanating from the gymnasium. Above the double doors, a great big painted-paper sign read BACK TO SCHOOL DANCE!

Our sanctuary came in the form of a student druggie, who traipsed outside to get high, and momentarily left the back door wide open. Scooting inside put us in a foreign land called High School Dance ... a pimple-populated frolic, coated in laser light and dry-ice smoke. Joker's 12-inch liberty-spiked hair, paired with Fingerbone's bleached fanning Mohawk, put security on our tail. We ducked behind social circles agilely, like dancers doing fancy footwork, then swerved into the bathroom. My pals wetted their hair down to make it appear normal-ish. I turned my green flight jacket inside out to fashion-forward orange.

Re-entering, I urgently had to discover a way of averting further suspicion. We made sure to leave the bathroom, one by one, a couple minutes after each other. My fellow miscreants were all but lost in the dance, but knew a desperate situation called for bold measures. We looked around the school party, tried to fit in—but didn't. I felt eyeballed like never before; we were the only kids not moving. Then, the worst song in history came on:

Wham! "Wake Me Up Before You Go-Go."

Everyone started jumping up and down frenetically, especially the dorks wearing "Choose Life" T-shirts. After a few deep breaths, my tricks of the trade kicked in, and I started dancing with this fat girl. Fingerbone and Joker tailgated with her two even-fatter friends. Our beefy dance partners weren't what you'd call belles of the ball, but they were a perfect cover, and we seemed to make their night.

Two cops walked into the dance, undoubtedly looking for us. They spoke with a couple teachers then intuitively scanned the place, the way only pigs and rats know how. I grabbed my girl's yellow veiled hat and put it on. Joker buried his face in his partner's chest and Fingerbone did this weird androgynous face-obscuring hand-gesture move. I was beside myself furious with Joker the whole time for not finishing his victim off, putting us in this absurd predicament. That guy should have been worm dinner. Our situational buffoonery only made matters worse. In Joker's defense, it was miraculous the guy even got up. Like watching Lazarus rise, screaming for help instead of thanking Jesus.

The cops kept roaming around the dance. The three of us kept dancing, if that's what you want to call it. *Footloose* must have rubbed off on us more than we thought. Fingerbone actually started to look like he knew what he was doing. Maybe he was a closet New Waver? The cops came up short and left. We figured it would be smart to cover our asses even further, and insisted the girls leave with us. They didn't argue, probably figured we were their last shot at having a date for quite some time. Besides, I had to admit, they started to grow on us. The smoke screen worked. It was time to get beer and escort the ladies to our old reliable inspiration point, Errol Flynn's.

Once we settled in and knocked a twelver back, our dates looked even cuter in that chunky nerd-gal way. The allure of our little hideaway was irresistible, despite its overall filthiness. After oohing and aahing at the breathtaking view, their clothes and inhibitions disappeared. Mine was, in fact, the first girl I messed with since Madeline … and probably had a lot more to offer, but I was shallow. What can I say?

On our ride back home, topic of discussion centered on whose girl was the fattest, which most certainly was Joker's.

"Your girl's so fat, when she dances, people die in China."

"Your girl's so fat, she's the slam pit at the Olympic, all by herself."

"Your girl's so fat, she bounced Big Frank offstage!"

Joker couldn't decide what was the bigger bang ... the sex or the stabbing. Both gave him a hard-on.

As far as the verbiage on La Mirada Boulevard's chamber of commerce building stated, we were now running the show. For four full hours, the sign, high up on that giant white wall, read "La Mirada PUNKS Chamber of Commerce." It took visionary balls to spray-paint a government building. Stormin' Normin and I sat across the street and admired our handiwork. We watched people's reactions all afternoon, up to the minute they sandblasted it off. An inordinate number of passersby did double takes, while we imagined full-blown anarchy, with us in charge. Santino the Mayor, Frank the Shank Mayor Pro Tem, and our city council members ... Mongo, Pissed Chris, and Joker. Stormin' Normin was positively unelectable. We all knew he would spend the campaign budget on cigarettes and limo rides.

A small issue arose toward the close of 1984. One of the pretty well-known white-supremacist skinhead gangs was eagerly trying to recruit LMP from many angles. Their higher-ups knew we put death down on the big board. Politics now came into play. Santino and I had to confer with The Godfather and handle this gently. All of us understood the level of respect to which we would climb in prison and on the streets if we had them as an umbrella. But we weren't that kind of crew; besides, LMP was mixed-race. Our values were bottom-line hardcore punk. A conscious all-out refusal of conventional society—violence was the calling card. Racism and establishing a criminal network for profit wasn't part of the plan. We weren't interested.

January 20, 1985, Reagan was a sworn liar once again. America loves a cowboy. I had too much free time, so I got a job working swing shifts after school at a warehouse. Keeping an old Impala on the road took more cash than anticipated. The warehouse manager had it in for me instantly and leveled the same old rap.

"Nice boots, where's the war?"

"Don't start cutting yourself and wiping blood all over the boxes."

Every shift, he piled on extra labor duties, exhausting me with comment after obvious comment. In short time, I got the address to his apartment and paid him a late-night visit with a small-caliber hunting rifle. I set free a few hollow-points from my barrel into his living room window and drove off smiling like Lee Harvey Oswald. After school on Monday, I clocked in then went about my job, labeling and stacking boxes robotically. When the boss made his rounds, he avoided my area altogether and wouldn't even look in my direction. Paranoid for weeks, I waited for a Jack Ruby to come from out of nowhere, but Mongo came instead and offered me asylum. Perfect timing.

Located on the east end of my neighborhood was an automobile window-tinting shop that employed Mongo part-time. His boss was a born-again, state-raised ex-con named Indian, who understood our type, and gave me a job right after a brief introduction. He looked like a man who had walked through the fire and come out alive.

INDIAN (MIDDLE) WALKING THROUGH THE FIRE WITH HIS ROAD DOGS. SOLE-DAD NORTH, 1976.

"So you're an individualist like your buddy here. Fine with me. When can you start?"

Indian disarmed all my preconceived notions of born-again Christians and tyrant bosses then and there. I made it a point to work diligently and always show up on time. Putting that custom touch on mini-trucks, bugs, and lowriders was somewhat cool, for the time being. To my surprise, Mongo was as punctual as me. Then I got a call from Indian one weekend to cover Mongo's shift.

"Your buddy couldn't make it in today, Frank. You should come in."

I hung up right away, dialed Mongo and got nothing but 15 rings, two times.

"Lazy fuck!"

I powered down a half-quart of milk and a bag of stale chips, then rolled by Mongo's house, assuming he got drunk and unplugged his phone. I knocked and knocked, then went around back to find the house empty. Weird, he was never out this early unless working.

My fuel gauge read empty as I pulled into the parking lot an hour late. A number of cars were standing by to be customized. Indian said they could wait as he took me aside…

"Looks like you're gonna be busy for a while. Mongo decided to take care of business, and is now being held on two murder counts. Nothing will happen with his case this afternoon. Let's get going and black these windows out."

Indian was right, except I had a virtual laundry list of questions and concerns that thudded my melon. What did the cops have on him? Mongo was crazy, of course, but he never started anything, only finished—must have been self-defense.

When I finally made it home and got in touch with Pissed Chris, he broke down the whole story.

"Mongo went to this house party in Norwalk with a bunch of hothead kids from La Mirada. Some older guys started talking their Norwalk shit out front of the house. Those La Mirada kids mouthed off back, then it got nuts. All those dudes jumped on Mongo. Guess they were a bunch of grown men and, with no real backup, Mongo started stabbing his way out. Then a couple of them kids started stabbing too—when it all ended, there was two dead Norwalk guys in the driveway and a ton of blood. Someone there said there was so much blood, it was carrying leaves down the driveway into the gutter."

The verifiable truths of the case were still fuzzy. A lot of hearsay, and actual facts, came trickling down at a snail's pace. On a positive note, one of the victims made it out of ICU. Mongo escaped the double murder rap. Also, an autopsy on the dead guy revealed multiple stab wounds from other knives; they couldn't pin it all on Mongo now. On a negative note, the petition hearing didn't go so favorably. The judge took one look at Mongo's humongous size, reviewed the brutality of the incident, and decided he was unfit as a juvenile and should be tried as an adult. Unless he played the lawyer game and pled it down, a significantly stiffer sentence would be the end result. LMP prepared for blowback from the investigation into possible accomplices.

Mongo wasn't saying a damn thing, prompting detectives to question every known LMP member, along with their parents. It only took them a week to reach my mother. A lead detective, with an overly determined voice, promised to arrest her if she didn't cooperate. He explained the details of my life as "The People" saw it: a known gang member, thief, and accomplice of Mongo the Murderer.

"Where was Frank the night of the attack? Where is Frank right now? Where is the knife Frank carries? We know he's part of it."

La Mirada punk rock party

By MICHAEL LEONARD
Staff Writer

For his 17th birthday, Scott decided to have a party with two punk rock bands at his home in La Mirada.

To make sure the word got out about the party, he and band members put out several hundred fliers announcing the party.

What he planned on was a good time with a lot of friends and acquaintances.

When it was all over Friday night, a 24-year-old Norwalk man had been stabbed and fatally injured, and a 17-year-old La Mira-da teenager was later arrested on suspicion of murder and attempted murder.

Domingo Payan, 24, a warehouse worker who was married with one child, was pronounced dead shortly before midnight Friday at the Medical Center of La Mirada.

The teenager was ordered by a Juvenile Court Judge this week to be detained until a fitness hearing in juvenile court on Jan. 9 to determine whether he will be tried for murder as a juvenile or as an adult.

"The party didn't get out of hand," said Scott, who spoke on the condition his last name not be used. "It was after the party broke up that it got out of control."

Scott said he and his friends decided to celebrate his birthday by having the party at his parent's house in the 15600 block of Elmbrook Drive.

They arranged for two punk rock bands, "Fallout" and "Sign of the Cross," to play at the party and decided to charge admission — $1 for girls and $2 for boys.

Scott said he distributed 250 fliers at La Mirada High School

ends with slaying

and El Camino Continuation School.

A friend put out another 250 fliers at California High School and at Fullerton High School that he didn't know about, Scott said.

When the party began at 8 p.m. Scott said he quickly realized that he didn't know most of the people who were showing up.

"The Sheriff's Department asked me to give them a list of who attended the party," he said. "There were about three-quarters of them I didn't know."

About 300 teenagers arrived for the party, almost all of them dressed in punk rock outfits.

Despite the large number of newcomers, Scott said he was unaware of any problems occurring before the gathering broke up about 10 p.m.

There were varying reports from residents in the area, who refused to give their names.

One neighbor said that while there were a lot of partygoers sitting on curbs, gathering in the street and drinking beer, they weren't causing problems.

Other residents, however, complained that there were so many teenagers in the street that they were blocking traffic and making it difficult, if not impossible, for residents to get out of their driveways.

"It took me 10 minutes to get from my house to the end of Elmbrook," one woman said.

Several residents said they called the Sheriff's department to complain about the crowd and the streets being blocked.

A patrol unit was sent to the scene at around 10 p.m., said Deputy Wes Slider.

Slider said no further action was taken because the deputies Please see PARTY / A2

PARTY

From A1

found the crowd was celebrating in an orderly fashion."

That all changed shortly after 10 p.m., Scott said, when he and his friends shut the party down.

Most of the people simply left Scott's house and backyard and started milling around in the street and neighbors' yards.

When he tried to get people to leave, most didn't listen to him, Scott said.

"They just stayed out there in the streets and that's when the fights began," he said.

Scott said there were several fights between the partygoers, with beer bottles being thrown out at around 11 p.m.

Homicide Detective Gary Kotler said Payan had been visiting a friend in the neighborhood.

When the last fight started, Payan and several other residents tried to break it up. But then Payan was stabbed in the shoulder, severing an artery, and another man was injured, Kotler said.

Deputies called to the scene found more than a 100 teenagers at the scene and the two men lying on the driveway where they had been injured.

Paramedics treated the two at the scene.

My alibi was genuinely ironclad. Mike McIntosh and I were out in Hollywood that night and later stayed over at his home. His mother could verify it. She made us fried eggs and corned beef hash for breakfast. Nothing pacified or deterred the detective's verbal assault.

"Do you really know this Mongo and what kind of monster he is? His assault cases, weapons charges, and probations are numerous. He's responsible for beatings that have left kids hospitalized. Mongo even punched a young woman unconscious."

My mother sympathized, but didn't quite see it that way.

"I know this young man very well, detective, and he might be slightly awkward due to his size, but he wouldn't do anything like that. You are wrong, malicious and, quite frankly, very rude!"

The detective pulled the same "I'm looking out for your best interest" crap with all of LMP, and yielded the same result—diddly-squat.

Meantime, Mongo's dad Stinky Ed engaged in a follow-up investigation of sorts amongst LMP. He believed that his determined efforts could help his boy Mongo beat the rap. His methodology was something torn from *Black Mask* magazine. Stinky Ed showed up on doorsteps, interrogating, and attempting to make deals.

"Whoever might be involved, or knows anything, I want to see them! Were you there, son? Was a dame involved? If so I'll give you some money so you can get out of town for a while. Don't worry, this will all blow over soon."

He did a lot of figuring, tied things together, used his razor-sharp intuition, and at the same time played the guessing game. Unfortunately, Stinky Ed came up leadless, and decided to go tit-for-tat with me. He knew I was Mongo's best pal and he even knew my mother, so the visit wasn't a hardball scenario. With no real drink to offer, I handed him a glass of water, and we both took a seat.

"Frank, what can you tell me that I don't already know?"

"Shit, Ed, nobody's talking. People are scared. None of the guys knew those other kids involved—bunch of wannabes who got stab-happy. Witnesses couldn't make out who was who, except for your son. He's hard to miss."

Stinky Ed furrowed his brow and exhaled.

"This is all wrong. He's up for murder fuck-one and not solely responsible for it—they're railroading him! I did close to ten years for something very similar, but that was a long time ago. Prison out here today's a fucking free-for-all, and he just turned 17. For Christ's sake ... I had better plans for my son."

I knew the story of Stinky Ed all too well; Mongo told it over and over any chance he could. Stinky Ed was a convicted murderer facing life, but caught a break on a technicality. He wore the face of a killer the same way a baseball player holds a wad of tobacco in his cheek—a perfect fit. Stinky Ed was thoroughly worn thin from the whole ordeal and it was only beginning. I always saw Stinky Ed emotionless and hardened as they come, but his son was his son … wonder if my father would do the same?

CHAPTER 16
"IT'S OVER FOR ME ... IT'S OVER FOR YOU"

T'S NOT LIKE I WAS GONE OR IN PRISON or hibernating. Maybe I just opened my eyes, or started paying more attention ... but something in the scene changed overnight.

Some batty chick, in all black, came up and handed me a flyer to some new venue in Hollywood.

She told me punk was dead and "It's all about snuff-rock and grave-yard music."

I had noticed for the last couple years that odd bands, mostly from over-seas, would pop up randomly at punk venues. Weird stuff with weird names: Bauhaus, Sisters of Mercy, Sex Gang Children, Jesus and Mary Chain. None of which I paid any mind to. However, our old Hollywood spots, as well as new places, were holding these types of shows with increasing frequency. The new shows easily outnumbered the punk gigs at Music Machine, the Roxy, Alexan-dria Hotel, and even Fender's Ballroom. First they were calling it "post-punk," then "goth" or "death rock," and then it was "industrial."

Someone tried to educate me, "It's all post-punk, man."

Someone else told me, "Trash rock is really glammed-up punk."

What a pile of confusing shit. None of it made any sense, but two things I did notice: these shows were happening and the people going were hardcore punks, or should I say ex-hardcore punks, who adjusted their look, or changed it alto-gether. When I ran into old familiar faces from the scene, a lot of them looked different. Some grew out their hair and put together a dapper Brit style with tall flattops, dressy creepers, and suits. Other guys had longer hair—Harley-Davidson meets junkie cowboy, with open long-sleeved shirts, vests, and lengthy necklaces with medallions, dog tags, or dangling crosses. GQ shit. Girls started doing a more salon-inspired glamour look of spikes and bleached blonde or black hair. Gone were the extremes of shaving out sections, teasing it up to no end, and dyeing it off-putting colors. Their outfits incorporated lingerie tops with fitted black leather jackets or skirts. Ripped fishnets held strong, boots were high-heeled and up to the knee, and eye makeup was dark. All of it evoked sex over violence.

Fetish Club opened on Melrose off the 101 freeway. If you couldn't park in their lot, you had to deal with the Latino gangsters on the side streets, throw-

FRANK (LEFT), BARNEY
(RIGHT), SANTA MONICA
PIER PHOTO BOOTH.

ing bottles and rocks at your car if you didn't buy their crack—fun stuff. Fetish was where I first heard all that eclectic-rock shit. I only hung there for the sleazy girls. Underground clubs magically appeared in the middle of downtown L.A., where you had to know the right person to get a pass. These illegal after-hours clubs were hidden in some tall building or warehouse, and for a small fee you could drink and dance till dawn. All these new outlets just left me feeling powerless. These people didn't know who I was. So naturally, with my king-of-the-hill mentality, I just re-devoted myself to LMP and what was left of hardcore.

Easy Street assembled 40 deep, along with our ringleader Santino, for a can't-miss show at Fender's Ballroom in Long Beach. Even Youngblood rounded up his bunch. Hardcores dedicated throughout the southland got the same dispatch. Fender's was packed well beyond what any fire marshal would allow … unless they were on the take. Punks that belonged to gangs were busy collecting their numbers. Packs of 20 increased to 30, then to 40, posting up in various dim-lit corners of the now ramshackle landmark. Each and every one had that glower you front when enemies are surrounding. Play at your own risk, and we all knew the rules.

Agression were headlining, a "Nardcore" band from Oxnard. My ears were either getting more sensitive or it was much louder than usual. You had to yell to get your point across. Cigarette smoke clouded the room from piss-poor ventilation. From the rafters, punks kamikaze-dove on top of the crowd to punish unlucky partisans. Maybe Agression was playing too fast, or their youthful skatepunk disciples were too wound up over their sound ... either way, we had to turn it up. Those of 'em who didn't know LMP's rep absorbed our punitive measures with masochistic glee regardless. You ended up in the pit to avoid being nailed, whether you liked it or not—fine by us. High elbows, horse-collaring, forearms to the face, and open hand strikes. You name it—we pulled out all stops. Pissed Chris was rubbing it in the crowd's face with his arms raised in victory.

"Who wants some? Who wants some?"

Of course, somebody did.

A beach city specimen wearing tan Dickies, Suicidal hat, and no shirt decided to throw a sideways jab at Pissed Chris. He missed, hitting Santino right in the kisser, then disappeared into the imposing crowd. I took in Santino's anger up close. He was stuck in time as the world around moved on. Santino's jaw clenched, nostrils flared like an unbroken animal, and his eyes darted at light speed as he tried to locate the messenger. I knew what was coming. Santino pulled two screwdrivers from his jacket and walked inside the pit. In short time I lost sight of both him and the prize. After the pit cycled around several rotations, Santino reappeared, sidewinding his way out of the fray, breathing heavy, tucking himself next to Popeye and me.

"Got that cheapshot fuck in both sides."

We searched the pit and at the same time braced for retaliation from Suicidal gang.

Pissed Chris guffawed at the top of his lungs, "No you didn't, look over there!"

We turned our heads to the action and sure enough, the shirtless Suey was skanking and goofing around with his pals. Santino showed me his hands; one held a screwdriver, the other was empty.

"Man, this is bullshit! I lost my dad's screwdriver in there for nothin!"

Possibly killing an innocent punk didn't even register. His face contorted in a memorable way I'd never seen before. The panic. The loss.

"He's gonna be mad as hell if he don't have it back—that's all he's got!" Santino exploded.

He jammed back into the unruliness; Pissed Chris immediately followed. Like paratroopers, we all jumped in. For that fastidious foot in time, LMP were unstoppable. Losing The Godfather's tool was something we all consciously agreed couldn't happen.

–Elbow to the cheek.

"Fuck you!"

–Short right hook to the chin, down he goes …

"Die fucker!"

–One-two to the chest and jaw.

"Who's next?"

–Head-butt down on the nose, blood inside and out!

We kicked punks left laying in our wake. That screwdriver was on the floor somewhere. It didn't matter; our moment had achieved a higher plane—high on violence. Family, respect, honor, brotherhood, being top dog, finding that tool, and wasting everyone around us symbolized LMP's entire existence. The casualties had no clue, probably figured it was time to get out of punk rock. Good times for everybody else in the scene were long gone and they weren't coming back … Que Sera, Sera.

The scene became a punk rock Vietnam; everybody had enough and wanted out, except the ones who couldn't let go. That was us. Our undeveloped minds had two ways of looking at our violent behavior: to most LMPs it was a joke, and blood definitely the punch line; the others merely treated it as sport.

Popeye went so far as to suggest, "Every time an LMP knifes, beats, or shoots somebody, they should get a patch like the biker gangs do."

Santino wasn't ready for all that.

"Forget that shit—we shoot, stab, and kill so much, there'd be no room on our jackets. Leave merit badges to the Boy Scouts."

Every gang worth their weight has at least one marquee player, all-star, difference-maker, or game changer. On the streets we called them legends while they were still active, performing feats of skill and brute force weekly. Witnessing these moments go down were just as thrilling as being at the ballpark for a no-hitter, or a walk-off home run. I was blessed enough to be playing the game while five street legends were in their prime—three were from LMP, one from Long Beach, and one from CV3.

Sailor and Mongo were both similar in size, technique, and skill level. Main difference was Mongo wouldn't level guys smaller than him, unless attacked. There was no action in it. For Sailor it didn't matter, he enjoyed combat all the same. Small opponents were "batting practice" as he called it. Sailor was a classic bully, and, as a rule, only fought drunk.

What set Santino apart was his hair-trigger ruthlessness, speed, and a willingness to shoot, stab, or gruesomely beat someone to horrifying degrees without hesitation. He was also known as the "Tool Box Murderer" after seeing the horror film where a maniac killed people with the contents of his toolbox.

"Bit by bit ... by bit he carved a nightmare."

MAD MANNY,
HOLDING DOWN THE
NEIGHBORHOOD

Santino pointed out, "Some tools are good for killing, others just for inflicting pain, and you can't get arrested for having a screwdriver or a hammer."

City of Long Beach had Tony Vermin. He wasn't especially big, but was hard-bitten, and uncompromising as they came. He had a rat tattooed on his arm, and a third eye emblazoned on the side of his head. Vermin swore he could see out of it when he fought. He also used to drum for LBC's Red Beret, though it took a back seat to his strong-arm comedy. Second time I ran into him in 1982, he was wearing a weird top hat and bell bottoms, leaning against a wall.

"Tony, what the fuck is that getup?"

Vermin wisecracked back, "I'm waitin' for somebody to say something smart about my stupid clothes, so I can fuck 'em up."

Tony Vermin achieved his legend status at the Vex nightclub, where he threw down with five bouncers, and dropped one after another, after another, with the final two getting the worst of it. He wasn't LMP, but ran with us for years. Vermin and Sailor were best pals in the early days, when they fought side by side; you didn't even have to put your beer down … they crushed all contestants.

And finally, there was Mad Manny, whom I considered to be the highest level of that lot, 6'2", 270 pounds, and veteran of the CV3 Tinys. Manny was smothered in black-and-grey tattoos, and handled business on Easy Street before he went away to prison. If it didn't come from The Godfather, it came from him. They saw eye to eye and respected one another immensely. Manny was a fundamental part of the colorful CV3 crew that dressed in 1930s suits, trench coats, and fedoras. The Tinys stood shoulder to shoulder with us at punk gigs when CV3 joined forces with LMP in the original days of hardcore. Mad Manny put his own twist on how to broadcast street power.

GANGSTER'S PARADISE, FRANK IN FEDORA.

"Shoot at anybody full-auto, at any time—for whatever."

Manny was a scary guy who scared scary people. Now he was out of prison and back on the streets. Manny undisputedly enjoyed punk rock music, whether or not he looked the part.

He would commonly tell me, "I love the way it makes me feel."

LMP & CV3 threw him a Welcome Home party at Santino's house on Easy Street. What a great night it was for everybody. Uninterrupted R&B jams were spinning right after punk records, one after the other. Cholos laced on sherm, mixed with punks warped on fry or shitty kitchen coke, while neighborhood cholas were cross-pollinating with city and suburban types, doing the freak. Gangster's paradise.

Mad Manny was up to something and waved Santino and me over to the front window. A suitcase rested against his leg. He opened the window and pointed down Santino's driveway.

"Look at Tops. Homes is fuuuucked up, ay…?"

Tops, one of the CV3 soldiers, stood wobbly at the edge of Santino's half-cement/half-dirt driveway. Tops smoked his cigarette in an effort to keep from falling flat on his face. I chuckled mildly. This was nothing new.

Manny opened the black box, brandished his AK-47, and stuck it out the window yelling, "Dance, you pinche pilgrim! Dance!!"

Manny squeezed multiple machine-gun bursts near Tops' feet, ricocheting noisy bullet clusters off the concrete. I spit-showered my drink at the calamity, finding it hard to catch my breath. What was this new level of sadistic humor? Tops double-timed it. He jumped and stomped like an electrocuted marionette while Manny directed his rhythm…

"Dance, Tops! Dance!! Yeeehah!!!"

As the clip emptied, the party patrons froze speechless.

"Should I reload for an encore?" Manny questioned.

I reined in my laughter when The Godfather stepped forward.

"No, Manny. This is a cruel and pointless game going nowhere."

Tops didn't find it funny, nor did the other CV3 vets standing right out of Manny's range. Nor did the off-duty Norwalk sheriff, who momentarily stopped by for a beer and small talk with his CV3 cousin. Regardless of Manny's antics, the sheriff humbly got in his car and drove off.

I was vet'd out at that point and realized why the sheriff didn't draw down or call for backup. It made perfect sense. He knew exactly where he was and what could happen. That sheriff understood he could easily get smoked, become a missing person, and nobody on the block would say shit. Cops, who were raised in or patrolled these formidable neighborhoods, also knew the rules.

Mad Manny was gun-happy and that was that. Most accepted this and just made sure to stay behind his gun. His rep, however, couldn't reach every natural rival, avowed enemy, or cursed fool. As fate would have it, these dynamics somehow played out nearly every instance we hung together.

I was quietly catching up after work with Mad Manny on Santino's porch. A cherry '52 Chevy came driving down our block, cranking Art Laboe jams beyond speaker capacity. The car was moving at a suspicious five miles an hour through the fog and dark. Manny disappeared inside the house, while I took cover behind a hedge. I ducked down right as the car creeped up. VLM, Carmellas, or South Side Whittier, looking to get some type of payback on CV3, was just part of the business. The music got louder as the car slowed down, right in front of me, almost coming to a complete stop. I buried myself even lower, held my breath, and waited for the lead to start flying.

Where the fuck was Manny and why wasn't he shooting?

I felt the sweat arrive under my arms and brow at an accelerated pace. What was I thinking, hiding behind a bush?

Did I just get got?

Was this it?

These guys were just as ruthless as us and obviously came to make a statement.

Fuck!

Could I make it into the house if I bob and weave? Guess I had to go for it.

I counted one ... two ... on three ... the music faded, and the car pulled away. Holy shit, they didn't see me.

Before I could even smile, Mad Manny marched past me, walking tall and pulling the lever into lock position on his AK-47. He stopped in the middle of our street, carefully shouldered his firearm, and then unloaded his full 30 clip...

Brrrraappp! –Brrrraappp! –Brrrraappp!

Bullets showered the car, obliterated the rear window, and painted holes across the trunk. We stared and waited in anticipation for the smoke to clear. Somehow, the Chevy miraculously kept putting along, dripping bits of glass until it reached the end of our cul-de-sac and started to turn around.

"What the...?" we both said out loud while reverse-stepping.

Distorted doo-wop tunes again got louder as the '52 lurched its way back to us.

Manny turned tail and bolted toward the side yard, yelling back to me, "No más! All out of bullets!"

But I was already past him, holding the gate open.

I wasn't in the dying mood.

Sure retribution from the vatos in the Chevy was mere car lengths away. I peeked through the wooden planks in the fence and guessed bullet caliber, rate of return fire, and possible shooters.

My heart was pumping, pumping.

The Godfather was gonna be pissed if they shot out his windows and doors ... again.

Come on already, let's get the show on the road.

"Oh, little darlin' Oh, little darlin'
Oh-oh-oh where ar-are you?
My love-a I was wrong-a
(la-la-la-la-la-la)
To-oo try To lo-ove
two
A-hoopa, a-hoopa, hoopa
Kno-ow well-a
That my love-a (la-la-la-la-la-la)
Wa-as just fo-or you Ooooonly yooooooooooooou."

Lo and behold, all it was, was this old VLM cholo, with his eyes barely open, whacked out on angel dust. Bits of interior were floating about his car while he moseyed along with no idea of what just happened. This guy was so dusted, he thought he was cruising Whittier Boulevard on a Friday night. How one bullet fired can accidentally kill an infant but 30 shots sprayed from a machine gun misses some drugged-out fool is only God's guess.

MAD MANNY (TOP LEFT) ON THE YARD WITH CV3 MEMBERS, CHINO STATE PRISON, 1981–82.

Manny's father was a half-Italian/half-American Indian from one of the oldest Great Plains tribes. He was semi-nomadic in nature, much like his ancient brethren, traversed the world as a pro wrestler, and eventually won a championship during the 1960s. Mad Manny Senior walked his own cross-country trail of tears, impregnated women, and married two prostitutes. In the aftermath, one put a .357 slug into his head. Too close to grey matter, doctors opted to leave it there. Unfortunately, he was subject to savage fits during lightning storms.

The city of Prescott, Arizona was hit with an unrelenting flash electrical storm on a night Mad Manny Senior was passing through. Story goes that he looked to the sky and started to speak in ancient tongues. He then stripped naked, punched a storefront window out, grabbed a spear from one of those tourist shops, and ran off into the hills.

He was back in the ring a week later and when asked about it he declared, "This is ALL my land and if I wish to go camping ... I go camping."

His bizarre odyssey finished in Las Vegas, where he worked as an outfit's leg-breaker at the Jolly Trolley Casino.

Mad Manny's shooting spree continued.

The CV3 shot-callers knew he was in the zone and figured, "Time for a drive-by."

Someone from Easy Street stole a nondescript sedan and gave me the keys. I brought a ski mask along and a backup pistol. Manny had his AK-47 stashed in the black box suitcase. I had no compunction about stabbing, shooting, or helping to kill chosen enemies. These were privileges bestowed by guys I would have done time for, or them me. Individuals held in such high regard were becoming few and far between, so I jumped at the chance. The LMP rank and file had changed considerably. *Mancanza di visione.*

Once we reached our objective and figured our escape route, Manny locked and loaded. I pulled down my ski mask while he made sure his fedora was on straight; Mad Manny liked to be recognized. From three houses away, I killed the lights, slowed the car at two, then on one, my man leaned out, and set free a full-auto burst that sent our opponents darting for cover.

The AK's sound was so distinct, so loud ... that's why they invented earplugs.

Mad Manny dumped off the rest of his clip on the neighbors' houses during our getaway, just because they lived near those roaches.

Many of these inspired moments of enthusiasm were outside gang protocol. Talk of Manny's exploits and possible reprisals bombarded the CV3 veterans, turning it into a touchy situation, not to mention the wasted ammo.

"Bullets don't grow on trees, Homes...."

Those guys got sick of continually being on the lookout and staying indoors, when it was good times outside.

"Let us borrow your cuete, bro?"

Manny figured it was coming right back and gave it up.

After sitting in juvie for months, Mongo finally got sentenced right around his 18th birthday. He caught another break. Three felony assaults with a deadly weapon charge and an enhancement of great bodily injury. Punishment: a six-year stint in Susanville. Mongo got a sweet plea deal for someone local cops thought was going away for life on an easy open-and-shut case. The autopsy got him off the hook, without some pricey downtown lawyer. The D.A. couldn't prove stab wounds from his knife killed the victim outright. All of Mongo's new pals, who were stabbing away that night, proved useful. "Any one of them could have been the maniac responsible," as the public defender put it.

Pissed Chris, on the other hand, didn't get so lucky. I was running out of friends quick. He got ID'd by an informant, and arrested for attempted murder for stabbing two longhairs. Pissed Chris stabbed so many people, it was hard to keep track of who was being knifed and why, but I'm sure he had good reasons.

Mongo and Pissed Chris' game of violence had ended before we could reach Helter Skelter. With those two gone ... punk rock lost out. Oh the times of change.

MONGO (LEFT) ON THE YARD, SUSANVILLE.

THE LAST DAYS OF CATHAY DE GRANDE.
ARTWORK BY DAVID MICHAEL BRANDT.

raduation came. Too bad I stopped going to school a month into my final year. Regardless of Mr. Bloom's persistence, it was too much of a drag; making good money selling weed and working full-time sounded a lot better. At the tinting shop, I would "accidentally" leave a joint or a bud in cars, to tip off customers that I was also the guy to see when it came to green. It worked mostly every time, and I was completely under my boss' radar. Being a legit businessman and devout Christian, he would not have tolerated it. I was saving for my own pad and had to try to get ahead.

Pissed Chris had an apartment for a little while and said, "It makes a big difference if you want pussy anytime, day or night."

He gave his girlfriend the key, and then got caught fucking someone else a month later when she walked in on him using her new key. The day before the cops rounded him up, she wrote "LIAR" in pink lipstick, red markers, and even in her own blood, on nearly every visible surface and object in the entire place.

"She must have been at it for 24 hours straight," he later explained in one of his many prison letters to me.

When the arresting officers took him away, they actually sympathized with him, saying "Maybe it's a good thing you're going up for a while; she'd probably end up offing you from the looks of it."

I made money and made women, pretty much whenever I felt the itch, but that one thing I had to look forward to was evaporating. Most bands I had respected, and made sure never to miss, looked and sounded like they were moving on from hardcore. Discharge sounded like trash rock, 45 Grave went metal, T.S.O.L. turned art-punk, 7Seconds got super-soft, Black Flag was a heap of stupid noise, and even Glenn Danzig started a new band called Samhain, which was plain off in left field. True hardcore punk shows were a relic from the past.

Out of desperation, Mad Manny and I decided to go see Tex and the Horseheads, playing with Legal Weapon, at the Stardust Ballroom in Hollywood. We had a serious thing for singer Texacala Jones. Girls copied her trippy eye makeup but never looked half as hot. Their music was part of the ridiculous cowpunk scene: a blend of country and punk, where everyone looked like Billy Jack meets heroin. We stood up front and perved out on Tex the whole set, while her crowd gave us the weirdo treatment. Those Hollywood snobs acted like Manny and me were from Planet Loser. Manny was beside himself. Stardust Ballroom had no action, and Manny was starting to get extra fucked up. He drank the same 12 or so beers, piggybacked with matching shots of tequila, but normally sweated it out going hard in the pit. The next band in the lineup was unlistenable, so we embraced the exit.

Manny and I walked the boulevard for blocks, trying to shake off our disgust for that crowd, and for everybody in Hollywood's current lack of intensity—a bunch of pretenders, strung out on their own look. We walked aimlessly, with much lighter pockets. Manny was still mad and suggested we go the fuck back to our neighborhood.

On the way down the 5 freeway, Manny jerked my steering wheel, putting us on the Long Beach 710 headed south.

"Let's roll a crack dealer."

What could I do but smile as I added exhaust to the already exhausted Maywood, South Gate, and Lynwood. Manny chambered his Ruger .22 auto when bad news tapped me on the shoulder, calling for us to exit.

East Alondra Boulevard, East Compton, I lit a cigarette, busted a right on Atlantic Avenue, then down a side street with no name. The unmanicured trees made it extra dark, masking the moon. We crawled past what looked like a hookup spot, shadowy figures and all. Manny suggested we pull over down the street and walk up.

We quickly went over our approach as we legged up the sidewalk toward the dealer.

"Whassup, whatcha need?" vocalized the hooded salesman.

"Rock," I pitched.

He looked closely at Manny and me, searching for details with some kind of extrasensory street sight.

"I got rocks—whatcha want?"

I reached deep into my pocket and retrieved a few bills. Clenching my hand, I proceeded to fork over the money, but dropped it at his feet at the last minute.

He gave me an unforgettable look of "Who the fuck you think I am?" that I'll never ever forget, took two measured steps back, and showed us he was packing.

"Pick that shit up!"

Manny knew the dealer was on to us and tried to play it off.

"You're blowing it, ese—pick it up."

I knew I also had to say something or that dealer was gonna walk ... or even worse, yell for his boys ... or far worse—start blastin'.

orry man, I'm just nervous," I put out for safety, as I went down on one knee to pick up the cash. The dealer took his eye off me to watch Manny. We were in deep. I had to take advantage of his misjudgment. I swiftly pulled my butterfly with one hand, pushed off with the other, and sunk my steel into his stomach. There was a pause of recognition. Stuck in mid-gesture, he tried to reach but nothing happened. Manny pushed him to the ground and fired two shots into his upper body. I watched the guy fall asleep while we went through his pockets. No tomorrow.

We ran back to the car and got the hell out as fast as humanly possible. Right when I was about to turn off the street our back window exploded from gunfire.

"Get down!" Mad Manny warned as he shot back.

The neighborhood lookout obviously made us. I felt my car take another hit as we rounded the corner to safety. I punched it to the freeway entrance, leaving the war zone behind. Manny jumped in the back and knocked out the rest of the window so cops wouldn't notice.

We got back to the neighborhood, covered my car with a tarp, and decided to count our score. I got close to $300 in small bills. Manny got another $100 and a nice bag of crack.

Manny's first words to me in over a half-hour were, "Hey, you're bleeding."

I felt the back of my left shoulder and realized he was correct. The pain came rushing in at that very instant. Manny took me inside a CV3 soldier's house where he was staying. We both gave my shoulder the once-over and were quick to discern a piece of glass must have hit me. No big deal. Manny got some supplies from the medicine cabinet and helped me with the cleanup and bandage.

After an earned amount of alcohol, I had to lay my head down and go to bed. Two sides to every shank, but more often than not, somebody gets my point.

innamon Roll Gang C.R.G. was a fake gang tag born out of the 1981 war we were having with Destructive Youth Gang D.Y.G. of Orange County. Youngblood and I ridiculed their limp-wristed name to the point of obsession, and ultimately decided to cross out their graffiti with the most sissy gang name possible—Cinnamon Roll Gang. We spray-painted Cinnamon Roll Gang, plus CRG, and a cinnamon roll symbol at every venue and hangout spot from OC to Errol Flynn's, until Youngblood and I were placed at Frontier High. There we met members of an actual CRG, Whittier's Canta Ranas Gang. It was time to quit that gag before someone in the real CRG got offended.

The Cinnamon Roll Gang's first reunion was actually going to happen—with me and my people from the days of old: Youngblood, Chemo, Stormin' Normin, Scary Sherry, and Sickness. Sure, I've seen some of them in passing or individually over the last two or three years, but now everyone was making a concerted effort to assemble, like some kind of holiday or to honor someone lost. I always held a soft spot for our little clique that was in on the joke. Everyone had drifted away through circumstance or fell off completely.

Youngblood's T-street crew disbanded after Mongo's murder incident. Turns out they were the young ones stabbing on Mongo's behalf. None cooperated with police; nevertheless, most got spooked out of the life, while the rest were absorbed into other LMP chapters. Without a crew to run, Youngblood's time became divided between his girlfriend, and people outside the gang like Mike McIntosh from LWP.

Chemo made new friends out in the Long Beach area once Fender's became a hotspot. These guys were a collective of "in it to win it" Irish crystal-meth dealers, and not your ordinary punk rock gangsters. Much like us, none had any qualms about killing, but their lack of sleep made them unpredictable company. A mutual love for speed was starting to suck Chemo in.

Stormin' Normin's emotional meltdowns increased in severity. Whenever an episode occurred, his folks had him locked up at the ding module that had so often housed Magnum. This condition arose more and more, making him uncommunicative and paranoid. I was sure he didn't have long before they zonked him out on meds full-time.

All three girls—Sickness, Scary Sherry, and Donna the Dead—developed no-nonsense drug issues. Sickness moved back with her mother in La Mirada, unable to keep afloat. Scary Sherry relocated a couple hours northeast to evade any kind of fast crowd while in detox. The exact location of Donna the Dead was unknown. "The Car" sat and deteriorated on cinder blocks in Sickness' mom's driveway, a most unfitting end for Lucifer's Limousine. I always hoped it would somehow spontaneously combust when Satan wanted it back. Instead, we corralled inside Scary Sherry's family wagon with extra windows. Not a chariot fit for kings and queens, but it had to do.

Hollywood here we come, back where it all made sense ... back where we belonged. Sickness broke out a community bag of mushrooms and we all gobbled the grams. I choked the dirty mold down with Sunny Delight to mask the awful taste and to activate their psychedelic properties. They tasted a whole lot worse than I remembered or re-imagined. How could hippie Deadheads stand it? Mushroom residue had poisoned everyone's taste buds except Sickness', of course. She still enjoyed anything gross out of principle. It was weird seeing her without Vitamin Ena though. He had taken off to NYC to chase his music career. The rest of us kept pounding vodka mixed with juice until we exited the 101. Scary Sherry missed the shortcut to Lhasa Club and got us stuck in bumper-to-bumper congestion on Sunset.

My fry trip began coming on as our car inched up the boulevard. Stormin' Normin's face had transformed into the Riddler from the original Batman, but instead of the question mark on his green leotard, it was smack center across his face. I guess the rest saw what I saw, or something even funnier, because the whole car was in tears. Reaching the stoplight provided a transition from the green villain. Each split second moved to a new trance, more captivating, more consuming than the last. An undiscerning buzz sound came into play. A motorcycle was coming toward us. My perspective switched to a frame-by-frame of the motorbike rider—blip–blip–blip–blip—as Scary Sherry started to turn left.

BOOOM!

The bike pilot struck our car head on and got ejected. He went flying—blip –blip –blip –blip—floating overhead.

His face freeze-framed above our windshield, his mouth was wide open, and his drool hovered an inch away. The terror was surreal ... then flew on by.

A shared "Ooooooh!" came from everyone inside, signaling true psycho-tropic entertainment.

Within seconds the accident evaporated from conscience, and we continued going forward, flipping the dial on our TV screen. The hit-and-run channel was over.

Our characterless vehicle provided safe passage across town while we continued to soak it all up. Scary Sherry found a neighborhood parking spot a short hike from our destination. Inside the Lhasa Club was for me a realization that Hollywood was filled with soulless ghouls who came to feed off the energy of the living. Where their eyes were supposed to be were dark holes that led to nothing. They walked around and pretended to have fun.

Drinking, dancing, fucking.

I could see the lie. I had to tell my friends the truth.

Where were they?

I found myself staring into a broken mirror in a disgusting bathroom.

My eyes were also gone.

I was them … subhuman.

Time to leave.

I pushed my way through the club straight out the front door. My crew was already outside waiting for me.

They had eyes.

We were off to Errol Flynn's to cool down. On the way back to our car, an automatic garage door opened like a curtain at a movie house, stopping us dead in our tracks. A woman, dressed like a man, wearing only a fake mustache and construction hat, was having passionate sex in the bed of a parked 4x4 with an old man in a Daisy Duke outfit, pigtailed wig included.

They froze.

We pointed.

The man-girl in the farmer's daughter getup jumped to his feet and frantically tried to get the door shut.

He couldn't.

"Turn the lights off then!" yelled Stormin' Normin.

Up at Errol's we drank beers and reminisced of times past as our trip subsided. I spray-painted a cinnamon roll symbol one last time for memories. This would be the last occasion we were all together. Trying to relive the old days was fun and all, but it sure didn't feel like old times. Those days were gone.

CHAPTER 17
"HOLY PIG"

I felt enough time had passed without suspicion for me to take my shot-up car into work. Before leaving, I painted a piece of duct tape the same color as my car, to hide the bullet hole on the rear quarter panel, and then drove directly to work. The glass company we dealt with sent a guy over to replace my back window. I told him the kids on my street were playing base-ball—blah blah blah.

My boss Indian and his old crime partner Grease were scoping my ride the whole time. Grease did a long prison stretch with my boss in the early '70s. They remained best of friends ever since. Indian warmly regarded his pal as "smelliest man in the joint, hands down." He refused to take showers; no one guy, or guard, had the balls to force cleanliness on him. Grease's stench got so bad someone hung a sign above his cell that read "SHOWER HOMES." He left it hanging there until they paroled him.

Grease was a lethal giant and known independent contract killer. He was currently trying to beat a first-degree murder case for killing a coke dealer that happened to be the son of Colleen Campbell, former mayor of San Juan Cap-istrano. Grease liked to chit-chat and told me he was hired by the guy's boss to kill him for skimming money. Time to clean house. All three—Grease, the boss, and the man with a price on his head—were flown out near Catalina Island in a small twin-engine plane to do a deal. Grease posed as the buyer, but instead of buying, he snapped that guy's neck and tossed him into the ocean.

He said the setup and hit "went like butter; body was never found, but that mother of his won't leave it be!"

She used her accumulated power to get someone to eventually talk, which turned out to be the pilot. Colleen Campbell used that same tenacity to later solve the contract killing of her racing impresario brother, Mickey Thompson, and his wife. Both were gunned down in front of their home in Bradbury, Cali-fornia. At present, the D.A. was arranging the pilot's plea deal, while putting the screws to Grease. His slim prospects at beating the rap were definitely wearing him out.

After the repairman replaced my back window, Grease walked straight to the taped-over bullet hole and tore it off.

"Somebody egg you with bullets, Frank? This is some amateur shit here. Saw it a mile away. You better bondo this clean if you wanna stay free, young brother."

My boss nodded along, expecting some kind of explanation from me. Indian was a devout Christian who never judged nor preached. If you had a question regarding religion, he would give you his best explanation in a way I could understand, not that scary, holier-than-thou, biblical babble.

"You want some peace? I got the hookup, I know somebody that can help you with that," was his favorite saying.

I told him a kind of half-truth about how I just drove down the wrong block. Indian had an ace bullshit-detector and the way he looked at me said, "You failed."

GREASE, PART-TIME COWBOY, FULL-TIME HITTER.

The Breakfast Club was a sham all along. I knew it. That was our pet name for San Fernando Valley's Fight For Freedom punk gang. Just like those kids in the movie: middle-class brats with sensitive teenager problems. FFF claimed recently in an *L.A. Times* exposé that we were one of their many enemies. Yeah, sure we were. In the article, they tried to take credit for what we had accomplished: the gang wars, the fear we spread, the power, the blood. Truth was, we rarely noticed FFF in Hollywood. Their crew tried to avoid LMP at all cost.

Not even a year ago, some FFF got all worked up when his disco platform creepers were made fun of inside Gino's/Electric Circus nightclub. Three LMPs were merely having a goof. Later that night, one of our soldiers wandered outside and got jumped by four FFF guys, backed by another outfit called the Ducky Boys. Both crews had no idea they were ambushing an LMP. There were too many to fend off; our soldier got roughed up pretty good. He managed to get loose and return to dish out justice with the two other LMPs, plus a tire iron. Knowing cops were surely on their way, my guys hopped inside a female LMP's revved-up-and-ready Dodge Dart. She punched her pedal, jumped onto the sidewalk, and ran over the four from FFF as they tried to flee. Bones cracked as screams of great bodily harm echoed down Santa Monica Boulevard. Three went to the hospital on stretchers.

FFF supposedly clashed with Suicidal from time to time according to rumor. Another Valley gang, more in their bracket, called BPO Burbank Punk Organization, were their rival. I guess they used to get it on over the hill.

Today, the Breakfast Club made headlines, crime scene photo and all.

Slaying a sign of the times: Mark Miller, ranking member of FFF, shot in head and killed outside Valley nightclub Hot Trax. Scrawled in blood next to his body were large letters, FFF.

The victim's father was quoted: "I knew it would happen before it happened, Los Angeles is changing. It's violent. It's become a very violent city."

A 16-year-old Asian kid showed Miller who was more gangster, and shot him in the back of the head with a .38. FFF finally got the fame they were looking for.

Mad Manny ran out of patience while waiting to get his machine gun back. He achieved little fulfillment by trying to ponder all the enemies it X'd-out in someone else's hands. Manny finally got wind that his AK-47 had been collecting dust since the CV3 vets "borrowed" it. They were still uneasy with his unpredictable shooting practices. On cue came Manny's rebuttal.

"This ain't some lightweight game I'm putting down. It's the only way."

The vets respectfully said "No."

Without a gun, Manny was a rudderless ship. He had to burn his .22 after the Compton incident.

Now a Ronin, Mad Manny somehow ended up in Orange County. He circled up and down the coast in an attempt to draw peace from the ocean. While sitting at a traffic signal, Manny witnessed an amateur crook snatch a lady's designer purse. The crook nabbed it right from her clutches and hopped into his partner's getaway truck. Manny swerved his car in hot pursuit. A mile into the chase, Manny jumped a lane and rammed his car into theirs. The force of his car sent the snatchers' truck into a disastrous roll; their momentum landed them upside down on somebody's front lawn. Manny's vehicle was still running, but wouldn't move. His front fender had bent down into his tire. He hastily abandoned his car, and left the crashed purse-snatchers to explain.

Later that night, Mad Manny had us in stitches as he recounted what went down. He made his escape via limping to a bus stop and working a free ride by lying to an RTD driver about how his walking cane fell down a drainage ditch. When he got home, Manny called his car in stolen.

"They got my car, man, those *pinche miates*!"

Mad Manny never let anybody fuck with a woman of any age. That was his breaking point. Good thing he never saw Captain Out of Hand in action.

A couple three days later, Manny wanted his car back and didn't feel comfortable getting gouged for that costly storage, on top of tow fees. Next thing I knew, I was driving him into deep Orange County, 3 a.m., dead of the night. I parked and before I could say anything, he jumped out with a crowbar and a pair of old bolt cutters. Five minutes later, Manny came flying around the corner, flashing his high beams, waving for me to follow. I couldn't suspend my disbelief of what just happened. This guy just stole his own car back from a police impound yard and didn't even bat an eyelash, then stopped for coffee and doughnuts only a mile away.

Manny really didn't need his car. He was usually too jacked up to drive anyway. What he did need was his trusted AK-47. Some of the guys said he slept with it under his pillow. Lost without it. Getting his gun back was going to require finesse and politicking, versus his usual strong-arm tactics. Manny knew he couldn't verbally abuse a CV3 vet. This matter had to go upstairs, higher than the vets.

Angel was in power.

Second in charge of CV3 was his brother and underboss, Paco.

Mad Manny brought the issue to them, explained his dire need for the machine gun, and a long list of fools that needed to get wasted. The CV3 vets pitched the same old rebuttal.

"Manny's too dangerous with that thing!"

A verdict got handed down right away.

Paco told the vets, "Fuck off ... Mad Manny holds down the neighborhood better than any of you dudes ever did."

The gun got returned, no questions asked, and another shooting spree was in the works.

I turned 18 and I was addicted to gang banging—who takes the blame? I needed it the same way the hype needs his shot.

Guns had become as easy to get as knives. My new source was an original PJ Watts Crip from the Blood-infested Nickerson Gardens project. His name was Ronelle, a military ex-con who did a stint in Leavenworth. I'm still not at liberty to say how we met. He sold us dirty pieces for dirt cheap that were left over from the Blood/Crip conflict in Watts. It was a big-time connection for my crew and a great way to make a quick buck, but I always preferred my knife.

Santino wasn't around much; he was too busy making babies, and hardly ever attended what few worthwhile shows were left in the scene. His house, and father, still served as our home base and mentor. I was covering all fronts in Santino's absence and just brought in a new soldier to the Easy Street regime named Check. Check used to run with the young ones from Belcher Street, six feet tall, half-inch shaved hair, tattooed, trademark Dr Martens, and above that, crazy loyal. Not only would he put younger punks in check when needed, Check would consistently rob checkbooks from his relatives, and sell them to the highest bidder. His loyalty didn't exactly extend to his family. Also, a new LMP member from another chapter was laying low with us for blasting some rival gangster in the face with a shotgun. Dude was funny as hell, always boning fat chicks, and when you hit him up about it, he habitually said the same thing.

"Ah man, just a slump-buster."

He was very musically on top of it and even played Manny and me the new English Dogs album. It was a far cry from punk. Matter of fact, the record was pure fucking speed metal. Any metal was just another flimsy excuse to grow your hair long and wear tight pants. It stood for nothing.

CV3 handed down a contract to me, personally. I was to carry out a drive-by on their neighboring rival; they'd provide the hardware, car, and exact location. Frank the Shank was more than up to the task, Check jumped at the chance for wheelman duties. I emptied a high-powered mini-14 clip all along the front side of my designated target home. Every single shot nailed it. Divine glass shards and sparks flashed all over. Check was outstanding, easy pedal on approach, sound acceleration during the cut and run. We ditched the car and were home safe in La Mirada within a matter of minutes. I made the confirmation phone call.

"Damn Homes, you guys don't waste any time...."

The thrill, however, came and went too quick. It was a perfect time to pay a cordial visit to some more LMP enemies. Check had a personal message he wanted to send, so without hesitation, we stole his mother's Volvo and got back on the road. A favor for a favor, this time I drove. Check guided us to his place of interest, then opened fire and lit up the front door with precision. Two blocks away, I turned into a semi-busy intersection, and stopped at a red light—right next to a fucking pig. Check still had the assault rifle sitting on his lap with no time to stash it. I did a surprised double take and the officer saw it.

Play it cool, Frank … play it cool.

Somehow I conjured up the balls to correct my nervousness and gave the officer a "You're doing a great job" nod of approval. After a million minutes, the light turned green, and he drove off in a hurry. Damn … he bought it.

We still had bullets and still more enemies. Fuck it, one more for the road. I drove small streets, and made as many turns as possible, just to be smart. Check ducked down in case there was a report of two shooters at large. Hyper-manic, my adrenaline was howling out of control.

You better watch out—I'll cut your fucking head off!

I pointed the target house out, and Check started busting shots…

POP –POP –POP –POP –POP!

We hit our target, plus a cluster of innocent apartment buildings. Oh well, those are the breaks, three drive-bys in under an hour. Message sent.

Better think twice before you look at me crazy—you motherfuckers!

My adrenaline lasted all night and kept me sleepless into the next morning, all the way to work. I was still a ticking time bomb. Indian handed me a cup of coffee and a breakfast burrito the moment I pulled into the parking lot.

"How's the neighborhood hot dog doing this morning? You doing good Frank?"

All my psycho-energy flipped on its axis to that calm space Indian inhabited.

"Sure boss, on time, and ready to work."

His calm had a way of seeping into your whole being. He had something I didn't.

The newest contender in the punk scene was a crew from OC called Pig Children. They also got their name from a band they followed and wanted what we always demanded—respect. Pig Children boasted more followers than actual gang members on their active roster. Sound familiar? They started throwing punk rock parties at a park in OC on Sunday nights, where different bands like Final Conflict, HVY DRT, Sacred Hatred, and Pig Children would play for free. The venue was gaining a crowd with other punk gangs from the area, like The League from Buena Park and a couple others we never paid any mind to. It was time for LMP to make an appearance.

Santino, our pimp-killing pal The Governor, and I decided to grace them with our presence—no need for numbers. After scamming on a few filthy chicks and drinking their beer, we decided to slam. People began whispering and looking in our direction, right on schedule.

All three of us doled out abuse to everyone in the pit until the band took a song break. Pig Children's crew gathered off on the side and began to demonstrate all the prelude symptoms of a good old-fashioned rumble. Now it was their turn to do something.

A new song revved up and the pit got re-energized. The three of us stood at the side and waited for their best shot. Pig Children's core soldiers were posing hard at the opposite edge, while the slam dancing pulsed along. They grabbed one of their fresh young punks, spoke in his ear, and shoved him in. We were dug in at the fringes of the action as the pit-ticipants boot-stomped and arm-flailed their way by. The young punk rookie came toward us, elbows up, ready to send us Pig Children's advisory. Santino easily handled it by arm-shoving the young rookie back inside the stampede, squashing their puny plan. Undeterred, the rookie cycled through and again zeroed in on us. Santino waited patiently. I could read his lips.

"Come to papa, come to papa."

BAM. Lights out!

The rookie punk tasted the dirt hard.

A section of the slam pit abruptly came to a halt and fanned out. Three Pig guys shifted away from their throng, and then another four moved on us, making it seven. Each one was a true Philistine: sizable, smelly, disgusting. Santino pulled his box cutter out and started slicing and dicing at the livestock. The Governor and I were pushing and kicking for space. A few guys ran off bleeding. One Pig Child got hold of Santino, they struggled briefly, but the inevitable always happened ... blood poured.

I counted six slashes to the chest.

The guy's face turned a shameful white, reality set in, and down he went.

"LMP! Want some, get some!"

Everybody backed the fuck up—the great equalizer once again proved its point. Shock seeped in as they surrounded their fallen.

Panic in Pig Park.

Santino, The Governor, and I stood tall—heads cocked back, eyes of evil. This was our show, the main attraction ... if only for a few moments. The Pig Children took an even harder look and realized there were only three of us, with no backup, and started to rally numbers. Next thing we knew, a good 30 or 40 guys became a rush of animals from every direction yelling "Get 'em!"

We went at it.

I dropped one and then two, steady as ever. The Governor was trading bombs and holding his own. Santino nailed a few with his fists then sliced another. Funny thing was, the Pig Children were hitting their own people as much as us. Happens every time you're outnumbered.

The Pig people kept coming and coming—it was time to retreat. We couldn't win and we knew it. Where the fuck were Sailor and Mongo when you needed them?

I pulled my butterfly, hoping to scare off the rest—but they didn't buy it. Out of the corner of my eye, a shiny metal object flashed off the orb of night, and then disappeared into Santino's back. His face showed recognition of clear-cut pain, but he somehow managed to fight off another ... and another.

I saw deep red.

Santino fell to one knee and then dropped out of sight.

Our blood in their water—Fuck that! Another minute and we were going to be in an all-out feeding frenzy.

I got a bead on the instigator calling for more guys to join the storm about to sink us.

He was mine, my special Pig.

I rapidly advanced within striking distance. He saw my knife, but it was too late ... closing time.

I shanked that dirty motherfucker, I stuck him deep, right in his sternum. My knife went right through. He let out a bloodcurdling scream at the top of his Pig lungs, then hit the ground convulsing—must have struck something vital, maybe his liver. His theatrics brought the party to a standstill. The Governor and I grabbed Santino and moved out. They were smart not to follow.

hat night, I lay my head to rest, knowing I did the right thing by saving my brother. But no matter how hard I tried, that screaming would not go away. I even had to turn the radio on to drown it out. No luck. If that guy died, that was the breaks. Those Pig Children should've let us leave and lived to fight another day.

Morning, I woke up to the sound of a car burning rubber out front and—presto, that unearthly scream came back with a splitting headache chaser. The phone started ringing off the hook. After the sixth or seventh series of rings, I threw a pillow and blanket on top to shut it the hell up.

I got a sick feeling inside.

I called Santino's house. No answer. No answer. No answer. Headache. Headaches. Headaches!

Why wasn't anybody picking up?

Why didn't The Godfather answer?

I had to get to Easy Street and figure this thing out. I knew something was wrong.

Wait a minute—what was that?

I tiptoed over to the window and pulled the curtain a millimeter. I saw shadows.

Somebody was there.

Phone wouldn't stop. Pounding on the door—pounding in my head!

I silently made a break for the back window and climbed out. Screw going for my car, how dumb you think I am?

After street-wising my way through the neighborhood, I finally stopped at our local liquor store's pay phone.

Zero change, I dialed zero and said, "collect." Zero, no answer.

"Listen you little brat, give me your bike or I'll kill your whole family!"

The kid dropped his Diamondback and ran off bawling.

I pedaled. Pedaled. Pedaled. My head was thumping. Thumping. Thumping!

I heard a siren behind me and ditched the bike, then jumped over a hedge. False alarm.

Rim was bent—piece of shit!

I tucked my hands in my pocket, tried to stay low, and walked at an accelerated pace—acting like it was all okay.

I finally reached Easy Street, drenched in sweat, and nobody was there.

Doors were locked. Weird....

The neighbor told me the cops came and they had picked up Santino. I nodded and walked away with my head ablaze. They got Santino. I was next.

Rays of light pierced through the soiled clouds overhead and it started pouring rain everywhere.

I had to get out of town. It was time to go ... fun while it lasted.

SANTINO (LEFT), THE
GOVERNOR (MIDDLE),
FRANK (RIGHT),
THROWING-UP LMP.

217.

CHAPTER 18
"10 – 15"

That night I turned myself in. Didn't want the sheriffs kicking my mom's door in. Didn't want a commotion out front for all the neighbors to see. Didn't want to shame my family and, bottom line, I wasn't the running kind.

I caught a ride to jail from this neighborhood girl I knew. The whole way there, I ran through all the possible low-down rats and snitches responsible. Once inside, the detective thanked me for surrendering, then booked me for attempted murder, assault & battery, and some flimsy charge of mutual combat, which made no sense. I mean come on, how is something mutual between guys a crime? With that, I knew law enforcement was trying to lock us up as long as they could. Stab LMP right through the heart. They knew they had the boss and his underboss by the balls. A giant file full of arrests, reports, complaints, and news clippings told our story. They had done their homework: a 10- to 15-year minimum was their planned conclusion.

In 60 minutes flat, Santino had bailed out to the tune of ten grand, 10% of the $100,000 bond, a lot of money for 1985. The Godfather must have drained his account, every penny. The Governor had slipped through the cracks. Police were only looking for two suspects. He didn't stab or slash anyone, but just in case, The Governor knew to disappear for a while. I made my single phone call to, of all people, my father, counting on his expertise in this type of predicament.

"Hey Dad. I'm in big trouble and I wondered if ..."

"You can go to hell, Frank." Click.

Next morning, I sat in a small, hot room handcuffed to a desk, and waited for the investigating detective to question me. That's when it all truly sank in. I was alone. LMP had my back on the streets, but in here it was just me. The detective came in and offered me hot coffee. I passed.

He gave me the prototypical "You really did it this time," and "You're an adult now. We can help you if you help us."

Yeah right.

They were thoroughly confused on who did what, even asking me, "Frank, in all the craziness of that night, isn't it indeed possible you stabbed Santino and they didn't?"

This asshole tried to manipulate the whole situation, thinking I was some chump.

"I want my public defender; I ain't saying a thing!"

He started laughing, as another officer came in the room laughing even harder. "Okay Frank, you got it, but you have no way out this time, you're fucked."

Lying in my cell that night, I found myself thinking of my life. How did I get so cutthroat, so evil, so hardcore? I just turned 18. What the fuck happened? I was totally out of control.

I started thinking of Indian, and what he taught me about peace. Peace of mind. God. I wanted what he had. To walk around knowing it was always going to be okay—no matter what. That nothing could hurt me.

After having my hands in so much bloodshed over the years, I most certainly had it coming. If you shovel shit at the circus, you can't complain about the smell.

I deserved whatever I got.

I didn't have the answers and didn't feel like making it up as I went along anymore. I was done.

It was never a matter of If, but only When.

Now that my time had come to pay up, I didn't want to do it alone.

My gang couldn't do a thing for me anymore.

Next thing I knew, I was down on my knees praying. I didn't ask to be released; that's what every prisoner asks for. Didn't try to strike some half-ass bargain, or promise to end my evil ways if he got me out of this mess. I prayed for forgiveness and forgave those who did wrong to me. I said sorry and made peace. I asked for Christ to be by my side.

Completely exhausted from the stress and release, I dozed off for a while. Slept like I never slept before. I dreamt for the first time in a very long time.

One of the many drunken times Dad forced me out in the backyard to fight, he was adamant. First exchange, Dad caught me with a quick shot to the breadbasket, sending me to the ground.

"Get up. Get yer ass up!

As I attempted to catch my breath, he grabbed me by my shirt, and stood me up to my feet.

"You got better blood in you than that. Come on!"

I took a halfhearted swing at him, missing by a mile. Dad planted and popped a couple jabs, causing me to take a knee. Way out of my league.

"Get to your feet. I'm gonna give you a free one. Aim for my chin!"

He stuck his jaw out. I tried to act uninterested, but put everything I had into my right hand. Dad ducked it, then countered, landing a clean shot to my cheek. I crumpled to the ground for good.

"Let that be a lesson, there's no mercy. None!"

I was stretched out for minutes listening to his rant. My pain was nothing. His eyes were filled with wrath.

"Now get up—Now! Never bow to anyone—Ever! Not even the man upstairs—He wants you to suffer! He wants to see you crawl!!"

I woke up centered with a new kind of focus. Got up ready to face what I had coming. I walked over to my cell door and pushed it open. Something inside told me it was time to go.

I just walked out.

As I strolled down the long corridor toward booking, an officer spoke up: "Hey, hey, hey buddy, I was just coming to release you. Charges were dropped. Wait a minute—how the hell did you get out?"

I smiled to myself knowing, without question, who unlocked my door.

"Guess somebody beat you to it, officer."

The officer shrugged his shoulders and escorted me to a counter. They gave me my wallet and belt back, made me sign a few papers, and released me.

I found the nearest phone and this time called my mom. What was she going to say about all this? She had done so much for me. My mother knew I was trouble, but she had no idea.

"Pick you up soon as I can. Please stay put. I tried not to think the worst, Frankie ... I'm so happy!"

Always could count on her.

I walked a few blocks for cigarettes, tried to figure out how all the charges were dropped. Okay, the guy lived, so why wasn't the D.A. coming after me for attempted murder? It made no sense, but perfect sense.

An hour later, a sedan that I had never seen before pulled up. My senses immediately established the person behind the wheel. My father. He looked me up and down, actually stared me dead in my eyes long enough to make me uncomfortable, then strained out a slight nod.

"Come on. Let's go, son."

We drove.

I deduced it had been over two years of no contact whatsoever. Nothing was said for miles. What could either of us say?

He broke the silence by turning on the radio and asking, "Did they feed you?"

"Yeah, they fed me. Tasted like shit."

After another considerable length of silence, my father pulled to a stop in front of my mom's, and put out his hand.

"Good luck, Frank."

He had a look of poignant agony on his face. Later, I would realize the look he gave me was acknowledgment, coupled with sadness, that I had become what he was ... a killer.

I walked up to my front door, more like floated. My mother heard me coming and opened the door. She hugged me. I knew she also felt responsible for how I turned out.

"It's gonna be okay, mom. It's over."

y first shower in three days felt baptismal. As I was changing my clothes, Mom knocked on the bathroom door.

"Somebody would like to talk to you, Frankie."

Mom handed me the phone and I said hello.

"I remember a young boy who used to take care of my dog and steal all my nudie magazines and tape the pictures all over his wall. Now I hear you have naked women tattooed all over you."

I was floored. On the line was my father's old employer at Lads Trucking Company, back in those days a "Capo," then underboss of the L.A. mafia: Sam Sciortino.

"I know it's a little late, Frank, but happy birthday, I owed your father a few. Now we're even. Try and keep your nose clean, at least for your mother's sake. Now go get yourself a steak or a hooker."

AFTERMATH
"NON-FILTER TRUTH"

TOO MANY PEOPLE DIED AT THE HANDS of punk rock violence. I got lucky, some didn't. As an ultra-violent punk rock gangster, I admit my part in ruining the scene. L.A. punk stood to be a magical moment of youth expression like no other and, for a little while, it undoubtedly was. The gangs ruined punk rock. I still have people telling me today that they quit punk because of LMP. Kids with talent in our scene expressed their anger through music or art. We, on the other hand, took our rage and confusion out on the streets. I'm far from that person today, but as that famous Black Panther said, "Violence is as American as cherry pie."

My relationship with my drunken abusive father changed little, except that in my heart I forgave him. I asked God to forgive him. He became ill with lung cancer and slipped into a coma soon after driving me home from jail that day. When he awakened, his faculties were limited. He still didn't want me around, but I showed up regardless. Spotty breathing and cracked lips, my father stared at me intently for a long moment. He was looking right into a mirror. I put out my hand, knowing this was the last time we were going to see each other. He mustered up a half smile and shook my hand. The next day, my father took a turn for the worse. A priest was summoned to perform last rites. The attending nurse said he refused and then closed his eyes for good—spiteful to the bitter end.

Santino's charges from the Pig Children incident were also dropped. Being he was stabbed in the back, the prosecutor didn't have much of a case. Not to mention Santino's Assistant D.A. cousin put heavy pressure on them.

He later told Santino, "The sheriff department's up in arms over the whole thing."

They thought they got rid of LMP for good ... instead they got nothing. Lucky for all of greater Los Angeles, Santino retired from the life a short time later. Right after his second child was born, he moved out of state.

The Godfather spends his golden years in a home close to the old neighborhood, smoking cigarettes, drinking beer, and tending his garden.

Sailor's alcoholism slid him further into the abyss. He passed out in the middle of Easy Street one day and couldn't be moved till paramedics came. Later that year, somebody hit Sailor over the head with a steel pipe, probably an old enemy. From then on he was never the same. Two years later, Sailor the legend died from alcohol poisoning.

Boxer disappeared, then re-appeared a paranoid schizophrenic, hiding behind window shades, staring out into the world he once participated in.

Captain Out of Hand still hates women when he's intoxicated, but hates trash even more. He works as a janitor somewhere in the Inland Empire.

Sickness stopped acting like Typhoid Mary, moved to Minnesota, and got clean.

Scary Sherry stayed clean and stayed in northern California.

Donna the Dead disappeared completely; no fan club, no goodbyes, no nothing.

Joker ended up doing a long prison stint for multiple violent felonies. On release, he overdosed on dope and died.

Magnum found a permanent home in a mental institution, where he parades around in his vintage three-piece suit, since "Hospital gowns are for sick people!"

Youngblood joined the biggest gang there is, the U.S. Army, and today guards political prisoners of the War on Terror.

Popeye came a long way, but went nowhere. He wound up a career convict and continues to steal shoes and jackets on the inside.

Chemo became a true ham-and-egger, making a career as a union electrician.

Stormin' Normin fell into a black hole of depression. After a number of suicide attempts, his fanatical parents had him committed to a psychiatric hospital, where sadly he found another way—*'Cause Stormin' Normin hung himself, Stormin' Normin hung himself—It happened just the other day—Jesus caught and pushed him off the shelf.* I always dug that D.I. song up until I got the dreadful news.

Degenerate enlisted in the Air Force sometime in 1986. Discipline suited him. Once his tenure was up, he got a badge, got a gun, and became a cop.

Bear moved to Florida during the late '80s to find his place in the booming cocaine industry, but ended up working construction. After he saved up enough money to build his dream home, a Category 4 hurricane blew it to kingdom come.

The Governor labors as an ironworker in a remote area of California, pounding steel instead of pimps.

Shitdick vanished completely.

Silent still remains silent to this day.

Pineapple Head stayed in the toilet and eventually flushed himself. He's been paying for it in the pen since I can remember.

Mike McIntosh had too much, too soon, and peaked too early. Following his father's death, he turned to heroin, and went downhill at an accelerated pace. Soon after, Mike passed away from a mixture of staph infection and heroin.

Mongo got out of prison after four years, became an accomplished tattoo artist, then someone got in his way and he went back upstate. In and out for the last 20 years, Mongo now resides in a padded cell for the criminally insane.

Pissed Chris had a few more narrow escapes from the law that landed him on the countywide police shitlist. He wound up railroaded by a malicious D.A. who put him in Pelican Bay on an accessory charge. Pissed Chris was subsequently stabbed to death inside. It's still very upsetting for anybody who knew him well.

Mad Manny somehow eluded the penal system and got the fuck out. He now lives happily with wife, kid, and machine gun.

Indian relocated to Tennessee and has a thriving concrete business. Still teaches, never preaches. His old crime partner Grease died in prison of hepatitis.

During the early '90s, Sam Sciortino retired to Palm Springs to live the good life of golf and grandkids. He got another dog named Frank to keep him company.

Today I'm closer than ever with my beautiful mother and two teenage sons. I dig graves at a small cemetery just outside Los Angeles. Plots and plots of quiet reminders. What else would you expect for Frank the Shank?

The whereabouts of "The Car" remain unknown. Some swear Satan himself finally reclaimed it. †